£1.50

Then and Now, This and That

First published in Great Britain in 2013
Published by the Larks Press
Ordnance Farmhouse, Guist Bottom
Dereham, Norfolk NR20 5PF
Tel/Fax: 01328 829207
E-mail: Larks.Press@xlnmail.com
Website: www.booksatlarkspress.co.uk

ISBN: 978 1 904006 67 1

Phototypeset by Transforma Pvt. Ltd., Chennai
Printed and bound in Great Britain by
Page Bros (Norwich) Ltd

Then and Now, This and That

Logie Bruce-Lockhart

Contents

Introduction

I am keenly aware that for a man of over ninety to expect people to be interested in an account of his life and times may be an optimistic delusion. It reminds me of Dr. Johnson's view of a woman's preaching: "Sir, a woman's preaching is like a dog's walking on its hinder legs. It is not well done, but you are surprised to find it done at all!"

This elderly account of the ups and downs of life for me and my family through the bewildering changes of the last 100 years is inevitably not free from the faults of old age ... periodic repetitiveness, frequent unreliability of memory, a tendency to bang on at excessive length on a few favourite themes.

But at least I am not concerned with being politically correct. I and my family have lived through the fastest changing times in history. I have hugely enjoyed it all and have seen it from some unusual angles. I hope that, if there should be any readers, they will find some bits interesting, or amusing or even ridiculous.

Dedication

To my beloved Jo: for sixty-four years the source, for all the family and many others, of courage, kindness and generosity.

"Life is mostly froth and bubble
Two things stand like stone.
Kindness in another's trouble
Courage in your own."

(*Adam Gordon*)

Chapter One
Sex, now and then

"Logie ...", said my Dad. A long pause followed, while I wondered why I had been called into his study. Why was he looking so uneasy? Was there bad news?

"I want you to be sure that you know all about how babies are made ..."

I swiftly reviewed my limited twelve-year-old knowledge, mainly based on the well-thumbed pages of the novel 'Anthony Adverse', which had given a detailed account of a torrid sexual encounter and had somehow avoided the eagle eye of the censor of the school library.

Fortunately, before I could overcome my embarrassment sufficiently to formulate a coherent reply, my equally embarrassed Dad summoned up the courage to forge ahead.

"I expect you've seen a cock climb up on a hen and seize it by the back of the neck and pass the sperm into her?"

Another pause. Although this description had utterly confused my previously fairly clear ideas about this procedure, I felt that a non-commital nod was called for. It was evidently enough to give Dad an excuse to draw the uncomfortable interview to an end.

"Well ... it's the same with all beasts and birds and with us too." He smiled with relief, and I understood there was no more to be said. As I made my escape I was deeply puzzled. Although I was beginning to enter on a lifetime's interest in birds, it had not yet taken the form of research into their sexual habits. Dogs? Yes, I knew that they had penises that grew when sexually aroused, and I knew where they inserted them and what consequences ensued. But cocks and hens? I had never seen a cock's penis and had never been sufficiently curious to look for an extra orifice under the mass of almost impenetrable feathers at the back end of a hen. Was it possible that, by some special arrangement, a cock's sperm could be conveyed to the hen's ovaries via the cock's beak and the hen's neck?

Fortunately a nascent interest in sport diverted my mind from the problem.

* * *

I start with this account of sex education in the early Thirties because, although it may have been an extreme example, it was typical of that time. My father was a wonderful teacher, an intelligent person, but could not overcome the almost universal inability to talk about sex.

Fear governed nearly everybody's attitude towards sex. Fear of illegitimate babies and the grim consequences in a society for which that was the ultimate sin and disgrace. Fear of sexual disease (remember that in the 19th century syphilis killed almost as many as Tuberculosis). Fear of homosexuality, which could land you in prison and ruin your career. Fear of masturbation, which, without any proof, was widely believed to be responsible for all kinds of ills and weaknesses, even blindness.

Although the First World War had gone far towards liberating women and had thrown young people together in circumstances which made promiscuous affairs inevitable, it didn't do much to banish these fears. Venereal diseases, although no longer life-threatening, and unwanted children caused as many problems as ever. In the Twenties and Thirties teachers and parents still tried to deal with the problems of sex education by turning their backs on them. Open discussion was very difficult in a setting in which small boys experimenting with the overwhelming and unexplained pressures of dawning sex were punished as if they were criminals. By convention sex was unmentionable: the young understood that it was the One Great Sin.

It took another war, the Pill and a social revolution to change sexiness into the One Great Virtue: the indispensable subject of conversation. Its variations and perversions were widely admired. Finally, the earlier and the more children were told about it, the better, until five-year-olds were encouraged to use make up and waggle their hips. Now Britain produces more early teenage unmarried mothers than almost any other country in Europe.

Whether either of these extremes makes for a happier society, or whether there can be a compromise better than either is a question which may become clearer in this book which looks at family, education and society in the 20th Century.

Chapter Two
The Background

From the beginning I must confess that I was brought up in a public school setting. My paternal grandfather was Head of Eagle House, now the prep school for Wellington. My mother's father was a Housemaster at Wellington. My parents met on the playing fields of Wellington. My father was a Housemaster at Rugby, then Headmaster of Cargilfield and finally Headmaster of Sedbergh. My brother was a teacher at Harrow, a Housemaster in Canada, a Headmaster of Wanganui in New Zealand, and then of Loretto near Edinburgh, and I taught at Tonbridge before serving twenty-seven years as Head of Gresham's.

This will be enough to deter many from reading any further. "What does a privileged, posh accented ivory tower toff from an outdated institution think he knows about real life or real people?" Most writers had the advantage of being unhappy at school and unhappy in their home life: too clever for teachers or parents. I admit to having enjoyed school and to having been enormously grateful to my parents and for the schooling they gave me. Some independent schools are bad, most are good, a few are brilliant: but they are certainly varied, and that is their importance and their strength. Whatever the schooling, however, the most important factor in shaping a child has always been the family home. And in that respect I count myself and my brothers extraordinarily lucky – in spite of our strange lack of sexual advice or education. Nothing – no family and especially no school – can escape the influence of time and place. I remember a Yorkshire Headmaster saying: "If the parents want their children to speak Swahili and have hairy legs, hairy legs and Swahili are what I'll give them."

Environment and fashion are the big factors in our lives, but nobody could be a teacher for long without realizing that genes are equally important. The British have the great advantage of being mongrels: the white Anglo-Saxon is a largely mythical being. We are all mixtures of Picts, Scots, Irish, Danes, Norwegians, Spaniards, French, Normans, Saxons and varied admixtures of colour from all corners of the Commonwealth – even though it is surprising, as Norman Davies tells us at the beginning of his great 'History of the Islands', that a present-day inhabitant of a neighbouring village has DNA linking him as a direct descendant to a long B.C. skeleton found in the Cheddar caves.

There are more recent skeletons in most of our cupboards, and the present fashion for looking into our family trees finds that everybody is not necessarily who he thinks he or she is.

So we should be less prone to racism than most other nations. Certainly that is one way in which we have markedly improved in the last fifty years.

In the case of myself and my three brothers the most powerful influences have been: a German granny (my mother's mother); Irish (my mother's father); Lowland Scot (my father's father and my wife's Agnew forebears); Highland Scot (my father's MacGregor mother) and English (my wife's Bradshaw mother).

My mother used to say, "John is the Irishman, Rab the Scotsman, Paddy the German and Logie the mixture of all three." Certainly we all felt divided between the rather wild and adventurous but charming MacGregors, who made fortunes and lost them in Malayan rubber and tea and Speyside Scotch, and the canny Presbyterian lowland Bruce-Lockharts. And I have always been crazy about the German romantics and Goethe, Schubert, Schumann and even (with a touch of shame) Wagner.

I was, however, given a wonderful start on life by the astonishing blend of freedom and discipline evolved by my mum and dad.

Chapter Three
Father's Influence

How did they bring me through childhood in the Twenties? Was it typical of the times or different?

Dad, wonderful teacher though he was, did not play a major part until I was eight and was taught by him at Cargilfield. He was too involved in the all day long task of teaching other people's children. But in the long school holidays he was a huge inspiration through his many enthusiasms, his example and his rare but telling bits of advice, some of which were found to be invaluable in later life.

"All you need to be happy is something worthwhile to be enthusiastic about."

"If you are tempted to be gloomy or depressed or going through a bad patch, find something to do which will help someone who is worse off than you."

"Success is 1% inspiration, 99% perspiration."

Dad had a strong Puritan streak, inherited from his father and his Scottish youth, but it was relieved by an unexpectedly Puckish sense of humour. Above all he taught us that to enjoy games or work we had to be competitive and practise. "You can learn to kick left footed, but not after a mere hundred attempts; you can only be really good after a thousand." He acquired a number of exceptional skills. Red, and then sandy-haired, he was neat and nimble-footed: a gold medal for figure skating at Wengen; highland dancing; a reverse spin service at tennis; water colours which made him a master of atmospheric painting, especially of the Highlands; he exhibited in the Academy; the first man to exploit the newly invented googly in English first-class cricket; a variety of unusual skills on the rugby field, which led him to be chosen for Scotland just before and after the war – which interrupted his international career, as it did Rab's and mine in the next war. He was also a much sought after singer of Scottish songs. People thought he was naturally gifted. Perhaps he was, a little, but his secret was that he thought and worked and practised as few others did in that amateur age, because he loved doing things well.

When walking back from school on a summer evening he would practise the finger work involved in bowling the googly by spinning the cricket ball and flicking it onto the back of his hand, where it would carry on spinning. His reward was to clean bowl Jack Hobbs, who thought the googly was a leg break and didn't offer a stroke, and to take thirteen wickets against Yorkshire, who were then county champions.

For the first two days of his holidays he would sleep and read Edgar Wallace thrillers. Then he would reach for his paint box or fly rod, or play tennis or squash with his four sons, or work at planning his wonderfully successful way of teaching French. He was incapable of being bored – a gift which he passed on to us and was a source of life long joy. Because we always had the school's facilities at our disposal we were able to swim and to play games against each other from an early age. He was about 5ft 10″ and slightly freckled, neat and precise in all his movements, twinkle eyed and with a broad smile which periodically lit up a strong face.

Chapter Four
An Amazing Mother

Our real educator was, however, our mum. Always anxious not to be thought of as competing with Dad, she hardly ever let it be known that she was a good linguist and historian, a competent pianist and singer, a useful water colour painter, a bit of a poet and a great story teller. In the home she was unquestionably the power behind the throne. She had an amazing ability to teach troubled or difficult children. I never heard her raise her voice, and they never tried to resist or to disobey. She exerted an iron discipline, but it never seemed to be so, and even the most tiresome children soon began to enjoy lessons with her. If they fell behind in school, she would take them for an hour per evening in the holidays, and they would learn more than the school could teach them in a term.

When I was five she took me without fail at 6 o'clock, when the church clock chimed, and taught me until an evening meal, followed by a story to which I looked forward hugely, and a short prayer. My bedroom had stars correctly arranged by constellations painted on the ceiling and a wonderful array of books, and if I wanted to read until midnight I could. The 'Children's Encyclopaedia' in ten volumes, French stories, 'The Wind in the Willows', 'The Scarlet Pimpernel', 'Winnie the Pooh', books on birds, flowers, fish, astronomy. So the fact that I didn't start school until eight didn't matter at all. Of course she couldn't have done it without the help of a maid who did a lot of the domestic work: we were indeed privileged in many ways.

Many years later she was doing the same things for my children and grandchildren, not to mention nephew and nieces. Once they had got into a good school, she stopped teaching, but still ruled the routine within the house with effortless calm. My eldest brother, John, for all his C.B., C.M.G., O.B.E, kept a very good portrait of her next to his gin cupboard. One eyebrow was faintly raised as she looked up from her knitting – and John would change his mind about a third glass. If we were staying indoors for most of the day, we had to observe a silent period after lunch for reading or sleeping and then join in highly competitive games, sometimes followed by music: a family quartet, or piano practice. Beautiful compassionate eyes, and a bosom made for comforting.

What was the secret of her success with 5–12 year olds? Although she was an exceptional person, it was an art which was much less rare in the Twenties and Thirties than it is now. Computer games and television have now replaced family games, family music, family meals and family fun. Mum studied children and what fascinated them, and built games, lessons and stories round that. She was utterly reliable, finding ready cures for cuts and bruises, asthma attacks and migraines and had a gift for knowing when there were troubles which we had thought to conceal from her. She enjoyed competitive card games infectiously and was a fountain of common sense. A spectacularly high speed knitter, she would churn out ornately patterned pullovers while playing a game or reading a story.

Chapter Five

Freedom to take Risks

This all seems very organized and perhaps restrictive for a family of four rumbustious boys. Not so! Outside lesson time she encouraged us to go out of doors. We were allowed to go where we liked and do what we liked. If the weather was vile we had a room, where we could make a mess and play our own games. We had complete freedom to a degree which would now be impossible. We were taught to swim and to fish at a very early age. No warnings not to talk to strangers, not to go near the lake or not to walk along the top of the wall or climb trees, in case we fell. We were given dangerous toys, and when they were not dangerous enough we made our own in a way that would now attract visits from social workers or the police. When we came back bruised or cut, Mum would mend the wounds without questioning or criticizing us.

Our freedom gave us the chance for enormous fun. Rab was particularly fond of explosions, electrical devices and a chemistry set (he later became a gunnery officer in the war). He had a battery with four metal devices which we could hold in our hands while the voltage was gradually increased. We had competitions to see how many volts we could stand – individually or as a group! We used the chemistry set to make all kinds of concoctions, explosions and poisons. Rab found a section of drain pipe in a rubbish dump and discovered that it was just of the right diameter to accommodate a tennis ball. This at once suggested to him the creation of a home made mortar. We found a rotten tree stump, hammered the drain pipe onto the stump, drilled a hole near the bottom, put carbide from the chemistry set into the mortar, sprinkled water on the carbide, rammed the tennis ball down, then applied a match to the hole. To our delight the mortar not only worked, but propelled the tennis ball, accurately aimed by Rab, over our three-storey house.

Equally enjoyable was a large iron ladle, which we used for melting lead. John got hold of a mould for making catapult bullets and also found six feet long pieces of solid wood into which we drilled holes, which we filled with lead. They made excellent weapons, which we used to re-enact the legendary quarter-staff battle between Little John and Robin Hood on the bridge in Sherwood Forest. Hitting the head was excluded by mutual agreement: cuts and bruises were just part of the learning process.

We were very proud too of what we called a land yacht. A couple of large wooden boxes were connected to the wheels of a discarded old pram. Curtain rods and old curtains were ingeniously arranged as sails and masts. When the September gales came to Edinburgh, the school playing fields made an admirable setting. We achieved some very pleasing speeds; the only trouble was that we had not devised any effective brakes. Luckily the playing fields were bordered by a nine feet high grass bank which brought us to a stop with only minor crashes.

Looking back at it all, I suppose it was a very privileged, if relatively inexpensive and unusual kind of education. We had virtually no pocket money and most of our presents were educational: squash rackets, rugby balls, musical instruments, atlases, encyclopaedias, and, like most middle class families, Grimm, Hans Anderson and Hilaire Belloc – and Scott's Waverley novels.

We were not given expensive treats to enable us to keep up with the Joneses. No T.V., no radios, no computers . . . They were either not invented or at the stage when, occasionally and awestruck, we gathered round a crystal and cat's whisker machine called a wireless, which, with careful tuning, produced barely identifiable sounds. As for 'designer clothing' and 'fashion', such words meant nothing to me. When we reached our teens we made music together inspired by the 'Comedy Harmonists' from Germany, singing 'Gather ye Rosebuds', 'O Mistress Mine' or 'Sing a merry madrigal' and a selection of German quartets. At all times there were mum's Irish Wolfhounds to join in the fun, or to act as affectionate pillows when we returned exhausted to the fireside.

Chapter Six

Changes in Home Life after the War

The huge post-war changes have made such an upbringing almost impossible. Health and Safety restrictions limit freedom, while parts of Britain, especially in the big towns have become no go areas for unescorted children. As for the widespread education of children by mothers who exerted unquestioned discipline, it has become counter to all modern tendencies and pressures.

One reason is that our expectations have become so high. As a young couple teaching after the war, Jo and I had no car, no radio or T.V., no hoover, no fridge and found it very difficult to pay for our food. Wine was only for Christmas, and beer only at the weekend. Not until I became Headmaster at the age of 33 were any of these luxuries possible. Nowadays a young family could have all of them and still be reckoned to be in need of state help. I am glad we had the experience of being short of money. It would be good if all young people faced it for a few years. After the war most of our friends were in the same boat, which was some consolation.

'Keeping up with the Jones' has recently become an absolute priority. At an absurdly young age children are allowed to notice what their little school mates are wearing and what toys and gadgets are in fashion and to clamour loudly to have them. If they haven't got the right kind of trainers, they think they are being deprived of a necessity and a right. The concept that money and possessions must be earned is quite unfamiliar to them. Modern mothers no longer make the bringing up of their children their top priority. It is scarcely possible for anyone of average or low income to afford to stay at home to care for small children. They are obliged to earn money and to rely on nursery schools of very varied quality – even if dad does an equal share of house chores and they can pay for help.

Most mothers try to achieve a happy compromise. Some make a real success of their whole time careers, sometimes at a heavy cost to their children and their marriage. A few risk the disapproval of their friends and modern society in general by being old fashioned whole time mums, at dangerous cost to the family budget. A majority strive, usually through part time jobs and nursery schools or work which can be done at home, to have the best of both worlds; but they often end up being unhappy with the strain of a double life, which is not totally rewarding in either capacity.

Too often both parents return home exhausted at 6 p.m. They quarrel about who gets the meal, or who does what with (or for) the children, who have already been released far too early from school and left to their own devices. This ends in everybody grabbing something from the fridge. The parents collapse in front of the telly and the children play computer games, don't do their homework or tidy anything away or wash up, and watch highly undesirable programmes in another room. No games shared with parents, no story telling, no chat or family meals. By the time they are adolescent the children have never failed to get their own way and are hardly acquainted with the word "No!" The parents discover that their attempts to have a quiet life by leaving their children to be educated by the telly and the computer has merely landed them in a state of inter-generational warfare, usually won by the young, "for the sake of peace and quiet." The gap grows beyond repair. The children only talk to and understand their contemporaries, while their parents become incomprehensible strangers. They almost speak a different language. Meanwhile Britain slides down the global graphs of educational achievement and the number of children born to unmarried mothers in their early teens is a way of life sometimes deliberately preferred to further education.

The student revolution of the late Sixties was in many ways responsible for this state of affairs, and so were we – by which I mean the post-war Establishment: the teachers, the parents, the Church. We dreamed of returning to a peaceful life watching films of jolly Jack Hawkins at the helm in 'The Cruel Sea', or village cricket matches. We took little account of the huge issues which arose after the war: the bomb, the Pill, women's lib, the violent death throes of racism, the end of Empire, the use of drugs, the threat of communist dictatorships, the challenging of religious certainties. We did not face up to these problems soon enough, and did not understand as quickly as the young how important it was to give guidance and examine these new problems in school.

But the revolutions brought harmful results in many ways. Various slogans spread through educationists in the Civil Service and the teachers: 'Child centred education' and 'pupil power' became fashionable. Discipline, elitism, punishment, prizes, authoritarianism, paternalism, competition all became terms of condemnation. The condemnation of elitism meant that clever pupils were held back, and even that excellence was suspect because it made the slow pupils feel inadequate. Paternalism was condemned because it was believed that teachers had "no right to try to impose middle class values, because all ways of life are equally valid". Sheer crap, most of it, especially at a time when family life was in need of every possible form of support.

As might be expected, what I have said so far is that the middle classes had a good education before the war. What about the workers? They were hit hard by the financial crash at the beginning of the Thirties: a lot of unemployment and poverty. Nevertheless they had high standards of family life, strict discipline in the home and in most of the schools. In some parts of Britain they sought education as a way of escaping poverty. The grammar schools provided a good ladder to a better way of life, and the best of secondary moderns were not far behind. Marx and Engels had prophesied that the proletarian majority would blow the "superincumbent minority", (the bourgeoisie) sky high. They never really understood that before long the proletarian majority would become a minority. In Wales, Scotland and Yorkshire, especially, the working class had a strong culture of their own. Not only were there highly skilled craftsmen among them, but their shelves at home were often packed with the works of Dickens, Lawrence, Scott, Burns and Dylan Thomas rather than 'Das Kapital' and 'The Communist Manifesto'. Welsh choirs and northern brass bands set high standards. Marriage was just as respected an institution as it was in the middle classes and probably much more than in some parts of the aristocracy.

That is not to say that working class life was easy. The Thirties provided a decreasing standard of living, grim unemployment and discontent made worse by competition from abroad and stirred by Trotskyite influence.

The shrinking aristocracy has always been a law unto itself. Its reputation was harmed by the prevalence of ineffectual, immoral, lazy and snobbish 'Hooray Henries'. Shielded from the necessity to work for their living many of them drank their way through life, being rude to their superiors in the middle and lower classes, and not even helping to preserve their large estates. On the other hand, many of the old aristocracy worked hard to keep up their estates, lived quietly in a wing of their lovely old houses, made an objective and sensible contribution to the much maligned House of Lords, gave to charity and were happy to drink with the locals and get beaten at darts in the nearest pub – which you would be unlikely to find German barons or French counts doing, in spite of the French Revolution. Since the Second World War, they have mostly lost any power they had; but a few are still huge landowners, and some, in spite of high taxation, have proved to be shrewd business men and made their possessions the source of considerable profit.

So far I have stressed the good side of family life in the Twenties and Thirties. In my own case I am extremely grateful for the wonderful happiness and effectiveness of the upbringing I owe to my mother and father and some excellent schools. But, of course, there was a downside.

In a family of four boys and no girls, in an all-male boarding school, no attempt was made to give us any guidance on the subject of sex: it was scarcely mentioned, except for dear Dad's one failed attempt. Mum had a sharp eye for any developments, but never gave any advice. She always supported her boys, right or wrong, and we never plucked up courage to question her about sex – or religion. The house was cheerfully free of all tensions, largely because these matters, together with Death, Disease and Poverty were hardly ever mentioned. Although Mum and Dad clearly loved one another and were occasionally seen to give one another an affectionate peck on the cheek, we could not imagine our parents bringing four cheerfully randy boys into the world. If they mentioned sex at all, it was to condemn it as sinful. Mum went a little way towards explaining this to us on her death bed at the age of 83, when she opened up quite startlingly.

She told us she had fallen in love in her late teens with a man who turned out to be not only unfaithful but totally unreliable in other ways. She soon realized that Dad ("Dear Man" as she always called him) was a better man, and she grew to respect him hugely and to love him. The Lothario's proposal was refused and she had a happy marriage. But ... sex had never meant much to her. It seemed to give him great pleasure, so she was content to "lie back and think of England" (her own words) and was pleased to be able to please him. That was not the way (I hope) that most of our wives felt.

This lack of any advice about sex and human relationships had a bad effect on us, and was very widespread in those days. Curiously enough I heard the same kind of complaint from a couple of distinguished Old Greshamians. Lord Reith, the founder of the B.B.C., became quite a friend of ours , and, encouraged by my Scottish background, would occasionally open up, when he visited his old school every now and again. Coming from an even more Presbyterian background than my dad, he was told nothing about sex, except that it was sinful. He had been sent to Gresham's in the time of that great Headmaster, Howson (of whom more later).

In the meantime I and my three brothers were brought up in single sex schools in the Thirties. We all enjoyed our schooling, except that John, the biggest and most self-confident, was bullied and unhappy at the prep school Eagle House, run by our Bruce-Lockhart grandfather. That was in huge contrast to his later happiness at Rugby, where he never heard an unkind word and became the ultimate 'Boys Own' magazine schoolboy hero. In one respect, in spite of the excellent all-round education we received, these schools failed us. Because they were all single sex schools and we had lived in remote places without sisters or any contact with young females, none of us had much understanding of girls' thoughts and feelings. At parties for teenagers, the boys stood at one end of the room talking about games, and the girls stood at the other end talking about the boys. When it came to dancing, conversation became virtually impossible, because of the volume of the music. So it was not surprising that most of us became male chauvinist pigs or giggling nitwits. We were beings from different planets.

Years later it was these experiences which led me to be one of the first to welcome co-educational boarding as the common sense solution to these problems. Girls and boys should grow up together: the shock of being suddenly exposed at University to contact with girls at the age of maximum sex drive without any previous experience of ordinary social meeting was too great. I never saw any girls except for fleeting glimpses of my elder brothers' girl friends. At my first dance, at the age of 17 I was invited into the rose garden by a vicar's daughter 10 years older than me and experienced my first kiss. She had, I remember, a suggestion of a light fuzzy moustache. We must both have been very desperate and never met again.

Chapter Seven
Changed Religious Attitudes

The other shortcoming in our education was religion. My life time has seen great changes in attitudes to religion; we were never able to discuss it at home. Dad was a good man, who lived by Christian standards. He preached well, sometimes inspiringly, to boys. But he skated round the supernatural, unhistorical or superstitious elements of fundamental Christianity. I suspect he was doubtful about the after-life, and too intelligent to accept the infallibility of the Bible, let alone the Pope.

Mum was determined that we should all be regular in prayer every night and be familiar with all the best biblical stories. Theological discussions were, however, not her thing: she carefully avoided them. Anyhow, we thought that we knew their views without being told . . . their example spoke better than words, and practice seemed more important than waffle.

The First World War shook many people's faith, and the second even more. How could anyone who saw the German concentration camps pray to an "Almighty and most merciful Father"? Plainly no Almighty God could tolerate Belsen or Auschwitz and be considered merciful. Yet, strangely enough, many soldiers who were involved in the fighting resorted to prayer. I certainly returned to the prayer my mother had taught me, when we were advancing into Germany, although I certainly didn't believe in an Old Man in the Sky. Sir Tommy MacPherson, the most highly decorated officer of World War II, still miraculously alive, did the same and found it gave him strength in terrifying circumstances.

Between the wars relatively unquestioning faith was, surprisingly, not uncommon, but doubts were increasingly voiced. Many of the priests ordained at that time found that by the '60s and '70s it was becoming increasingly difficult to defend a faith that accepted miracles and religious beliefs which belonged to a very different time. Many continued to accept the teachings of Christ, but found it hard to support the practices and fundamentalism of the modern church. I only dare generalize about these things because, between 1948 and 1982, Jo and I entertained more than five hundred priests, from young curates to Archbishops, to dinner or lunch after hearing them preach: an interesting if rather overwhelming experience. A few were remarkable people whose spiritual strength was obvious even to the most atheistic observers. Among the cheerful rubicund vicars, the gloomy and austere grey-faced priests and the delightful array of characters recognizable from 'Barchester Towers', at least three made a lasting impression.

Pastor Alfred Schultes had a quite unique power to communicate with teenagers. His background was aristocratic East Prussian and Lutheran. He had been outspoken in his criticism of the Nazis, which led him to incarceration in a concentration camp. A brave campaign by powerful friends led to his release, but he could not remain in Germany, and he escaped to Weston-super-Mare with very little money and hardly any possessions. From this unlikely base, he set about a mission to the young. Wherever he could find young people (schools, prisons, youth clubs or universities) he would go and talk to them about life and their problems. His reputation spread by word of mouth. He never asked for money – it was just sent to him by admirers. You would think from his initial appearance that he might be an unlikely person to cast a spell over teenagers. Smartly dressed, always with highly polished shoes, about 50 years old with a quite strong German accent, he preached a short sermon and invited any boys and girls interested to join him in the Headmaster's drawing room. Although my room was very large, I could hardly squeeze the audience in. They were sitting on each others' laps, on every corner of the floor and even on the window sills. Within a few minutes they were opening up about their home and family difficulties to him with extraordinary frankness. He would put his head on one side and consider the reasons for the unhappy situations, put one or two questions and then put his finger unerringly on the spot and offer the solution, even if it involved strong criticism of the questioner. Many former pupils of mine who met him have talked to me about his remarkable impact long years afterwards, saying that they felt he had some extraordinary power of intuition and of inspiration – which Alfred himself attributed to the power of prayer and (he didn't seek to avoid the word) to the help of God.

There were a few more who were able to communicate the reality and force of a spiritual life to pupils. Aubrey Aitken, the Bishop of Lynn, and Bishop Wilson of Birmingham were two others. Aubrey had a special gift for communicating with boys. Built like a front row forward (which, indeed, he had been) he suffered for many years from cancer of the throat. He had to speak with the aid of especially high-powered microphones, which carried his unearthly hoarse voice, like Darth Vader's, to every corner of churches or chapels. It commanded instant attention. He always seemed to be positive and cheerful: a great man to have at a party. His points were vividly, sometimes eccentrically illustrated. I remember him talking of the difference between ease and simplicity. In mid sermon he took a golf club (a number 7 iron), ingeniously concealed beneath his voluminous robes, and a golf ball from his pocket, placed the ball on the floor and chipped it towards my pew so accurately that I was able to catch it.

"There you are," he said. "In all things, including a golf swing, the supreme excellence is simplicity: but it is by no means easy and requires a lot of hard work."

The Bishop of Birmingham just told us the story of how, in a Japanese prisoner of war camp, he was tortured, flogged and put in a small cage in solitary confinement, because of his help to maltreated and starving "white scum". He told us that the strength which came to him through prayer during the floggings gave him an exhilaration which thrilled him with the power of God . . . After the war his torturers wrote and asked him if he would forgive and baptize them "because they had seen something extraordinary in his face."

So, whatever Richard Dawkins may say, there is something more at work in the universe than the Darwinian survival of the fittest, based on pure self-interest, undoubtedly true though that is. There are beauty and ugliness, truth and falsehood, cruelty and kindness, strange powers for good and evil, which cannot be weighed and measured.

Strangely the key to the power of those things seems to lie in a factor common to all three of the Christians I have mentioned: experience of acute suffering. I treasure a most understanding letter from the Bishop of Birmingham, when he heard of the death of my little seven year old daughter. It is not easy to be of any help in that situation, but he was.

Chapter Eight
The Family and Religion

How did our family cope with this shift in attitudes to matters religious? I was, perhaps, a shade less precocious than

> "John Grubby, who was short and stout,
> And troubled with religious doubt,
> Refused about the age of three
> To sit upon the curate's knee."

Nevertheless by about five or six years old I had worked out that Noah's Ark would have had more than a little difficulty in accommodating two of every kind of bird and beast with adequate feeding and sanitary arrangements. I can and could at an early age only agree with the words of the song

> "The things that you're liable
> To read in the Bible
> They ain't necessarily so . . .
> Jonah he lived in a whale –
> He made his home in
> That fish's abdomen –
> It ain't necessarily so."

In the Forties and Fifties John, Rab, Paddy and I and, to some extent, our parents and millions of other people were trying to find our way through what felt like a thickening mist. To begin with, we still didn't discuss these matters much. Later, under the influence of our wives or when fortified by a little drink, we began tentatively to exchange views. We admired the Christian teaching, we respected the good work of the Church; we felt that there were forms of good and evil at work in human society, but increasingly rejected the miraculous and superstitious elements. The atheists who refused to countenance any spiritual side to life seemed to us almost as unsound as the fundamentalists who accepted everything in the Bible and rejected well-proven scientific facts. And we were no more attracted by the astonishingly numerous British people who tried to fill the gap in moral and spiritual guidance left by the Church of England, which seemed to have lost the ability to give firm yet acceptable leadership, with all kinds of strange sects. There were and still are many genuine believers in communication with the dead 'on the other side', and even in ghosts, fairies and winged angels, prophets of future events and people who remember the long past. Belief in the power of prayer to heal even physical wounds and 'incurable diseases' was widespread.

Chapter Nine

Difficulties of Religious Guidance in Schools and Church

For priests and Headmasters, especially in boarding schools, it was particularly difficult. Although most parents had by about the Seventies abandoned churchgoing except for weddings, christenings, Easter and Christmas, most of them still wanted their children to be taught a credible form of Christianity.

Bright teenagers are very quick to pick up any sign of insincerity. On the other hand they are receptive to guidance on the moral and spiritual side of life, and it is important that they should see the importance of the role Christianity has played in forming our relatively civilized society, as well as the harm done by the entirely unchristian behaviour of fundamentalist Muslims, Roman Catholics, Protestants and Puritans. It has been a difficult path to steer. I was lucky in that for most of my time as Headmaster I had a good partnership in my Chaplain and assistant Chaplain. Group Captain Ray Bowen had been No 2 in the R.A.F. hierarchy of Chaplains, responsible for a large area of air force bases round the Mediterranean. He thoroughly enjoyed the common room life, which was very like an officers' mess. He had a simple faith with no great intellectual pretensions, a lot of common sense and an interest in young people, Wales and rugby football. He made it his job to see that the boys and girls knew the Bible and behaved themselves, without letting himself become entangled in theological arguments. He enjoyed a glass or three of gin, but avoided excess under the eagle eye of his wife. His assistant, David Hart, was a young man (Ray joined us in his late fifties) of a quite different kind. He had worked in a slum parish, knew what the effects of poverty were, and was deeply concerned to work out an intellectual and acceptable interpretation of Christianity which could help solve global problems. Some of his ideas were beyond the normal ground covered by the Church, but he was a real help to some boys and girls who were puzzled or concerned about the significance of Christian teaching. He went on, appropriately, to become a university chaplain and to write books about the complexity of modern interpretations of Christianity. Anyway the greatest tribute I can pay both of them is that they managed to get my, at that time, idle and hearty rugby playing son, Bede, an A grade A level in divinity and a lasting interest in spiritual values. For that I shall always be grateful.

The four brothers reacted to these matters slightly differently, although I think we all (with varying success) tried to follow the Christian code of conduct. John married a Bishop's highly intelligent, not aggressively holy and markedly beautiful daughter. At Saint Andrew's University he did the same kind of course as the one I followed at Cambridge: French and German literature and culture. Its influence on our thinking was, however, different. He was particularly interested in the French Encyclopédistes: Descartes, Helvétius, Condorcet, Voltaire, Diderot and all the rationalists, who believed that the human mind could solve all the problems of the human race, if it could free itself of emotional and other prejudices. I was more drawn to the German philosophers, most of whom believed that the mind was an undependable tool of more powerful sub-or unconscious forces, and that it was almost impossible for any human being to rid himself of, or even to be aware of, the forces that shaped his thinking, whether they were genetic or the result of his upbringing.

John's rationalist outlook excluded any belief in God or in any religious sect. But he retained an admiration for the work of the Church – after all, he had a Bishop for a father-in-law! Much later (in the Seventies) I had one or two conversations with him about these matters and he confessed that he was, in old age more puzzled about the source of his strong feelings about beauty and ugliness, good and evil. Strangely enough, he was a real Romantic at heart.

Rab was a saint, incapable of a mean word or act. Completely faithful to his wife Pip, he wrote to her every day of their long war-time separation. He uncomplainingly looked after our eventually immobile and helpless mum, although both he and Pip were dangerously ill themselves. If you wanted to know whether a course of action was right or wrong, he was the first person you would go to, yet there was never any trace of priggishness about him, and he never raised his voice or made any assertions or criticisms that were not invited. He was cheerful at all times, in spite of what must have been horrifically painful gall bladder trouble and a failing heart. Greatly gifted for all ball games, he was always modest to a fault. I benefited greatly from his encouragement and coaching, to which he devoted a lot of time. He never talked about religion, he just lived it. He was deeply influenced by the stoics, particularly Marcus Aurelius and some of the modern Christians like Bonhöffer and Tillich. He would have been mildly offended if anyone had called him an intellectual, but read widely, especially the classics, having a great admiration for the ancient Greeks, which I always found hard to understand. He was always great company, and never critical of other people's idea of fun – even on London-Scottish rugby tours, on which bawdy songs and heavy drinking were common practice, he was not disapproving. A couple of glasses revealed a sly sense of humour and warmth, which contrasted with the first impression of shyness. When it came to any decision he made as a Head, if he thought it was right, no matter how strongly it was opposed, he stuck to his guns.

What did Paddy, the great surgeon, think? Although he spent his life healing and working to improve medical services for the poor, and was an admirer of the Christian way of life, he was never a believer.

Becoming President of the Medical Association of Ontario and Speaker of Canada's Medical Parliament, he loved delivering babies, more than 10,000 over his long career, and he soon began to be sent all the most difficult cases. His calm decisiveness in a crisis was legendary, and he gave everyone confidence.

But he was not a believer in souls and spirits, because he believed that character and characteristics are the product of our brains and that brain surgeons are on the point of being more successful in changing our attitudes and ways of life for better (or worse) than any priests or teachers.

As for me, increasingly influenced by Jo and our children, I was impressed by the teachings of Gurdjeff and Ouspensky, without becoming in any way a disciple, also Goethe, Thomas Mann and Hesse, and some other German philosophers and the best parts of Buddhism. I became obsessed by the question of how a country which had produced Bach and Beethoven could also be responsible for Belsen and Auschwitz. I came to realize that, if I had been brought up in Germany by my German grandmother, I would have undoubtedly have been recruited (blue eyes, fair hair, fond of games and drinking songs!) to the S.S. For every school in Germany in the Thirties was run on strictly Nazi lines, and any books were banned and burnt, which went counter to the anti-semitic Aryan superiority themes, or to the teaching that the supreme virtues were to lay down one's life unquestioningly for the Führer, and to be obedient to him under all circumstances. Once in the S.S. and discovering the extent of the persecution of Jews, communists and dissenters what would I have done? I will look more closely at the reasons for Germany's fanatical support for Hitler later.

Would England's gift for distrusting and mocking leaders have saved it if it had been faced with similar circumstances? I suspect that any nation under a ruthless dictator would be capable of going off the rails. The late 'dear Leader' of North Korea, playing his first ever round of golf on his new championship course, managed to persuade his numerous admiring escorts to put their signatures to a statement that he had done eleven holes-in-one. It was said that the whole nation accepted that a miracle had been done. It is either ludicrously funny, an invented story, or frighteningly tragic! Is the human race's gullibility limitless?

As a father and a Headmaster, I felt that it was very important to support the best Christian values, without either saying things I did not believe, or trying to inculcate the more questionable official Church teachings to young people, who genuinely found some of them impossible to believe. For many Headmasters it was a difficult task. It involved all sorts of other questions. Compulsory chapel or voluntary? Prayers at assembly? What to do for Muslims, Jews or Roman Catholics? Introduce them to brief outlines of the other great religions?

Chapter Ten
Childhood Memories

Old men are supposed to have vivid memories of their early youth, but very shaky memories of recent events. I don't have clear or reliable memories of childhood: hardly any before the age of 5. It's hard to know whether the few incidents change over the years, because somebody else witnessed them and saw things differently or because we think of them from an adult point of view. Most of them are mental pictures, like photographs, grown a little dim with age.

I remember one incident clearly, because it caused me a deep embarrassment lasting some years. I was, in spite of my cheerful and confident brothers, a rather shy and timid little boy ... well, perhaps not so little as I weighed 12 pounds at birth, but with fair and curly hair and tiresomely precocious: "Quite unnaturally keen on Athalie by Jean Racine", as Hilaire Belloc put it. I was frightened of people outside the family and what they might think of me. One day my parents decided to leave me at a tea party given to 4–7 year old children by some friends. They all seemed very grand and good and exquisitely dressed. The children all knew each other well and ignored the shy newcomer. Eventually I felt an urgent need to pee, but didn't dare or know how to ask where there was a loo. After enduring an hour of agony, I just burst, leaving a conspicuous puddle on the floor, and dissolved into tears. It must have been a couple of years before I could face any form of party without remembering my disgrace.

Other memories of Rugby, where my dad was a Housemaster until I was 7 or 8, were mostly pictorial. The house yard, lit up in the Christmas holidays, was occasionally flooded when there was a sharp frost to allow a first attempt at ice skating. My bedroom with the dark blue ceiling with the stars and planets printed in bright yellow. The lawn on which my three brothers and I learned to play cricket with a tennis ball. The Rugby chapel and playing fields, and the first sight of rugby football. The tuck shop, where I was taken for a treat in summer to eat a 'Royal ice cream': thick cream, strawberries and a double ice. Most exciting were our first wireless set and our first car. The car was an early version of a Vauxhall with running boards. Dad took the wheel and drove us carefully to the 'straight mile' near Dunchurch. Greatly daring he reached 60 miles an hour with the four of us cheering as the speedometer reached that undreamed of figure.

My own particular Heaven was a crude tree house, about 14 feet up a poplar tree near the front gate. The base of the tree was surrounded by a yew. The top of the yew combined with a fork in the poplar afforded a framework for most of the house which we extended with collected sticks. It was well placed; we could spy on everybody walking down the road, while remaining invisible. Inevitably I fell out of it, but the branches of the yew broke the fall, and I escaped with slight bruises. It also provided me with a fascination with birds, which has been a life-long joy.

Chapter Eleven
Cargilfield

Dad was then successful in his application to become Headmaster of Cargilfield, at that time one of the best prep schools in Scotland. About 5 miles from Prince's Street, situated in lovely grounds between three well-known golf courses, and only a little way inland from the Forth Bridge, it provided our family with a very happy setting for the most important years of our upbringing. Dad was spectacularly successful and, for the first time, was reasonably well off financially – at Rugby he was still experiencing the money worries that even the best schools inflict on their staff, but were eased by his years as a Housemaster. I still remember the magnificent Scottish breakfast we had: choice of fish, eggs, bacon, mushrooms, kidneys and sausages.

John went to Rugby School – Rab and Paddy, when they had finished at Eagle House, Camberley, under my grandfather's Headmastership, went to the Edinburgh Academy. I went to Cargilfield, and then to Sedbergh. I had the good fortune to be a member of Dad's most brilliant little French class. Before and during the First World War he had worked with a French professor at an entirely new approach to teaching French. There had for some time been attempts to use the 'direct method' which insisted that, from the beginning, the English language should never be used. Unfortunately most of the varieties of the 'direct method' avoided the complication of French grammar. The originality of Dad's method was that, while he used French only, a large part of his lessons were devoted to practising and learning grammar in French. He also invented a number of amusing little phrases, which we had to learn by heart in a perfect accent, illustrating at the same time common idioms or grammatical rules. We never were allowed to waste a moment, as he fired questions at us sometimes demanding a reply from all, sometimes from each individual. "L'adverbe suit immédiatement le verbe. Donnez-moi des exemples". When we hesitated he laughed and repeated the rule, pointing out that it was an example too. We never forgot. "Georges est socialiste malgré que son père soit définitivement Conservateur."

"As-tu eu du sucre?"
"Le bonbon fondit entre les dents du bon bandit."

"Le perroquet du Président est parti pour le Paradis."
"Ton thé t'a-t-il guéri ta toux?"
"Joffre et Foche adorent les Boches."

That little group of pupils consisted of nine boys starting at the age of 8 and ending in every case with a scholarship to a leading public school at the age of 13. They were not specially selected as guinea pigs: just the first nine entrants to the school when he arrived. The later careers of those nine pupils were so remarkable that Dad was made a Chevalier de la Légion d'honneur years later for his 'services in spreading the love of French language and literature'.

The class of nine were taught for five periods a week, with two periods of prep and a daily French table for lunch at which English was forbidden. If Dad was absent the senior boy (usually Pat Rodgers) had a Larousse dictionary to look up any word for which we were at a loss. Dad also had a book of pictures as a basis for conversation, and there was a French play to be performed every year.

Perhaps Pat Rodgers was the best of us. Later, as Bishop of Manchester, he addressed a meeting of European priests for half-an-hour in French without a note. But the others were equally remarkable. Sir Tommy MacPherson became the most highly decorated officer of World War Two (3 M.C.'s, a D.S.O, Croix de Guerre, Legion of Honour, Papal Knighthood, two Italian awards and a Polish top honour), for his exploits behind enemy lines, aided by his command of languages. Then there was Freddie Luke, Professor of French at St. Andrew's and then Oxford. H.M. Gee, who, funnily enough, became Her Majesty's Government's Chief Inspector of French teaching. The two Barbour brothers were very fluent: one became Moderator of the Church of Scotland and the other a Professor at Aberdeen University. Graham Cobb was helped by an exceptionally musical ear. He became Head of French at Rugby School and a distinguished organist and piano player. Then there was myself, who got a Wright Prize for modern languages at St. Johns, Cambridge.

There was a boy who was prominent in all our French plays, whose name I've sadly forgotten, perhaps because he was killed in the war in his early twenties. He added to a lovely French accent a delightful mimicry of French gestures and faces.

We all enjoyed Cargilfield, although I can't say that the religious education quite matched its French. On arrival at the school we queued up to give various details to the staff so that they could be put on record: telephone number of homes, numbers of brothers and sisters, dogs, cats and special interests.

One question puzzled me. In a strong lowland Scottish accent the master was asking each boy: "Pisky or Presby?" I hadn't the faintest clue about what he was talking about. The boy next to me dug me in the ribs and said: "If you're a true Scot, it's Presby." So I obediently signed on for the Presbyterian Kirk. For all

I knew it might have been Polynesian devil worship. Anyway I attended Cramond Kirk with the majority of other pupils under the scholarly eye of the Minister, Dr. Stott. His sermons were invariably half-an-hour long, and they were far over the heads of boys of our age. The only thing I remember about them is that Caleb is the Hebrew for dog – but in what context or even how spelt I know not.

One of the other decisions we had to make was which Division or Clan of the school we wanted to join. I think there were four: Bruce, Wallace, Stuart and Graham. Even though about a quarter of us were English, it was thought that everyone could find some relationship to one of those great clans. At least that was not a hard choice for me. The teaching was good, even if not particularly politically correct by today's standards. I well remember one master, explaining in answer to a question about class divisions in Scotland compared to England, "Everyone in Scotland is upper class except for a small lower class which lives in Glasgow and is Irish and Roman Catholic!"

One of the greatest benefits of Cargilfield was the opportunity it gave us for enjoyable holidays. The school itself was like a holiday camp ... indoor swimming bath and gym, tennis courts, golf courses, rugby fields, long and high jump pits. No wonder we all became crazy about sport. When Dad and Mum felt an occasional corrective dose of culture was due, the wonderful facilities of Edinburgh were only a few minutes away. But, certainly for me, the summer holidays in the Highlands made the most lasting impact.

We were taken to some of the most beautiful, and, in those days, wild and remote places that the heart could desire. The Isle of Harris was at that time almost entirely Gaelic speaking. Old ladies sat before their thatched houses singing old Hebridean songs as they worked at their spinning wheels – not for the benefit of tourists, because we were almost the only ones outside Stornoway some 40 miles to the north. The fishing was great, the scenery unforgettable, the few people to whom we could speak (I have no Gaelic) were charming and hospitable. Ardnamurchan was almost as remote and as beautiful ... it was only attainable by the wild old road through Glencoe and then two ferries at Ballachulish and Ardgour. What with Bettyhill in the far north, Applecross, Loch Maree, the Spey Valley and the Aberdeenshire Don, Perthshire and Argyll, we got to know and love the huge variety of scenery, to marvel at the shifting colours of the sunsets behind Muck, Eigg, Rhum and Skye, framing the dark blue islands in a blaze of turquoise and scarlet sky and sea. And every kind of water from the green and purple sea to the mountain lochs and the tumbling bluebell, primrose, heather and gorse banked rivers. We were free from the age of 8 upwards to wander with fishing rods and binoculars where and as far as we wanted, delighting in the strange calls and beautiful plumage of the divers, the curlews and the golden plover. With all the pleasures of this amazing world to look back on, none has kept the power to heal and to cheer in the way that fishing in the Highlands has done ... the one infallible cure for the darkest of times.

Midges and rain? Yes, it must be admitted that they can be devastating. But the rain, though ruthless and penetrating, lifts at intervals. And there are, usually in May or June, three weeks of glorious spring which no other country can rival – and an elusive echo of that in a brief September Indian summer, when the colouring of the glens is unique. Happy days indeed.

We were all happy at school too. John had not enjoyed Eagle House. It is not always a sinecure to be a Headmaster's grandson or son in his own school. But as soon as John went to Rugby School he started to enjoy life hugely. He told me that on his first day he was trying to open the common room door, when carrying a cello. A sixth-former leapt to his feet and opened the door for him saying: "Dashed difficult things to handle, these expensive instruments". From that moment on he claimed that he never heard an unkind word from anyone at Rugby. He had a great admiration for the Head at that time: Vaughan.

The press tended to be more interested in David and Lyon, who came before and after Vaughan, because they had unusual and 'progressive' ideas about teaching. Vaughan was just a great schoolmaster, who was respected and firm, but fair. He truly understood boys. He would talk to new pupils to find out about their hopes and fears. Then he would say: "Here are the school rules. If you break them you will be punished. If you do WRONG, you will have me to reckon with." Perhaps only an experienced Head can fully appreciate that sentiment. Rules are a rather tiresome necessity to be reduced to a minimum (Rugby had very few). Right and wrong are far more complex and important.

In due course John's exceptional powers as a leader came to the fore, and he will long be remembered at Rugby as the very pattern of a schoolboy sporting hero. He captained the 1st XV rugby team in a season when they not only were undefeated but didn't have a try scored against them. In the last match their record hung by a thread. In the final minute of the game, the opposition wing three quarter broke through and beat the full back just short of the corner flag. John, at wing forward, had anticipated the move and crashed him into the corner flag. No try, and the whistle went for time. Over 6 foot tall, curly haired and very dashing, he was better looking than the rest of us.

Some sixty years later I was being treated by a doctor. When he saw my name, he asked me if I was a relation of John, and when I pleaded guilty, he told me the above story and said it was the most exciting sporting moment he had ever seen!

Rab too was very fortunate in his schooling. He was the shortest of us, but wiry and quick in all his movements – the most like our father. Even at Eagle House his reputation for games had saved him from bullying. At Edinburgh

Academy not only did he get a good Scottish education (as ever, better than English schooling), but he rose to be Captain of an undefeated rugby side, and of the cricket side and was the record-holder for the 100 yards. He caught the eye of the Scottish selectors for his exceptional acceleration and handling, and was capped at the age of 22, after playing for the Scottish schoolboys. Both he and John and indeed myself lost the best years of our rugby to World War Two, when there were no international matches and not many first class fixtures. John lost the years between the ages 25 and 31, Rab between 22 and 28 and I between 19 and 25. Sadly the same was true of our dad in World War One. He was capped just before and after hostilities.

In those days it was not customary to kiss and cuddle try scorers. Rab was playing for Warwickshire (on the strength of being born in Rugby) in the final of the counties championship. It was a closely fought game, but, in the last few minutes, Rab broke through and scored a spectacular individual try to snatch victory. Harold Wheatley, the very large England and Coventry forward, picked him up as though he was a favourite son, and planted a huge kiss on him. It was the first time I'd ever seen such a thing!

Paddy joined the Edinburgh Academy too. Almost exactly the same height as me, depending on which leg he stood, he had darker hair. The difficulty of the troubles he had had to face because of his tubercular knee made him a more determined and ambitious man than his brothers. He had spent a couple of years largely on a truckle bed in his youth, and then at 16 another year in plaster from his chest to his toes. During that year I spent a great deal of time with him, fetching and helping in what way I could. He was magnificently disciplined, exercising his arms and wrists (the only parts he could move except his head and his toes) until they grew unusually strong. From an early age he had made up his mind to be a doctor. Every day he would work to make up the school time he had lost. I got to know him intimately in that year, and loved him for his cheerfulness and admired him for his sense of purpose. Almost immediately after being released from his plaster he took up playing games competitively with his brothers: squash, tennis and cricket and dancing to an extraordinary standard, considering his permanently stiff leg. His medical studies prospered too, and it was not long before we saw that he would have a great career as a doctor. He took up fencing as the one sport in which the stiff leg would not be a handicap, teaching himself to fence with an épée left handed so that he could lunge onto his flexible knee. Unable to become a rugby international like Dad, Rab and me, he managed to fence for Scotland.

The only trouble I experienced for the first year or two was asthma. I had some frightening attacks, when I really thought I was going to suffocate. The doctor recommended one pint of Whitbread's or Worthington's beer every morning at 11. It worked like magic, and I have never suffered since.

We were extraordinarily close in those years as a family, full of shared enthusiasms, delighting in each others' success, laughing over our failures, competing fiercely and joined by a dad, still young enough to pass on skills and share the fun. My mother quietly pricked the bubble of our growing conceit. She coined the expression B.L.G. – Bruce-Lockhart Genius – not as praise, but as a warning that we should never think we were so good at something that we didn't need to work hard at it. She would hear one of us say something mildly conceited, raise an eyebrow and say "Watch it, John ... B.L.G. again". Years later my eldest daughter heard her use the expression and imagined that mum really thought her sons had natural genius, and was naturally indignant as she (Jenny) had a closer and more realistic view! It also gave her an exaggerated inferiority complex: unjustified, because she had very different and sometimes more important gifts. My nephew Jamie has written about the 'indoctrination' of our Clan get-togethers. I think that the fact that we joked about it showed that we didn't take it all too seriously. But family success remained our top priority.

Chapter Twelve
Sedbergh

At the age of 13 I was sent to Sedbergh, which had been Dad's old school. It was my first experience of boarding, and I was still something of a Fotherington-Thomas, frightened of big rough boys and unsympathetic to those who might not share my enthusiasm for butterflies, flowers, classical music and French. Sedbergh had a reputation as a tough school, supposedly sending its pupils out to run up Winder (a 1550 foot fell dominating the school) every morning before breakfast, and being unbeatable at rugby, because the rainfall was so high that no visiting team ever mastered playing on mud with a ball as slippery as a bar of soap.

It was some time before I settled in. The reputation for before breakfast runs was much exaggerated. The rugby was brilliantly coached by Collison and Brooks. Collison was a small, neat ex-Cambridge blue fly half with wonderful hands and a great gift for making half-breaks which released the centre outside him. Brooks was the ideal man to exploit the space he was given. Tall and long striding, he had deceptive acceleration and was a difficult man to tackle. Although for my first two years I did not shine particularly, I suddenly grew six inches in a year and fell in love with games, to the detriment of my art and music, which I regretted later, broke the record for shot putting, knocked down my former tormentor and started to enjoy school again.

I had not enjoyed those first two years – I was bullied, not successful in my school work and fed up with cold baths every morning (later abolished by Michael Thornely on the advice of the school doctor!). The Headmaster, G.B. Smith was unwell and getting near retirement and he had let the discipline get out of hand, although I believe he had been a good Head for most of his time. I came across a certain amount of homosexuality, which disgusted me (I suppose nobody is allowed to be disgusted now). Homosexuality and bullying are an ever present danger in single sex boarding schools, more dangerous in prep schools. I have been a governor of three prep schools and one public school. In all three of the prep schools, one of the masters was found to have been taking advantage of his position to seduce not one, but several boys under 13. There should be no delay or hesitation about bringing these cases to the notice of the police and sacking the offenders. But there must be certain proof, and to take action on suspicion only was difficult. It is a minefield in which the Head is quite likely to be the sufferer, but also in which an innocent master can have his career ruined by a boy making false accusations. In no case should the children involved be regarded as in any way guilty, as they might once have been.

Chapter Thirteen
Bullying

Bullying has always been the biggest threat to the excellence of boarding schools: it is the fear of every parent and the major problem facing every Head. Although in girls' schools it seldom finds expression in physical aggression, it is often more subtly unpleasant and just as widely prevalent. It is not directly connected with homosexuality, but is often indirectly linked to it.

In single sex boys' schools it is often most common between 14 and 13 year olds, or between 15 and 14 year olds, although it may happen at any stage. The older pupil is usually uncertain of his newly acquired virility. He is frightened of not being 'in' with the majority. Eager to try to gain popularity, he looks around for a victim who is unpopular – because he is different and defenceless against the gang, and sets about transferring the unpopularity he fears for himself to the weaker boy. The 'gang' consists of an age group, which acquires a pecking order soon after arrival at the school. Much depends on the character of the leader: a good Housemaster will identify him and make a point of cultivating him and combatting the bullying through him. The victim is liable to be anyone obviously vulnerable: a few boys seem to be irresistible magnets attracting unkindness. A nasty nickname is attached to them, any unusual habit is studied and mocked until their life becomes a misery. In a very good school it may be rare; but, given the nature of teenagers in a crowd, any Head claiming that he has completely eradicated it is being extremely rash.

To combat this the Head should make it the primary duty of every Housemaster, House Tutor, and, above all, Prefect to ensure that every case comes to light and is nipped in the bud. Boys should have the reasons explained to them, particularly at the beginning of their school career and when they become Prefects. A close relationship between the Housemaster and the top of the pecking order can go far to reduce the risk.

The best cures are privacy, busy enthusiasms, and above all co-education. The reduction in the number of day rooms and open dormitories was a huge step forward. A pupil must have a private study, where he can pursue his own interests without being overlooked continually, and he is free from gang pressure.

Enthusiasms leave no space to be filled by being a bully or a victim.

Co-education provides an almost complete answer: the experience of most co-educational schools is that manners, kindness and every form of civilization – music, art, drama – improve out of all recognition.

Curiously enough, there is another form of bullying to which I have not referred. The bullying of masters by their pupils. Nearly every single sex boarding ex-pupil can remember examples of teachers who were singled out for ruthless and brutal 'ragging'. It may have been fun at the time, but it ruined the careers, the happiness and the lives of many teachers – often because of insignificant eccentricities.

Nor should it be thought that bullying is confined to schools. The Big Wide World has firms and organizations, where the bullying is just as sinister and unpleasant. Human beings, when confined in a group, are unfortunately prone to beating down the weak. And we should not forget that some of the nastiest cases occur in the home and on the street.

It was just when I was beginning to enjoy life at Sedbergh that a thunderbolt landed. Dad was appointed Headmaster. That is always a hard situation for both! I think Dad handled matters quite well, but I always felt I could be open to the charge, if I scored any notable success, of being favoured by the Head man.

Dad quickly set about putting things straight, good order and enthusiasms were not long in arriving, but his ambitious plans for change were made difficult by the outbreak of war. The good young teachers nearly all joined the armed forces, although teaching was initially a 'reserved occupation'. Replacements of quality were hard to find. The supply of builders ran out too, and domestic help was almost impossible to find with a munitions factory not far away. Rationing of food and clothes provided yet more difficulties, as did the rationing of fuel, with many parents having to travel long distances. Central heating was limited and the dormitories cold. There were even worse epidemics than usual: whooping cough, flu, chickenpox, measles and mumps. As the war went on the school doctor decreed that the rations did not supply enough vitamins to combat these diseases, and that everybody should take supplements during the 11 a.m. break: Radio Malt and Virol. All this placed a heavy burden on my mum, who was responsible for domestic service, catering and clothing, and also had to cook if the cook didn't turn up, and darn all the socks and do the job of nurse and matron for School House.

I remember vividly how mum and dad and the four of us turned on the radiogram and listened to the announcement that war had been declared. All of us were thinking of the horrors of the First World War, and wondering how many of us would survive. It was a grim prospect.

Another difficulty followed the declaration of war. There was an outbreak of pacifism among the staff – understandable, because their generation had been brought up on the horrific accounts of mass slaughter on the Western Front; the war memorial in the Sedbergh School chapel had more names on it than there were boys in the school. The life expectancy of a young subaltern going to the front had been not more than three weeks – my uncle Norman, aged 19, only lasted two.

Pacifism was understandable. But trying to spread opposition to the 1939–45 war against Germany among the boys brought objections from some parents, and Dad decided to support their views. A difficult situation, and it brought resignations from two of the most prominent pacifists. It is hard to know retrospectively if it was right. I think it was a matter for families and their children to decide rather than teachers.

There were still, in spite of the war, some outstanding masters at Sedburgh. Collison and Brooks were great coaches, and, a little later, Hammer was a German teacher of legendary efficiency. Sumner was a wise Headmaster, and Crawford helped my squash. Ward had a rare ability to make Maths clear. Coldham was a good cricket coach, Christopherson and Chawner were memorable performers in Gilbert and Sullivan. Art and Music were always strong. First MacCurragh then Cowan and his beautiful wife set the highest standards. Lyons Wilson was a fine landscape painter. In a rather elderly staff Len Taylor was one of those schoolmasters who seem never to be young or old: stuck at about 45 for ever. Ray Cooper provided youth and enthusiasm.

Carl Bishop was teaching German under Steinberg. He was no great scholar, but a modest, kindly and thoroughly nice person. He invited a few of the Sixth Formers into his house in the evenings, where we read and discussed Goethe's 'Faust' over a glass of cider by the fireside. I have loved Goethe ever since, and we were hugely grateful for those evenings. Dear old Bill Gairdner, teaching Sixth Form French, was a far better scholar, but was occasionally not on the same wave length as the rugby hearties. We were delighted, however, when he asked us home, where we were enthralled by his very gifted wife's playing of Chopin.

This informal interplay of staff and boys was a notable strength of Sedbergh - and still is. I believe it is the most important part of education: it teaches the 'spirit of the extra mile' and makes the difference between a community with a life long influence and a mere school.

Among my rugby playing contemporaries I was lucky to have as my scrum half Arthur Dorward, who, like me, played for Scotland later, as did his brother Tom with my brother Rab. Willie Wood was a fast wing forward, who joined me later at London Scottish. John Leybourne was another robust forward, who remained a good friend. Birtwhistle proved to be an outstanding number eight and Pat MacSwiney a fine wing three-quarter.

Nearly 60 years after that great school side I was amused by a letter from the Archbishop of Westminster, Basil Hulme, enclosing his book 'Basil in

Blunderland'. It said: "In the closing years of my life, there is one sin from my past for which I find it hard to forgive myself. I was wing forward for Ampleforth [he was later to be their coach], and I was too slow to break from the scrum in the closing minutes, thus allowing you to drop the goal that cost us the match." A delightful man, and a great enthusiast.

I often wonder what has been the reason for Sedbergh's astonishing success at rugby football – now (2009–2012) better than ever. I think that dad's insistence on practising individual skills was something to do with it. He didn't leave the acquisition of a dummy to chance. We had to practise it with two attackers and one defender. A decision had to be made by the ball carrier, whether he was to pass or sell a dummy. The defender made his own decision as to whether he was going to tackle the ball carrier or the recipient of his pass. It takes repeated practice to learn exactly when and where the ball carrier must make up his mind. All the details of technique must be right if you are to sell the dummy. You must not snatch the ball back too quickly after extending your arms towards the recipient, you must raise your thumbs and keep your head towards him. You must simultaneously time your side-step and accelerate, neither too early nor too late – and practise repeatedly against different defenders. It was the same with kicks: if you try 1000 times to kick with your 'wrong' foot, you can. If you try only 100 times, you think you can, but you can't.

It seems that Sedbergh went on finding great coaches ever since then. For a school of less than 400 there was always a surprising strength in depth. The second XV, strengthened by a couple of highly skilled staff, could usually be relied on to give the first XV a very close test and was usually unbeaten against other schools. There were good coaches for the under 16's and under 15's as well as some savagely contested House matches: too savagely, because some comparatively frail players were caught in the clash of the Titans and were injured.

I was invited to speak at the Sedbergh Speech Day by Chris Hirst, when, a few years ago, he had just persuaded the school to go co-ed. I can only think he asked an over 80 year old because I had taken that brave step myself, and he knew that I had become a great supporter of the idea. A substantial number of Old Sedberghians were afraid that their great rugby tradition would suffer. I reassured them, telling them that the rugby would actually benefit from the presence of admiring girls. About four years after the arrival of girls, we at Gresham's had had an unbeaten season and were declared 'Rugby World's' school team of the month. My prophecy was right: a few years after Sedbergh went co-ed they had three successive wonderful years, which enabled them to add to their forty international players.

I don't know what role the Sedbergh school songs still play in their traditions. We had to learn them by heart as new boys, and there were three that we used to enjoy singing: a little like the New Zealanders' Haka, though we did not actually sing before the matches to intimidate opponents. On the occasion of their ten mile cross country run we sang:

"At Olympia far away in the boyhood of the world
There were glorious games they say
Discs were thrown and spears were hurled
Came the athletes strong and stately
Leapt and ran and wrestled greatly
While a nation stood and wondered
And a shout to Heaven was thundered . . .
Strain and struggle might and main,
Scorn defeat and laugh at pain,
Never shall you strive in vain
In the long run."

The rugby song had a thumping rhythm to it:

"Charge like an elephant
Run like a stag,
Grapple and hug like a bear.
Keep cool, never scrag,
Keep warm, never flag,
Play fearlessly, Browns, play fair.
Though bespattered with mud
And bedabbled with blood
And never a man of you whole,
Bear them away like the Rawthey in flood,
Sweep them away to the goal!
Chorus Play up bonny Browns
For House and for cup
For the fame of the school, play up!
Never say die, make it a try
Carry it through to the goal line."

and finally 'Winder'

O Eton hath her river
And Clifton hath her down,
And Winchester her cloister
And immemorial town . . .
But ours the mountain fastness,
The deep romantic ghylls,

Where Clough and Dee and Rawthey
Come singing from the hills.
For it isn't our ancient lineage,
There are others as old as we;
And it isn't our pious founders,
Though we honour their memory.
'Tis the hills that have stood around us,
Unchanged since our day began;
It's Cautley, Calf and Winder
That make the Sedbergh man!

Most writers recall the many discomforts of their school life in grisly detail: insanitary conditions, bad food, cold dormitories, harsh punishments, continual infections and epidemics. Except for a brief period of bullying, none of those things loom large in my memory, perhaps because there was so much fun and games, and because I was not very sensitive to those inconveniences. 'Dura virum nutrix' was Sedbergh's motto: 'stern nurse of man.' Conditions probably were fairly hard: it didn't worry most of us, and I have never fussed about comfort since!

I am not sure how many Old Sedberghians confessed to taking these songs seriously. The British have become easily embarrassed by unashamed heartiness, and it is so easily mocked. But we were less cynical in the Thirties, and I think that, among many rather silly traditions which Dad got rid of, this was one that I am glad he kept.

Rather silly traditions? Such as the number of blazer buttons you had to do up depending on the number of terms you had been in the school. Such as the parade of juniors in the common room before prep; they had to stand in a row, with the books they were going to work from or with balanced on their heads. If any boy had forgotten his book or didn't know what prep he was supposed to do, he would be hit on the head by a prefect with a large book (usually the Bible) and set some work.

Even allowing for the fact that corporal punishment was almost universally accepted in all schools and by all parents, I had some doubts by the time I left school about the wisdom of extending its use to the prefects. Not that I was greatly worried – it was generally administered for ragging in the dormitories after lights out, or leaving the house during prep time. Three strokes for a lesser offence, six for a repeated or major offence. It was generally fair, quickly over and the result you expected if you were found out. But I now realise that for some sensitive people it can be a real ordeal. Although I didn't come across it at Sedbergh, there is always the possibility that there may have been cases of sadism and abuse.

It is a strange fact that few of us can escape the fashion changes of public opinion. Until about 1969 almost all schools had corporal punishment. The student revolution and the psychologists gradually persuaded schools that there were other, better ways of establishing discipline in schools as well as in homes. The difficulty was that many schools abandoned it without giving enough thought to what should take its place. Some decided that neither punishment nor rewards and prizes were justified. I began to give pupils the choice between being beaten and going into an extra period of work on a half-holiday. Then my decision to go co-ed solved the problem for me: I didn't fancy caning a girl, and the school was becoming good enough to make it superfluous in any case. But I'm still old-fashioned enough to believe in punishment and rewards, although within a minimal framework of rules. There is now no doubt in my mind that caning was misguided, although the horrific picture of misuse painted by its opponents was exaggerated.

A custom at Sedbergh which I disliked was sending us on house runs when conditions were too wet or cold for rugby. The whole house had to run between 3 and 6 miles in driving rain, hail or snow. I've always been heavy for my size, long backed and short legged. Although fairly fast over 100 yards and very quick over 30, fell running was not my thing. Small, weedy boys would pass me with effortless ease. I developed a protective theory that those lengthy runs – let alone the famous 10 mile run over the fells – would harm my acceleration on the rugby field. Even in my fifties I would dream that a red-haired boy called Campbell was sailing past me on the last corner. It may have been something to do with the long hatred between my MacGregor forebears and the murderous Campbells. It was rumoured that when my Uncle Rob MacGregor Lockhart married Madge Campbell, few people came to the wedding: Highlanders have long memories!

I have not explained why I came to love Sedbergh. Although I remember 12 inches of rain in the first week of one October, when the sun shone it was an enchanting place. It often shone in May and June and sometimes in September. We were from time to time given extra half holidays in fine weather. We escaped regularly on Sundays, and in the holidays, to watch peregrine falcons on Black Force or buzzards and ravens at Cautley, or to climb the Calf and clamber down beside the spectacular waterfall near Cautley. We refreshed ourselves with huge slices of ham and eggs plus a glass of sweet red Vimto at the isolated Cross Keys pub. The four local rivers, Lune, Rawthey, Dee and Clough, all provided trout fishing and wonderful bathing. The Rawthey's banks were lined with buttercup, kingcup, bluebell woods and meadows; grey wagtails, dippers and sandpipers abounded. My naughty nephew Sandy, later to be knighted and then elevated to the peerage as Baron Sandy of the Weald, used to escape from his house at night and poach salmon from the Lune ... Poachers always did make the best gamekeepers!

Sedbergh was emphatically not the place to meet girls. It did nothing to correct my lop-sided upbringing in an all male family and all male schools. The nearest girls' school was beyond the reach of even the most ardent walkers. My three older brothers had given me glimpses of girlfriends, but these were distant, if beautiful untouchables. A fishing holiday in Ireland landed me at the age of 13 in a hotel, in which the bathrooms were divided from each other by frosted glass. I discovered that the glass separating me from a girl of roughly similar age having her bath next door had an inconspicuous crack, which enabled me to have a good look without revealing my presence. It was the first time that I had had the opportunity to see the precise difference between male and female ... my sudden passion for cleanliness ought to have alerted Mum and Dad, but it didn't. On reflection it is not quite true that it was my first glimpse.

Marie de Montoussé, who looked after the four of us, when we were between 12 and 17 and she was 19, was a remarkable person, and some time later secretary to the French Ambassador. She introduced me to the love of strange fungi and told me thrilling goodnight stories as well as improving all our French. On one occasion she took us all to poach a great trout loch, while the owner was attending Kirk on the Sabbath. Her method was to attach a 3 fly cast to the back of a toy yacht, and she thought nothing of completely stripping in order to rescue the yacht, which had got stuck in the reeds. It made a memorable impression on the four of us, although I believed, perhaps naïvely, her motives were entirely innocent!

It was inevitable that, when my uncle, General Sir Rob, entrusted his very attractive daughter, Betty, one year younger than me, to my parents, so that they could look after her, while he was fighting on the North West frontier, I should fall in love with her. After a few weeks of desperate but unrequited 17 year old passion, we were firmly told that between first cousins it was NOT ON. We were parted, and only ever saw each other once again. Thirty years later, when we met again, she was married, curiously enough, to an officer of the Life Guards (my regiment during the war). He was a good squash player. They had three children and she died of cancer at a sadly early age. My mum thought she was a wicked schemer seeking to lead her innocent lamb astray. In fact I believe she was quite as inexperienced and bewildered as I. We held hands, danced and kissed and, as first loves know, it hurt a lot at the time...

Sedbergh remained my home and base, until I was fully employed and my dad retired. On leaving school I tried to join up and registered for army service, but was told that I was too young and should put in a year at Cambridge first. I had been accepted at St. John's College and given a choral scholarship. But that still left a gap of 6 or 7 months with no specific job. Together with my brother Paddy, who, like me, was waiting for a job, we decided to answer an appeal for volunteers to work on farms to replace agricultural workers, who had already joined up. Extra food was already needed because of the shortages caused by the increasing U-boat campaign. They called it 'digging for victory'.

Chapter Fourteen
Rigmaden Farm

We looked back on our time at Rigmaden Farm as one of the most valuable lessons of our lives. Right from the start Paddy and I knew it would be no bed of roses. The farmer was some 60 years old and as strong as a gorilla. He had a very attractive wife of 20. There were two farm labourers, too old to join the forces. There was no machinery. Milking was done by hand, and horse and cart took on any job now done by tractors and harvesters. The two labourers might have been any age between 35 and 55; they were smaller than us, slim and weatherbeaten. They were men of few words, and, when they spoke, it was in a dialect so broad that Pad and I couldn't understand more than a word here and there, although brought up to hear a ripe combination of Yorkshire and Cumbrian accents. The old farmer took one glance at our white hands and young faces and grunted. You could see he was wondering what sort of creatures the crazy government had inflicted on him. Relationships were not improved by his instinctive dislike of our posh accents and our tendency to use long words and unfamiliar expressions. Very soon he made it plain he was going to get the best possible value for money out of us.

We started the day at 6 a.m., one of us mucking out the cow byre and milking, the other catching the uncooperative horse in a vast paddock, harnessing it to the cart and starting the main day's work. There was a short break for a very good breakfast, and another at one o'clock. Rook and pigeon pie, prepared by the old man's wife was a welcome reprieve from scything the prickly barley, stacking and binding it, loading it in hundredweight sacks onto the cart, climbing up a ladder with the sacks and emptying them into the loft. Alternatively we were set to weed 400 yard long rows of mangolds or pick potatoes. It is surprising how much skill some of it demanded. No-one showed us how to catch a horse, which always seemed to be in the most remote corner of the field, and how to harness it. Tolstoy wrote movingly about the pleasure of scything in rhythmical unison at harvest time. We were young, strong and fit, but after 10 hours or so we were exhausted. The two professionals, half our size and strength, managed it with enviable ease. The old man, although he didn't work with us, showed us how he flicked two hundredweight sacks over his shoulders without any of the bending and struggling that we found necessary. Just try it!

Anyway we got a good late meal. The farmer's wife was not above giving us flirtatious looks, but we were too tired and too scared of the old man to respond. I remember being woken up by Paddy in the middle of the night. He was stacking his pillows on the floor, half asleep. A couple of years later, I was doing a 36 mile competitive route march at Sandhurst, and carrying a bren gun in addition to the usual heavy equipment. It was a piece of cake, compared with Rigmaden. Paddy and I both agreed, when reminiscing about it in our old age, that it was the hardest work we had ever experienced. When I hear anyone criticize farmers or say they wish they had taken it up, words fail me. But times change, and modern farming, if hardly a doddle, is not so physically demanding.

For this we were paid 7 shillings and 6 pence a day. At the end of the week, we had a Saturday night break and went down to the village pub. There the old boy played an unusual variety of dominoes, of which only he knew the rules. He always won and Pad and I had to buy the drinks: in his case double scotches. Goodbye 7 shillings and sixpence. The old boy had to be supported between us for the walk back and, on one occasion, even carried up to bed.

When we had finished our spell we went down to the pub for a last time. He actually paid for the drinks, winked at us and said: "Tha didn't work sae bad after all." We have never valued a compliment so highly.

Chapter Fifteen
Cambridge

Cambridge was the next stop, although I knew it would be interrupted by military service. In early war time the whole country had changed. All the young, male or female, were waiting to join the forces or munition factories, and watching to see what turn the war would take next. There was the rape of Czechoslovakia, the evacuation from France in Dunkirk, which even Churchill's oratory could not quite present as a victory. Then the humiliation of France. This was followed by the excitement of the Battle of Britain. For the spectators in the south, it was a thrilling experience although, for the young pilots, the odds on survival were fairly thin. It took the place of the score in the suspended Test matches, and, even if the score was sometimes a shade exaggerated, it was much more reliable than Germany's version and a considerable morale booster. It gradually dawned on us that the U-Boat campaign was causing serious problems. The casualties at sea became increasingly serious and rationing became very restrictive.

But morale was extraordinarily high. There was a togetherness which was never repeated after the war. Young men and women were freed from the rather severe social restrictions of the Thirties, and the girls, especially, revelled in their freedom. Everyone felt they were serving a good cause. Hitch-hiking was universal, and we never heard of any abuse of the practice, which has made it so dangerous today, when the price of fuel ought to make it a near necessity.

Cambridge University was, as ever, overwhelming in its beauty. Its history and elegance made us feel very small. In the first years of the war, however, it was not the distinguished centre of learning that it was in peace time. Most of the young Dons had joined the forces or had been offered jobs in intelligence. The students knew that their studies would be interrupted and, brought up on the horrific accounts of World War I, thought that it was likely that they would not survive. For them it was "Eat, drink and be merry, for tomorrow we die". The best of the Dons were putting their minds to solving the problems of how to win the war. The old ones were called upon to work after the retirement age to take their places.

I played games, joined the choir, punted on the river and got to know some remarkable people. Not all the Dons had abandoned their students, but it was the undergraduates who influenced me most. I did not spend much time chasing girls; there were only two ladies' colleges: Girton, whose undergraduates had the reputation (probably unjust) of being blue stockinged, virtuous and scholarly, and Newnham, which was thought to be a refuge for insufferably 'jolly hockey-sticks' girls of aristocratic background. The competition for the attractive ones was fierce. Cambridge men outnumbered the girls by over ten times. Even my dear friend Sandy Smith, whose good looks and popularity with the female sex were legendary, had a rest from womanising, although it was only a case of "Reculer pour mieux sauter".

Some great Dons were left. There was Pat Charvet who lectured in French or French literature and commanded a big audience. Dr. Knight introduced me to Nietzsche and was both amusing and instructive. Frank Thistlethwaite, later Vice-chancellor of the University of East Anglia, took the trouble to get to know his undergraduates. Charlesworth was reported to time his boiled egg every morning by the time it took him to finish 'The Times' crossword, and swam a few lengths every day, during which the long lock of hair (with which he concealed his baldness by arranging it in a double circle) gradually unwound. It streamed out behind him like a tow rope.

It was a sad indictment of our undergraduate frivolity that we did not always treat our Dons with due seriousness. There was an elderly lady of considerable distinction and with a profound knowledge of 16th and 17th Century French religious literature. She had written some authoritative books. Her lectures were the best attended of all. To begin with I couldn't understand why, because she had such a soft voice that a only a few, seated directly in front of her lectern, could hear a word she said. I was soon enlightened as to the reason. She had an extraordinary habit of periodically telling a joke in some rare language – usually Provençal, Basque or Catalan – which was quite incomprehensible to her audience; she would then lean forward, smile contentedly, and say, loud and clear, "Watha". What this meant, or why she did it, we never found out. However, nearly all her modern language students were involved in a high stake betting operation, based on the number of "Wathas" there would be in each lecture. I hope she never discovered the reason for the popularity of her lectures.

Partly through my fault, partly through the lack of any advice from the tutors and supervisors about how to spend my time and organize my work, I largely wasted this first year. My supervisor for German was Dr. Brock: a dear but excessively Teutonic and slightly peculiar man. He took three of us every week for an hour-and-a-half. The other two were Wilfred Brown the wonderful tenor who later became famous for his performances in the Bach passions and as an interpreter of Schubert's "Schöne Müllerin" and "Winterreise".

Not a big voice, but sweet and flexible and squeezing the last drop of meaning out of the words. He was a true romantic, easily moved: he once told me that he re-read Goethe's best selling 'Werther' every year, and that it still always reduced him to tears. The other was a very nice but rather shy man, whose name I shall not record as he surprised us all by committing suicide shortly afterwards. Dr. Brock never set us work, or gave us any advice, or asked us for any of our opinions. He seldom strayed far from his favourite subject: Immanuel Kant, on whom he was a world expert. Unfortunately he never succeeded in conveying his unique understanding of that complex and difficult philosopher. He would stand, eyes closed in ecstasy, musically declaiming page after page of Kant's 'critique of pure reason'. We did our best to follow his thought, but none of us could make much sense of the seemingly endless thirty-line sentences in which he concealed his apparently vital lessons to the world. Nor did we have any explanation from Dr. Brock, whose only communication with us was to welcome us, invite us to sit down, and then declaim. He ended an hour later by smiling at us and saying "Goodnight, gentlemen. Was that not the most beautiful thing you have ever heard?"

It soon transpired that Dr. Brock was having a mental breakdown, because of a persecution complex. He thought that, as a German in war time, he was the intended victim of a racist plot. I'm sure that he received nothing but kindness in Cambridge, but he had to be taken to a mental hospital after a few weeks.

When I returned to Cambridge after the war I found that I had again been allocated to his care. Sadly it was again only a short time before he suffered a relapse and returned to the mental hospital . . . I hope that this was not linked to my return and my continued inability to understand Kant's philosophy!

Chapter Sixteen
Sandhurst

My education was interrupted by an answer to my request to join the army, and I exchanged my course at Cambridge for Sandhurst, which I enjoyed equally. For public schoolboys, accustomed to being away from home and submitting to strict rules, discomfort and plenty of exercise, it was not a strange experience. It gave me a chance to play some rugby for the college and the army. In a way it was a shameful advantage for public schoolboys, because many boys from the state day schools had never left home before and were somewhat bewildered by army life.

Sedbergh, like most independent schools had run a training corps, which had taught us how to shoot and a certain amount of drill. At the beginning of the war I was still at school, when the corps was asked to help the home guard in hunting for a German parachutist, who had supposedly landed near Garsdale a few miles from Sedbergh, which was one of the places we knew well from our dreaded house runs. It was, of course, a false alarm, but we spent an amusing night searching the countryside, with live ammunition specially issued to us. It had been more like 'Dad's Army', with more Pikes than Mainwaring's, than Sandhurst.

Work on the farm had been a good preparation for Sandhurst, apart from the spit and polish. The physical demands, which were quite an ordeal for many of the young cadets, were mild compared with the barley harvest at Rigmaden.

How effective Sandhurst was in preparing young adults for leadership in a modern war I am not sure. It taught us quick automatic obedience, how to handle small arms efficiently, how to use cover and camouflage and to be smart on parade. But it was still based on the experience of the First World War, and had not learned the lessons of Blitzkrieg techniques from Germany: it was of more use to infantry than to future armoured regiment officers. I owe my survival and that of those under my command to later training.

Nevertheless most of us enjoyed the daily drill on first parade. It is something which the British have always done well, and Sandhurst can certainly take a lot of the credit for that. Once a week, when we thought we were nearing perfection in every aspect of foot stamping and arms drill, the three company sergeant majors gave a demonstration. It was sheer, beautiful impeccable harmony, such as I have never seen since. When they shouted at our inadequacies later on, we accepted it humbly: they had every right, for they were unquestionably masters of their trade.

Our relation with staff at Sandhurst was quickly and crisply established: "I'm Sir to you, Sir, and you're Sir to me, Sir – and don't you bloody well forget it, Sir."

A sergeant would creep up behind a new cadet. "Am I 'urting you, Sir?" "No, Sir". "Well I bloody well ought to be – your 'air is so long that I'm treading on it!" My favourite quote came from that most formidable of men, the Regimental Sergeant Major, who took the young officers on a refreshment course on drill to keep them on their toes. "Mister my Lord Marquis Blandford, Sir, you're marching like a ruptured rook, Sir!" It encapsulated the whole class system of the Forties so neatly!

While the drill sergeants were getting on with first parade, Major Tom Hardy walked up and down, watching, followed by a batman with his three white Pekingese dogs.

Chapter Seventeen

Sherwood Foresters

While we were at Sandhurst we had to make up our minds what kind of unit we wanted to join. Various officers came down trying to recruit for their regiments. Family traditions were pulling me toward Highland regiments (the Seaforths, the Argyll and Sutherland Highlanders, the Cameronians etc.). My French and German might have given me some advantage in an Intelligence role.

The Highland Regiments seemed to need infantry, which I did not fancy greatly. Nor was I attracted by the prospect of spending the war interrogating German prisoners and translating documents. I was attracted by the eloquent picture Colonel Juby Lancaster M.P. presented of his newly formed armoured reconnaissance regiment, the 9th Sherwood Foresters. The men and officers were mostly from the mining district near Nottingham. There was a sprinkling of horsey officers from the racing world to keep up a pretence of cavalry traditions. He explained the role that a modern armoured reconnaissance unit would play, leading the way after a break-through. My languages would be useful and they would teach me all the mechanical skills necessary. It sounded very exciting. It would, he said, need quick decisions, there wasn't time to be afraid. You would be in a safe harbour area at night. As a troop commander, you made all the decisions after contact was established, and you would be the first to make contact with the enemy every day you were on duty. I liked him, he seemed to like me, so when I left Sandhurst I joined the Sherwood Foresters near Mansfield and stayed with them, training for the next two or three years.

A troop consisted of two large Daimler turreted armoured cars and two smaller scout cars. I knew as little about engines and mechanics as I knew about horses, but enjoyed learning. I had had a little experience of driving at Sandhurst, but mainly on motor bikes. My first lesson on motor cycles had been a disaster. My instructor had shown me clutch, brakes and gears and told me to follow him. He took me on paths, which wound their way through the

Sandhurst Woods. He suddenly disappeared round a blind corner. I accelerated instead of slowing down and hit an old man standing by the side of the track. I hit a tree, dismounted and picked up the unfortunate victim who was heavily bleeding. It was the instructor who was punished, not me – evidently those forest paths were out of bounds! The old man recovered surprisingly quickly, but it was not a good start to my driving career!

My training took me to Bovington for driving and maintenance instruction. In Pembroke I learned about gunnery, from stationary positions and on the move, for two-pounder guns and the Besa 792 machine guns, which were co-axially mounted in our turrets. Then to Yorkshire (Pickering, Moulton and Knaresborough) to practise tactics, use of smoke, troop control and use of wireless. Then to Weymouth, where another officer, called Primrose-Wells, and I experimented with methods of waterproofing armoured cars sufficiently well for them to drive ashore from landing craft in three feet of sea water in case of need. I never found out Primrose-Wells' first name, because he was never called anything else but Petal.

We worked in a garage all morning, fitting waterproof bags round electric parts and sealing the rest with a variety of materials. The exhaust pipe was extended upwards like a periscope. In the afternoon we took the armoured car down to the beach and drove around in three or four feet of sea water. Then we would take it for an hour or so's drive to see whether it had survived without damage. Sometimes it stopped; if there had been a small leak, we had to trace the trouble and put it right. If we were successful we drove to a pub to celebrate . . .

My penultimate course was in Croydon with R.E.M.E (The Royal Electrical and Mechanical Engineers) for a more advanced course on mending and driving armoured cars. I had to tackle all the repairs that could be rectified after damage by mines or enemy fire. I don't think the major in charge liked my posh accent, and he seemed to take a special delight in seeing me doing the oiliest jobs. But I was (to the surprise of my family) awarded a grade one pass in driving and maintenance. I was better at tackling exams than tracing faults, but eventually knew my stuff. Croydon was, for some reason, the target for a heavy attack by V.1's and V.2's, so I was quite happy to spend a large part of the day under nine tons of armour. They did a lot of damage, but I didn't find them very frightening. V.1's were clearly visible as small short-winged fighter planes. Before they exploded, the engines shut off, and they plunged to earth continuing in a straight line. You could tell where they were going to land. If it was anywhere near you, you lay down flat. There was very little chance of you getting a direct hit (most casualties were caused by the collapse of buildings); armoured cars were the right places to be.

V.2's caused yet more damage, but weren't frightening, because you couldn't hear or see their approach and were either blown up or not. Worrying about them would make no difference.

My last posting before the invasion was to Kent for a more advanced course on wireless communication, including Morse. It also brought me a phenomenal stroke of luck which changed my life.

Chapter Eighteen

Wild Oats

The time has come to talk about the unscraped corners of the sardine tin of my life. My children, watching me scribble away at something which might end up as an autobiography, do their best to nag me into a pornographic description of my activities during the most disreputable period of my youth. They probably imagine that if a raunchy enough truth emerges, they will profit from good sales after my death. I, on the other hand, have too much Scottish blood in me to like confessions. My upbringing made me ashamed of parading the details of what I still regard as my weaknesses. I think of all the autobiographies I have read. Hardly any wrote well about their sexual encounters. Gloating about "successes" is cruel and undignified, shedding romantic tears about "failures" boring. To mention names is a breach of trust. Apologizing for something I enjoyed is hypocritical. To attach a number to one's liaisons smacks of a bad batsman inventing a batting average.

So I will just say that my days with the Sherwood Foresters provided me with more than one kind of training in many different parts of England. I am not proud of it; but the idea of the Great Sin no longer prevented me from great sinning.

Although not good at gloating or apologizing, I am tolerably good at making excuses. Britain was ablaze with girls straight from school or university, completely free and independent. They took advantage of their early escape from ultra respectable parents. They were eager to comfort males, who thought they might only have weeks, months or a year or two to live. There was tremendous excitement in the air: impending battles are notorious aphrodisiacs. There has seldom been a time when temptation was greater. It was easy come, easy go. We clung to each other as the irresistible current swept us towards our Niagara. There were seldom any long range intentions, because we felt there was no future.

So much for the excuses. 'Je ne regrette rien', except for having upset one or two relations who found out enough to disapprove.

For the sake of my children I will describe one rather unsuccessful adventure which took place when I was with Petal. It was, in the often quoted words, a long time ago, and the wench is long since dead. Petal had a most attractive blonde, curvaceous girl friend, whom we called H.M.S. Juno, because she was in the WRENS. One day she turned up in the flat for a date with Petal, only to find that he wasn't in and I was. We got on surprisingly well and were just in the process of undressing, when we heard Petal drive up to the door. Luckily the loo was half way up the stairs, and Petal stopped to pay a call. It just gave us time to reorganize our clothing. Though we must have looked flushed and dishevelled, I still don't know whether Petal had his suspicions, but certainly Juno put up a dazzling bit of acting the innocent. I never saw her again, but years later, when I was safely married with two children, I got a letter: "What do you do when you're not playing rugby? I am to be found on Saturday nights in the Bag of Nails." – signed H.M.S. Juno. I am proud to say I was not tempted to accept the invitation . . . well, not very much.

During this hectic time I still found time to play in a few of the war time games. International matches were suspended, but there were some inter-forces games that were of very high quality because there were lots of good players around. I remember some unusual and exciting matches. I played fly half for the army, notably in the last match in which Gus Walker figured, who had played fly half for England. He was to lose an arm rescuing a pilot from a burning plane, and became Air Chief Marshall Sir Augustus Walker, a much loved and feared figure. Small for an international, but neat and nippy, with lovely hands. I got to know Gus quite well later, as he too settled in Norfolk. He and I used to get invited to the same rugby club dinners, and he refereed a lot of matches in the East. On one occasion, when neither of us was in our first youth, we were invited to the very hospitable West Norfolk rugby club's dinner. I was to toast the game of rugby, and Gus the West Norfolk club. Gus was an amusing speaker, but on this occasion he must have had one or two too many. He puzzled his rugby playing audience by telling a number of golfing stories. We knew he was a good golfer in spite of only having one arm. The reason was revealed when he wound up his speech by inviting us to raise our glasses to "the West Norfolk Golf Club!"

I partnered Hadyn Tanner, the great pre-war Welsh scrum half, for a war time Barbarians side against Leicester: a lovely experience. Another exciting match was the only occasion on which the Rugby Union played the Rugby League. It was played under compromise rules: a very close game with high scoring on both sides. For the army against, I think, the R.A.F., I achieved my best kicks ever: two penalties from inside my own half. We (the army) also played the New Zealand forces in England – and lost! It was a lot of fun and many of the players who survived the war kept in touch for some years.

Chapter Nineteen
Travel by Train

In about March 1944 it became clear that the day for the invasion of France could not be far away. I was given a few days' leave after the devastating news that Monty had decided to take only one armoured car regiment, and that it would be the 2nd Household Cavalry and not the Sherwood Foresters. We were disbanded without being given any advice or help as to where we might find a berth. We felt very bitter – was all that training going to be wasted? We thought we had become highly skilled and could have done a great job. I had been on the verge of being promoted, but had to give up that idea and find someone who would let me start again in some other sphere. I still didn't fancy a job at Supreme Headquarters, but, by a stroke of luck, got offered a job as a troop commander with the Household Cavalry, who had been chosen for the invasion by Monty. I would initially be a reserve, but would be called on at the first vacancy. That was a polite way of saying the first casualty.

I got a week's leave and said goodbye to my parents as I was unlikely to see them again before D. Day. I returned to my new quarters in Kent. The crowded troop train left Oxenholme in a depressing, drizzly fog. Everybody seemed to be smoking, and there was little space. Barging my way down the corridor looking for a seat, I saw a vacant seat in a first class carriage opposite an extraordinarily pretty girl in a smart civvy suit. She had amazing eyes and legs which seemed to go on for ever. Although she was sitting next to a dragonly lady, who I took to be an aunt or a chaperone, who looked at me with obvious disapproval, I sat down. I was dressed in my new cavalry uniform and looking distinctly less scruffy than usual. I was getting tired of my wild oats period, and I somehow knew that this was a quite different prospect. I spent the first 50 miles wondering how I could establish contact, only managing a few words and a little careful, mainly silent flirtation. I was desperate not to let her get out of my life. At last I could restrain myself no longer. I happened to be reading Rupert Brooke's 'Grantchester' and saw her glancing at it. Greatly daring, I underlined some passages, and passed the book over to her saying: "These are my favourite lines, what are yours?"

Was that the origin of the expression "shooting a line"? I felt as though my whole future depended on her reaction. To my huge relief she accepted the book. After a swift perusal she underlined a few passages and wrote a few observations ... she returned it, and, to my delight, had written her name, Jo Agnew, address and telephone number. From Crewe to Liverpool Street we talked, regardless of the scowling dragon (who, it turned out, was her Godmother) and a fascinated group of travellers.

My impertinence was rewarded by the Powers That Be. By a bizarre stroke of luck she was posted to the same small town as me. We fell deeply in love. She was one year younger than me, and on the rebound from an unhappy relationship to an officer to whom she had been engaged, but who was sent to New Zealand, from where he wrote without warning, that he had married someone else. She was a high speed morse expert in the W.A.A.F.s. Within weeks we were married. 64 years later I still fancied her. She always managed, even after 50, to look at least 15 years younger than she was. When she was well past 40 and had given birth to five children, I was hugely proud to overhear two Cambridge undergraduates exchange low wolf whistles as she walked past them on the boundary of the cricket field. One said to the other "Phew! Whose bit of totty is THAT?"

What I could not have known was that she would turn out to be kind, artistic, brave in the face of some really grim times, great fun and an amazing mother with a knack of gaining the trust and love of everyone from the domestic cleaners to Peers of the realm.

Some people get the luck they don't deserve!

Chapter Twenty
The War

So far I have only written about war time in Britain. As D. Day got nearer life speeded up and got more and more confusing, exciting and bizarre. The precise date was an astonishingly well kept secret, helped by wild rumours, which may or may not have been deliberately sown.

Three close friends of mine became real heroes. Sandy Smith, who was my neighbour and constant companion at St. John's, got an M.C. for leading his platoon to capture Pegasus Bridge, thus preventing a German armoured division from crossing and attacking our troops on the beaches on D. Day. He was a truly unique character of whom I shall write later. Then there was Robin Robinson, another St. John's friend, who had a great influence on me. The son of working class parents in London he was at one time a communist and a pacifist. He gradually moved towards the centre, did outstandingly well in the academic world, joined Bomber Command and got a D.F.C. for repeated and dangerous raids on Germany. He later became Professor of Modern History at Cambridge, specialising in Imperial History of Africa. The most amazing of the three was Tommy MacPherson, who had been to school with me at Cargilfield, played with me for London Scottish – and then earned 3 M.C.s, a D.S.O., Croix de Guerre, Legion of Honour, two top Italian awards for gallantry, a top Polish medal and a Papal Knighthood, in fabulous exploits behind the enemy line, recorded in his book: 'Behind Enemy Lines'.

I was definitely not a great war hero. But I got some valuable front line experience of what it is like to kill and to be shot at. It was against a generally demoralized and retreating enemy. I am, in retrospect, grateful for the experience. Armoured car warfare is strange, and I think it is worth describing in detail. Our job was to be the first to go down the road to contact the enemy at dawn and, if possible, find out what weapons he'd got, what strength in numbers, and what positions he occupied. To do this we rose at about 5.30 a.m., checked our wireless communications, our guns and our ammunition. The advance was down a centre line, given us by orders on the preceding night. The regiment advanced with three troops each on its own centre line, like a three pronged fork. Of the five troops three were on the attack, one was rested and one was in reserve protecting H.Q. We were in permanent contact with H.Q. by wireless, and they in turn were in contact through the 'rear link officer' with Divisional H.Q., who could provide help for us with mine clearing experts, tanks and air support, if we had bumped into heavy opposition. Headquarters was usually in a field, preferably with a barn, some miles behind where we made contact with the enemy. The first minutes after contact were frantically busy with drills we had so long practised. If the opposition was light we would either speed past them and report their position and strength. Or we might decide to shoot at them. Or we might decide to retire to a position from where we could scan the countryside thoroughly to find out more about them. Everything depended on speed of action.

As detailed scanning of the countryside ahead was vital, we could not operate at night, so we retired to the harbour area, where the Sergeant Major (he was called Corporal Major for some strange reason) had organized as good a meal as possible. We got together with the squadron leader to receive orders for the next day and enlarge on what we'd seen. Then it was orders for my troop, cleaning guns, netting the wireless sets and early bed. This was in a tent formed by stretching canvas from the car. It consisted of an army bed roll – wonderfully warm and waterproof. I shared that tent with my driver and my gunner-wireless operator. We slept well, although I remember waking up to find that my hair was frozen solid ... Northern Europe can be cold in winter.

Of the five troops, one was always resting. The fact that you slept with your crew meant that there was a different kind of discipline to that prevailing in the Infantry, and I think that, in our circumstances, informality worked better than apartheid. When we had our turn for a rest, we gathered in a barn and enjoyed playing poker or racing the aces. Two officers who had been racing correspondents worked out the odds at lightning speed and took large bets, while the rest of us perched on bales of straw looking down to see fair play and place our bets. Those evenings were a blessing often denied to the Infantry. The reverse side of the coin was that to meet the enemy, even if he was demoralized and retreating, every day at dawn was very wearing to the nerves. We weren't conscious of fear at the time, because everything happened so quickly that you acted on a wave of adrenalin. It was when you got back to the harbour area that a reaction set in. My predecessor in charge of C. Troop was involved in some fierce fighting before the break out from Normandy, which should not strictly have been the function of armoured cars. He got an M.C. but the Colonel wisely decided that he should not continue and got him a job away from the front.

Before I describe the 'snake patrol' method of advance, I should explain what an armoured car troop consists of and how it is equipped and armed.

B-L's and Mac Gregor Clans gathered round great granny at Balmenach Distillery shortly before I was born. Speyside 1921

Francis Hamilton-Moore Married great aunt Mavora Mac G.	J. H. (Rufous) B-L My dad Headmaster	Robert B-L My grandfather Headmaster	Jim Mac G. My great uncle Ran Balmenach (Distillery)	Alastair Mac G. My great uncle Malayan rubber and tea	John Gardner Family friend lawyer	General Sir Rob Mac G. Lockhart Last C-in-C India	
Mavora Mac G. Then Hamilton-Moore	Eunice Mac G. My great aunt Jim's wife	Florence Mac G. My granny Married Robert B-L	Great granny Jean Mac G. (who ruled them all with a rod of iron)	Winnie Mac G. My great aunt (and considered rather fast)	Fanny Mac G. Alastair's wife Nee Cunningham	Dodo Mac G. Jim's daughter	Mona B-L My mum Alwine Ivy nee Brougham
Rupert B-L My uncle Actor and singer	Rab B-L My second brother Headmaster of Wanganui and Loretto Scottish International Rugby and cricket	Freda B-L (Winnifred) Actress, film critic, Roman Catholic	On her knee Mavora Gen. Sir Rob's Daughter	Lady Madge B-L (nee Campbell) My aunt, married to Gen. Sir Rob	Douglas Hamilton-Moore Brother of Francis	Dacre Mac G. My great uncle Brigadier Cameron Highlanders Died on the same day as my grandson Dacre was born	Paddy B-L on her knee My 3rd brother Canadian Doctor [I am discreetly present in Mum's tum]
			John Mac G. B-L My oldest brother No. 2 in MI6 Personnel Manager Courtauld's CB. CMG. OBE				

J. H. Bruce-Lockhart (Rufous)

Mona Bruce-Lockhart (in the 1st World War)

Rab Bruce-Lockhart

Josephine Bruce-Lockhart

Jenny, Logie, Fiona, Jo, Rhu and Bede at Gresham's

Kirsty with Big Bear

John, Rab, Paddy and Logie at Sedbergh

Logie, Rab, John and Paddy, 43 years later.

London Scottish Rugby Team 1952 Captained by L B-L

Sandy Smith, Rab and Carole Smith

The Daimler armoured cars weighed about 8 tons. They had a turret with a two-pounder gun and a Besa machine gun co-axially mounted. On the side of the turret there was a smoke bomb projector, which sent the bombs about 100 yards. There were two more attached to the front of the car, to create a local smoke screen to hide the whole troop. Inside the turret the gunner sat on the left and the commander on the right, while the driver was in front and below. There was also a rear steering wheel. When the decision was taken to reverse, the 5 automatic gears operated in reverse at the same speed as forwards, (up to 60 m.p.h.). The commander had to drop to his knees to steer the car and control its speed, looking through a small slot with a rather inadequate field of view. This operation needed a lot of practice, particularly tricky if you had to drive through some of the smoke screen, or if somebody had obscured the port hole by bad stowing of the camouflage netting we carried with us. Round the middle of the car were stowed the 20,000 rounds of machine gun bullets of which one in seven were tracer bullets, which also served as incendiaries. The tracers showed you where you were firing and whether you were hitting the target. There were also 50 shells for the 2 pounder gun, some of which were high explosive and some armour piercing – effective against houses, personnel carriers and enemy armoured cars, but you were very lucky if you damaged a tank. On the top of the turret we always had a second machine gun, a Bren gun, in case we were attacked from above, or by enemy who had got too close to be shot by the main turret guns. And if somebody succeeded in getting right up to the car, we all had revolvers.

A troop had a leading scout car with a driver and a gunner. It had no turret, but was more manoeuverable than the armoured car. No two pounder: just a Bren gun Then came the troop leader's armoured car, followed by an identical second armoured car, and, lastly, the 'get away scout car', whose enviable job was to take any casualties back to H.Q., to make sure he didn't get involved in any ambush and could report on any disaster to H.Q.

We became greatly attached to our cars. Nearly all of our troop were N.C.O.'s, because you needed to be able to take over as driver, gunner or wireless operator if anyone was out of action. All the armoured cars were named after famous racehorses: B squadron cars had to begin with B, C squadron with C and so on. My two cars were called Challenger and Call Boy. The thick tyres were "run flat", so that we wouldn't grind to a halt if they were riddled by machine gun fire. Ordinary small arms fire didn't harm us, but we were vulnerable to any anti-tank weapon, including the Panzerfaust: a sort of bazooka issued to most German infantry units with a range of about 150 yards. It was not very accurate, and to fire it you had to stand up. Nevertheless it made going through woods where infantry were concealed a dangerous pastime. Experience taught us that the best defence against this weapon was to stow soft materials (like bedding and camouflage netting or greatcoats) round the turret, because the bombs could blast their way through armour, but needed to hit something hard to set them off, if they hit something soft they fell harmlessly to ground. In sudden contact with the enemy we had the advantage of being alert and having our hands on the triggers, while they were very often taken by surprise, so that it took them a minute or more to get to their weapons; it only took seconds for us.

The things that we feared most were the mines. Even in the last days of the war the retreating Germans found time to leave mines at likely places: cross roads, entrances to villages, gateways, road sides, bridges and any lay-by which our vehicles might use. We packed sandbags round the driver to minimize the effect, but it just meant that he would be wounded rather than killed. We had to scan the roads all the time for signs that mines might have been laid. The cars had four-wheeled drive: very important if we had to cross muddy fields or rough tracks. And big powerful springs helped too. The cars were fun to drive: wider than ordinary cars, the driver was seated exactly in the middle. Normal traffic was very quick to get out of your way.

The snake patrol was our normal method of advancing to find the enemy. The front scout car would select a place where he would be able to have a good look at the land ahead, without, as far as possible, exposing his car to view. He also looked for the next observation point, probably two to six hundred yards away, depending on the nature of the land ahead. When he was satisfied that the coast was clear, or if he had spotted something or somebody suspicious, he would signal to the leading armoured car, with the troop commander, his gunner and driver. The leading armoured car would take his place. He then headed off at top speed to the next observation post; the leading armoured car had to be alert to give covering fire in the event of an undiscovered enemy shooting at his scout car. In the meantime the second armoured car took the place of the first, as soon as the first had got the signal from the leading scout car to join him. The get away scout car followed at a discreet distance, hoping that the other three had done their jobs. Sounds like a Sunday Times mathematical puzzle, but it was quite simple really! Until we met the enemy, it was a fairly swift way of advancing, and of getting a good look at the land ahead.

First contact with the enemy, usually at dawn, was a time of hectic excitement when speed of thought and decision was all important and the whole vindication of our long training. It might be enemy spotted by binoculars a long way away, who hadn't fired at you because they hadn't seen you. It might be an anti-tank gun firing at you. It might be infantry running away behind a hedge. It might be an enemy motorcycle and side car or armoured car coming along the road towards you. Or it might be an army truck parked by the side of the road at the entrance to a village, while the crew were frying sausages for breakfast. Or, yet again, it might be an infantry platoon camped in a field, just waking up. Or a mine-laying party mining the approach to a bridge. Or a sniper in the top floor of a house. Or a group flying a white flag or waving a white sheet seeking to give themselves up. And, just occasionally, it might be a carefully planned ambush involving one of the few tanks they had left.

H.Q. already knew where you were, because you were in touch by wireless and reported when you reached prearranged map references.

The first thing you do when there is contact with the enemy:

"Hello, Gela One. Contact! Wait ... out" You then decide whether to advance, stop and shoot back, or retire to the nearest safe place and then have a good look and decide what to do.

Let's assume you have been shot at by an anti-tank weapon and the enemy seems well organized and expecting you.

"Driver, halt ... Driver, smoke! Prepare to reverse." You then give circular wave of your hand and pat your head, which means reverse and close in on me when I stop. You say "Gunner, traverse right". You pat him on the shoulder when he's pointing in the right direction. "Gunner, smoke." He fires, to provide the long distance smoke screen. "Gunner, traverse to front". You drop to your knees. "Driver Reverse." You grab the rear steering wheel, pray that the rear driving slot is not obscured and that the other cars are already under way.

When you are no longer in the line of fire, you halt, poke your head up from the top of the turret and summon the others for a quick consultation; the leading scout car or the other armoured car may have had a better view than you of where the enemy were and what kind of gun had fired. You contact H.Q: "Hello, Gela! We have been fired on by an anti-tank gun, we think an 88, from map reference so and so. We will try to find out more. No casualties. Wait . . .out." If there is good cover from bushes, undergrowth or trees, you dismount, leaving one car to protect you; you use your excellent binoculars to watch the enemy and try to establish whether there are any armoured or other vehicles, exactly where the gun is placed, and whether there are any troops on the other side of the road. You may decide to loop round: to continue the advance by using a side road. You may decide to make a dash: to get past the enemy position. If there is a lot of smoke, cars going at 60 m.p.h. are a difficult target. Or you may decide to keep them under observation until H.Q. provide tanks or air support, which, of course, would have to have approval from Divisional H.Q.

If the enemy are only infantry, with no proper dug out protection and no big guns you would probably resume your snake patrol.

There are a great number of things that can go wrong. You may be blinded by smoke and drive into a ditch or hit one of your other cars. The rear driving slit may be obscured by inefficient storing of bedding. Another nasty mistake, which cost the lives of some beginners, was to start driving either forwards or backwards, when your guns were still pointing sideways. If they consequently hit a telegraph post or a tree, the whole turret would swivel abruptly – but not the floor; the gunner and the commander would be half twisted, sometimes with fatal results.

I was summoned to join the operations in France, when the first casualties had been suffered by the regiment. They had been used, unfairly in my view, in the Bocage country in Normandy, before the break out for which they were designed, and they were made to join in slow advances across unsuitable country against infantry supported by tanks. By the time I was sent for, they had already broken out and were heading the advance across France. I and another officer, Bill Pooley, with whom I kept in touch after the war, because he lived in Norwich and sent his sons to Gresham's, crossed to Mulberry Harbour and thence by cattle truck to Lille where the Colonel picked us up. Bill told his sons that we had played poker in the truck and that my "phenomenal memory" had ensured that I won every time. My 'phenomenal' memory had forgotten about that, but I certainly had a run of luck, which enabled me to surprise Jo by sending home some badly needed cash.

Memories of the war are strangely intermittent. If you asked me what I did on January 1st 1945 I wouldn't be able to remember exactly where I was or what I was doing. There are incidents and places of which I have very vivid memories, but I never kept a diary.

There were several different phases. The first was when the excitement of the dash across France, into Belgium and Holland ran out of steam, partly because we had outrun our supplies and failed to capture Antwerp, which would have eased that problem hugely. Partly because, as we got nearer the German frontier, the German army began to reorganize itself, taking advantage of our failure to seize the bridges over the Rhine and the Meuse, and fortified by the feeling that they were making a heroic last stand to protect the sacred soil of their Fatherland. We felt that Monty had let us down over his failure to seize Antwerp, and by the disaster at Arnhem. Our advance ground to a halt, and there was little for armoured cars to do while the infantry forced their way, with heavy casualties, through the Reichswald forest, and even General Patton came to a halt. Our regiment could only play at being infantrymen and send patrols to the edge of the Meuse river, the far bank of which was occupied by the Germans, now in quite considerable strength. The astonishing counter attack by the Germans in the Ardennes took everybody by surprise. Our intelligence must have failed. An attack by a good armoured division in cloudy, snowy conditions was alarmingly successful to begin with and caused real panic, especially when the Germans overran a lot of Sherman tanks and took them for their own use. We had no clear idea as to what was happening, and feared that they would swing north and cut off a large part of the Allied forces. I was sent to find a senior Allied officer who could put us in the picture, as communications seemed to have broken down. By the time I had found an American colonel, the whole picture had changed: the snow had melted, the cloud had cleared and Allied air power had inflicted huge losses on the German tanks. Hitler's last major victory turned into a wound from which they were never able to recover.

In the mean time (December and January) our regiment was stationed near the border between Belgium and Holland not far from Boxmeer, and, for a time, Nejmegen. You could usually tell when you were in Holland, because the windows were always clean and the people were glad to see you and reliably supportive. It was not the same in Belgium; although there were some great people. I always wondered whether there were notices hidden in the cellars, in case there was a change of fortunes in the war: "Herzlichst Willkommen". Their windows were seldom clean.

My memories of this "Sitzkrieg" as we began to call it are of a few odd incidents. One evening I was sent on a foot patrol to see if I could find out how the Germans were managing to send patrols to our side of the river. We made our way along a hedge towards the river in single file, with blackened faces and in silence. Suddenly I saw something move on the other side of the hedge. I gestured to the troop (ten of us) to lie down and keep quiet. It soon became clear that there was a German patrol on the other side of the hedge, and that they had likewise stopped. But they had not seen us, for they were chattering away. I was wondering whether I should leap to my feet, order the troop to charge and throw grenades and earn a Military Cross, or, more probably, remain in a 'position of observation'. Fortunately I didn't have time to decide before the Germans decided to go back to the couple of rowing boats in which they had crossed. The next night we organized our armoured cars to provide an ambush in case the Germans should follow the same route. They did, and the cars opened fire. But we were not trained for night fighting. We only wounded one, the rest got away, because although we had powerful headlights we didn't realize that if you switch them on suddenly in the dark you are as dazzled as the enemy and by the time you have managed to get your machine gun, in the dark inside of the turret, under control, the enemy have disappeared.

Another attempt at night patrol was nearly disastrous. We bumped into another group of patrollers and fortunately before anyone fired it turned out to be from another Allied unit – commanded by extraordinary chance by an old rugby playing friend.

Before we started to move again and do the job for which we had trained, Monty had another of his bright ideas. He decided to move the whole of our division some 50 miles north by night, in order to deceive the enemy as to where the attack was going to be launched. We were issued with infra red lights and glasses and instructions as to the route we were to follow. What Monty hadn't reckoned on was the weather. It poured with rain. The fields to either side of the only road were flooded, and the road itself was muddy, and visibility, in spite of the infra red, restricted to a few yards. It was a major shambles. In about five hours we had advanced about 2 miles. Tanks had slithered into ditches, broken down vehicles blocked the only passable road. As we waited for something to happen, I remember a bedraggled infantry platoon of Highlanders trudging past us. A Jock Sergeant went up to the armoured car in front of me and banged on the side: "What bluidy shower's this and where are we?" he enquired of the equally bedraggled officer, half asleep with his head sticking out of the turret. "This is not a bloody shower. It's His Majesty's Household Cavalry, and I've no idea where we are." There were more casualties to vehicles that night than in a month of advance in the weeks to come.

We were eventually moved to Nijmegen awaiting orders to resume our advance – into Germany itself. It was an eerie town a shade smaller than Norwich. The Germans shelled it every day with a regularity that was surprising even from them. It was not what you could call a heavy bombardment ... one shell every ten minutes, for a couple of hours twice a day. You knew by looking at your watch when a shell was coming and could hear its whine. There was the faintly comic sight of everyone on the streets lying down. The odds against being hit were comfortingly high.

At last the order came to advance. We crossed the bridge over the main branch of the Rhine, which splits into two or three parts thereabouts. It was held by anti aircraft guns and tanks, who waved us on as we made for the border town of Enschede. There was no indication of precisely where the border was, and the only German forces we saw on that first day surrendered without firing, and obligingly told us that there were no proper defending forces for 5 miles ahead. Although it was exciting to be first on German soil, it had not been a frightening experience ... in fact the first village we entered provided a friendly welcome: women bringing out sandwiches and drinks and hanging white sheets from their windows. None of the sniping from roof tops we came across later. Enschede itself had been bombed, which perhaps was why it had been abandoned.

However, the next night, the supply route to our harbour area came under quite heavy fire, and, after a nervous night, we had to resume our 'snake patrol' advance more cautiously. The next few weeks during which we headed the advance, which ended on V.E. Day when we reached the North Sea near Cuxhaven, became more and more confused and confusing, at its most bizarre when we crossed Lüneburg Heath. Thousands of refugees from the Russians' merciless advance were trying to get home to the big towns in the Ruhr: women and children; fleeing soldiers who wanted to be taken prisoner by the Allies, as the only way to get food and to avoid being slaughtered; people who had escaped from prisoner of war camps or concentration camps, when the remaining German forces abandoned them; Nazis pretending to be anti Hitler. Among them were the remnants of the still loyal Germany army, and a sprinkling of S.S. troops still believing that a miracle might save them. There were Germans who were genuinely relieved to see us, others who were still laying mines and shooting at us. It was not always easy to know who was who. Only two weeks before the end one of our troops blundered into an ambush prepared by a little group of heavy tanks and the commander lost his life.

Much of the detail of that chaotic time I have forgotten, but I remember, usually visually, a few incidents because they were funny, or frightening, or crazy. I remember going round a corner into a village and seeing three German soldiers eating sausages at a restaurant table on the pavement, with their personnel carrier parked just opposite. Their expressions of absolute astonishment I can still see. As I had my guns ready to fire, they had no choice.

Prisoners were a problem. To begin with I had a quick word with them to try to find out what resistance we would be likely to find ahead, and sent them back to H.Q. who disposed of them to the nearest P.O.W. camp. Later on there were far too many for that. We took a 15 cwt truck to collect their weapons and told them which way to go.

One day we were parked in a field, while I went up to a bridge, which I thought might be mined. It was, and while I was examining the mines to make up my mind whether I could remove them or whether I should call up the experts, a machine gun opened up from the edge of a wood on the far bank of the river. I sprinted back to the safety of my car, but in climbing back through the top of the turret got my shoulder strap caught in the wireless aerial and had what seemed a long struggle to disengage myself, while the bullets whistled by ever nearer. Then all the cars opened up and the machine gun was silenced. It was a lovely April day. The silence after all the clatter was startling. I remember that a thrush burst into song and a fox trotted out of the wood as though nothing had happened. I can see it as if it were yesterday . . . there was hawthorn blossom over on the right.

There was another vaguely similar incident involving a bridge and a mine search. We had seen one or two enemy around and were parked round the edges of a field overlooking the bridge. I took advantage of the pause to answer the call of nature behind a convenient bush. No sooner had I started than a German mortar ('Minnie', the Minenwerfer, which sends over several at a time) opened up. Without waiting to do my trousers up I raced for the cover of my car. As I passed the other car, Nobby Clark, the driver shouted, "Good luck, Sir", and then more softly, "On your way, bare arse!" Laughter can be a great antidote to fear!

I should explain at this point that there are two ways of entering an armoured car: one through a small door at the bottom, and the other through a closable hatch at the top of the turret. One of our officers, who shall remain nameless, was a bit older than me, and distinctly fatter. He had to be promoted to be rear link officer because he could no longer negotiate entry to the armoured cars. As Rear Link Officer he had plenty of room to accommodate wireless sets and maps, and no danger of being shot up when stuck in a small hatch. I remember he was a great and successful gambler, last heard of going to Italy to become a 'town mayor' and 'learning' to play poker with a lot of young Americans who were poorer in pocket for the experience. I have a very vivid memory of an incident, when we unexpectedly came round a corner at speed and saw a couple of German soldiers in a motorcycle and sidecar coming towards us at similar speed. I happened to be in the leading scout car and gave chase, when he turned round. I shot the driver, and the motorcycle veered off the road into the ditch. The NCO was virtually uninjured. I asked him where the rest of his reconnaissance unit was. He said it was a mile the other side of the village and would be willing to surrender. I made him ride on the front of the armoured car to make sure he was telling the truth. He was! I apologized for killing his driver . . . he just said: "It is the damned war". We collected the weapons and sent them back to HQ. It was the first mass surrender I'd experienced.

Periodically we would run ahead of our supplies. I remember not having a meal for two days: on return to H.Q. the Corporal-Major fried eight eggs for me . . . I had a nasty stomach ache next morning.

On another occasion the Major sent for me and said "We've completely run out of food for the squadron, Logie. Be a good chap and see if you can get some food from the Germans." "No shops will have enough to feed a squadron, Sir." "Perhaps not: it's meat we really need. Try the farms. I'll give you a bit of paper saying we're commandeering it for the army and asking the military government to give compensation later."

I didn't fancy the job. It wasn't clear which villages were still occupied by the Germans and I hate killing animals. One of my troop volunteered to come with me. We took a scout car and a machine gun and a pistol each, plus a 15 cwt truck to carry the meat. We tried the nearest village, but it was practically deserted, and there was nothing in the shop that would feed a troop, much less a squadron.

We drove into the country: not much farmland. At last we came to a small striking old farm, big outbuildings, a huge roof and massive beams, and some cows in the fields and – it was the first time I'd ever seen one – a stork's nest on a tall chimney. It reminded me of a setting for Grimm's fairy tales.

We drove cautiously up the drive. No sign of any human being, but the enclosed farm yard had stables, pigsties and chickens running around everywhere. We knocked on the massive front door and hammered at the windows. The place was completely abandoned. What a bit of luck! The corporal looked at me. "Shall we start, Sir?" I nodded reluctantly and decided to start with the chickens . . .

You can't machine gun a chicken. A revolver is not accurate enough to hit a highly mobile bird whose head is moving backwards and forwards at high speed. Fortunately there were two rifles with which we shot three or four birds thus avoiding having to run after them and wring their necks.

"Even if we kill the lot, it'll not feed a quarter of the squadron." We looked at each other. "It'll have to be the pigs."

Pigs meant machine guns. We hardened our hearts, and chose a three pig sty and the Bren. I have never felt more disgusted with myself . . . A terrible racket of squealing pigs and machine gun fire, made louder by the echo from the surrounding walls. We carried the three pigs to the truck, thanking God it was all over, when something untoward happened. Up the drive and round the corner came what was obviously a funeral procession. Everyone was dressed in black, and the procession was headed by a tall elegant figure in a top hat. My heart sank to my boots and I felt more like a schoolboy caught by his Headmaster than an officer commandeering much needed food from a defeated enemy. Regardless of the fact that my uniform was bloodstained, I saluted the leader of the procession and mustered what dignity I could explaining that it was an emergency, and that I had to find food for a whole regiment, and I handed him the piece of paper, saluted and made for the exit as fast as I could. I glanced back over my shoulder. The tall gentleman was screwing up the bit of paper and depositing it in a rubbish bin.

The squadron leader was pleased. Both the Corporal and I were deeply ashamed . . . It's a strange thing, but I was more upset over this peculiar incident than over the first Germans that I killed . . . "I was only obeying orders." Now where have I heard that excuse before?

One incident involved a narrow escape. We had just been in contact with the enemy and had gone to a hill top to scan the landscape ahead. I heard a message "Hallo, Gela One, Limejuice coming at 13.45, map reference x." Limejuice was the word for air support. Mildly surprised, I glanced at the map reference. It was precisely where we were! We had exactly five minutes to get a safe distance away and hide our cars in the woods. Exactly on time the air support blasted the hill top where we had been. Some ass must have seen us, reported us as enemy armour and done his best to finish us off.

The last weeks of the war became increasingly surreal. When we were wondering whether we could get to Berlin before the Russians, we were ordered to swing north towards Cuxhaven on the North Sea. Wild rumours of all kinds flashed around: some true, some not, some exaggerated. The S.S. were heading for the mountainous south, where they would fight to the last man. Himmler had been caught on Lüneberg Heath and was trying to negotiate a separate peace. Hitler was pronounced dead several times before his death. The Allies had struck a deal with Admiral Doenitz to unite with the last remnants of the German army against the Russians.

When we reached the sea we could go no further. The C.O. called the officers together and announced that there would be an unconditional surrender and a complete end to hostilities on the very next day . . . and this time it was true. There was wild rejoicing – but no supplies of drink to celebrate with had caught up with us.

Chapter Twenty One

The First Daze of Peace

Looking back on it all I was extremely lucky. Like most other young men I had been frightened by the stories of the First World War: the terrible scenes of the battles of the Somme; stupid generals ordering advances which everybody knew would lead to certain death; the Hell of the trench warfare. The great advantage of armoured cars was that you made all the decisions as to whether you should advance, shoot or retreat. Also that things happened so quickly that you had no time to feel fear until later. And, perhaps best of all, you could usually sleep in comparative safety and comfort. For some strange reason we all felt intensely alive: what was beautiful was more beautiful; what was exciting more exciting. On the other hand, it was a nervous strain, and the habit of being ready to shoot quickly at a moment's notice made us rather wild and unnecessarily trigger-happy for a time in the early days of peace. And there were moments when we were afraid and saw what a ghastly mess the whole business of war can be.

One evening in the early days of peace, we were sitting in a comfortable dining room in an improvised officers' mess, having a good and mildly alcoholic meal. About ten of us were seated at a long table. The regimental wines officer was seated on my right, cheerful, but with no sign of being drunk. A big moth flew in through the window and crashed in his wine glass. Unhesitatingly he drew his revolver and shot it. How he managed to miss our knees under the table, I don't know.

As soon as peace was signed the C.O. sent me as interpreter with the Wines Officer to Hamburg to see if we could replenish our empty stock of drink. We took a scout car in case of trouble and, optimistically, a large truck to bring back whatever we could lay our hands on. It was a fool's errand. Hamburg was a complete mess. The town had only been overrun a couple of days earlier. Nearly all the town was bombed flat: no houses with roofs; no streets open to traffic, because of the rubble; no shops and very few people; one or two survivors with carts, swapping farm produce for other bare necessities. Money was meaningless. We had brought packets of cigarettes, which, for the first weeks, acted to some extent as a form of currency.

To our surprise, however, we found a sailor, obviously inebriated. We stopped and politely questioned him. German brought no reply. He turned out to be French, not a whit afraid of us and willing to disclose the source of his good cheer. It emerged that a substantial ship, destined for the German High Command had docked, found chaos as the Allies entered the city; the crew had fled, abandoning the ship and its contents. Nobody had paid any attention to it and he had been able to get on board. It was full of good drink, as he would show us.

We went down with him. The docks were deserted. The ship was an answer to the colonel's dream: countless cases of Champagne, apricot brandy and Pommard. We rang the squadron leader: would it be looting, if we helped ourselves? There should be enough for the Division. Would the general authorize commandeering? If it had been destined for the enemy, surely it constituted 'legitimate spoils of war'? The squadron leader said, "Guard it with your lives; I'll consult Higher Authority." Higher Authority was not long about giving his verdict. I should fill my truck for my regiment; he would send a three tonner for Division.

It was that decision which enabled us to drink Pommard at 6p a bottle, apricot brandy at 3d. a nip and Champagne for a shilling a bottle for the next few months.

For some unknown reason we were sent to Schloss Brühl for a few days. It is not far from Bonn and was, and still is, among the most beautiful of Germany's many lovely Baroque palaces. We had no specific job except to help the elderly staff ensure there was no vandalism. We passed that week going to look at the devastated towns of the Ruhr and Cologne Cathedral, a little damaged, but still standing firm in the middle of an area that was absolutely flattened.

On a subsequent visit to those parts I noted that most of that space had been devoted to car parks. I reflected that the unexpected result of our over the top bombing of Germany was that, with their huge energy and efficiency, they were able to replace the out of date buildings, drains, water and electricity supply and factories from the days of Bismark with brilliant modern facilities. While we are only just beginning to face the bill for replacing Victorian slums and infrastructure.

With little success, I spent some time trying to shoot the big fat carp in the ponds. The Germans love them and they eat them at Christmas instead of turkeys. The biggest used to bask on, or near the top of, the water in the summer sun. Fortunately even a 30lb carp was too small a target for my revolver at a range of 50 yards. Don't believe those Wild West films – no-one can shoot a glass out of a drinker's hand at the other end of the bar 30 yards long!

After little more than a week we were summoned to what proved to be the most challenging and important task we had ever faced.

Chapter Twenty Two
Mariental

Mariental was couple of miles north of the main Autobahn from the Ruhr to Berlin, at the point where it formed the new frontier with the Russian Zone. The nearest sizeable town was Helmstedt and somewhat closer the little town Grasleben, just on our side of the border which then ran through heavily wooded country. There were as yet no marks to define the border precisely. I suppose somebody, Eisenhower or Stalin, had drawn a line on a map and sent copies to local commanders, but it was still a matter of debate which side of Farmer Braun's 100 acre field it ran.

Our new job was to prevent more refugees from crossing from the Russian Zone because the numbers were getting beyond the stage where we could find accommodation and food for them. Secondly, we were to look after the big 'Displaced Persons Camp', at the former Luftwaffe barracks which was to be our Headquarters. Neither we nor the 'Powers that were' had any idea of the extraordinary nature of that second task. Lastly we were to help man the frontier post on the main autobahn in the event of any trouble.

We soon discovered that the first task was impossible. To stop anyone from crossing an invisible frontier in miles of heavily wooded country was beyond our means. When we succeeded in stopping a small number of refugees, we discovered that they had been robbed of all their worldly goods and the women had all been raped, mostly by the Russians on the other side of the frontier. We could not insist on returning them to the people who had just been brutalizing them. They had often trudged for a hundred or more miles, almost without food or water.

It was the D.P. camp which presented the biggest and most urgent problem. Some 5,000 crammed into accommodation meant for 600 members of the Luftwaffe. The great majority were Poles, divided into prisoners of war and agricultural workers who had been taken on to replace the German labourers who had been sent to the front. Refugees from the East added constantly to the population. The small remainder was an assortment of other nationals who had fallen foul of the Germans and been forcibly recruited for a variety of purposes.

When we took over it was like a concentration camp suddenly freed from its guards, but also deprived of proper food and drink. The Americans had first liberated the camp, but had been ordered to hand over to us before they could bring many improvements. The accommodation was appalling: rooms 8 × 12 designed for single Luftwaffe men, without lavatories or cooking facilities, housed whole families. Lavatories were hopelessly inadequate: one or two per corridor. There had been a bulb for every room, but the electricity supply kept breaking down. The German authorities had at least provided regular supplies of milk, bread and potatoes and a few vegetables. But before the war ended they had disappeared and made no arrangements to fill the gap.

Because of my French and German a very large portion of clearing up the mess fell to me. I had the help of a Belgian doctor and his medical student assistant, a white haired but very competent Dutch business man and, best of all, a Polish lady who spoke excellent English, French and German, was built like Brunnhilde, had the courage of a lion, feared no man and dealt with the most ghastly problems swiftly and decisively. We called her Boadicea, and she was respected by the D.P.s, the Germans and our squadron. These four were members of U.N.R.A., the support agency which had been planned to deal with emergencies of this kind. She should unquestionably have been made a D.B.E. I was a kind of liaison officer between her, the squadron, the Germans and the two self-styled leaders of the camp. One was a Polish Captain who claimed to be the leader of the prisoners of war. I cannot believe that he could have been elected, for we found him totally unsuitable. To begin with he and the leader of the civilian Poles met Boadicea and me every day to determine what actions needed to be taken. He (I think Dziourjinski was his name) would spend all his time asking for special privileges for 'his' officers, and particularly that they should be allowed to carry arms. He would then offer bribes: the services of the prettiest girls (an endangered species) in the camp, and a supply of his specially distilled spirits: a potato peel concoction distilled in the cellars (which also served as overflow lavatories), and which was responsible for much sickness in the camp, even, according to our Belgian Doctor, blindness. He also smelt of expensive perfume and had somehow procured little luxuries when everyone else was on the verge of starvation. We soon got rid of him and gave Boadicea complete command, helped by the not very reliable but well intentioned leader of the civilians, who had the disadvantage of a passing resemblance to Adolf Hitler after a night out.

The Belgian Doctor got supplies of medicine to combat the venereal diseases which were rife and the troubles caused by malnutrition. Great help came to us through the Bürgermeister of Grasleben and the Landrat of Helmstedt. Whatever their history – Nazi's or not – they were polite, efficient and eager to please. They restored a regular supply of milk and bread ... in the first fortnight few babies had died. When we asked for some hundreds of shoes of various sizes, because quite a lot were reduced to going barefoot, they produced them within two or three days.

During our advance I had briefly glimpsed one of the concentration camps, Sandbostel, so I had no reason to doubt the horror stories which were emerging from Auschwitz and Belsen and the like. I asked the military government where and how I could get the right equipment for a massive clear up at Mariental. They suggested Belsen; all the brushes and disinfectants had been sent there, and they probably had some to spare.

So I went to Belsen some few weeks after it had been rescued. Even after that time it was unbelievable: the inmates were still there looking like ghosts from Hell, not yet fit for freedom. I spoke to the guards who gave me a full description of the horrors of those first days and showed me the men's graves. It made me more than ever astonished at what ordinary men can be taught to do. I made up my mind then and there to devote my time at Cambridge to finding out where the land of Bach and Beethoven had gone wrong. We looked at Germans with renewed suspicion. Could they not have known? Could that nice, efficient Bürgermeister have sent his Jewish shopkeepers to Auschwitz? Could my granny's father have failed to speak up? Might I have looked the other way if I'd been to school in Germany – and have sung proud nationalist songs with the rest of them? The human race managed to create hells on earth of an ingenuity that the Devil himself must envy.

I returned to Mariental with supplies. It had been on the way towards a Belsen-like destiny, but through neglect rather than through deliberate viciousness.

I suppose the lesson that Mariental taught us was that trying to bring order out of complete chaos involves quick action and, therefore, mistakes and risks.

In those early post-war days there was no social structure except the remnants of an overwhelmed German organization. There was no justice system in place. Our military government did its best, but had as yet no proper structure of support. This meant that, when we had to deal with extensive crime in Mariental – and I don't mean just pinching somebody else's cabbage, but rape and murder – we had to take immediate action on our own initiative without waiting for authorization.

So we had a hut set aside as a prison. The camp was an entirely lawless place. Abandoned by the Germans shortly before we took over, the Poles had thought they would at once be free. Somehow they had got hold of weapons, which they hid in the woods and used to hold up refugees from the East. They soon recognized that they couldn't be free. Nobody wanted them in the Western Zone, to return to the East was something they couldn't contemplate and the Russians didn't want them. We managed to thin the numbers a bit by getting jobs on the farms for them, but the vacancies were small. It was some time before anybody could afford to pay for employees, most of whom spoke no

German or English. In the meantime the camp was like a slum in the throes of gang warfare: the survival of the fittest. The sound of pistol shots was an everyday occurrence. Of course not all the inmates became drunks and criminals. There were remarkable families that had managed to keep their tiny rooms clean, and even to teach their children to play the violin and to learn languages.

The measure of our success was that the small children no longer died, and that conditions became just about tolerable. The measure of our failure was that, when I made enquiries twenty years later, the camp was still catering for a number of people who couldn't find a place in East or West.

One or two incidents are worth recording if only for their almost surreal nature. We (by which I usually mean Boadicea and me) were worried about the way in which some of the armed Poles went into the woods near the frontier and lay in wait for the refugees. They would search them for anything the Russians might have neglected to take, and they would rape most of the women. It was a daily occurrence. We announced that anyone found guilty would be imprisoned and, later, tried. I formed a hare-brained scheme to catch the offenders. I decided to dress as a refugee with two volunteers who spoke a bit of German, and hoped that we would be set upon by the errant Poles, produce revolvers from underneath our shabby coats and arrest them. It didn't work out quite so smoothly. We chose a forest path that seemed to have been trodden recently, but, as there was nothing to indicate the exact location of the frontier, we were not sure where to stop and turn round. We had gone out early, and hoped to hide for a time. We had brought a wheelbarrow in which we'd put bundles of unwanted rubbish: old clothes and pots and pans.

Unfortunately before we could call a halt, we blundered into a Russian patrol. We must have crossed the invisible frontier. Not a nice situation. There were ten of them, fully armed: shouting at us. The commander was waving his rifle in our direction and seemed to be considering shooting us on the spot. He didn't speak German or English and we had no Russian speaker. Moreover we had weapons and no means of identifying ourselves or of explaining the situation. One of the extraordinary things which could only happen at that Alice in Wonderland place and time came to our rescue. A tall and imposing figure came down the path from the Russian side. He spoke German, Russian and English with equal ease and was smartly dressed in civilian clothes. The Russians must have known him, for he was received in respectful silence as he raised his hand. He asked me who I was and what I was doing: understandably disbelieving at first, when he found that we all spoke excellent English he suddenly realized that it was true and burst out laughing – as did the Russian patrol when he explained it to them. I never found out who he was or why he was there, but he had saved us from a highly dangerous situation.

Later we saw more of the Russians. There were a couple of meetings to settle little arguments over frontier disputes, like the ridiculous "Battle of the

Brewery". The brewery in question was in Russian territory, the shop which was its main outlet was in ours, as was the electricity supply for the brewery. It took childish threats to cut off the electrical power before a sensible compromise was reached. It would be silly to judge Russia's heroic forces by one small infantry unit at the end of what must have been history's most horrific campaign. Nevertheless we were astonished at their primitive lack of education, mistrustful attitude to us, and continual maltreatment of the German refugees. Practically all of them were illiterate. We asked the officer in charge to come and have a drink with us. After much hesitation he accepted our offer to look at our equipment and join us in our mess – provided he could bring an armed man as protection. So while he drank and communicated with difficulty with us through an interpreter, a large uncouth soldier sat on a bar stool with a revolver in its holster staring balefully at us while he lowered pint after pint. When he saw our Daimler armoured cars and our 3 tonner trucks, the officer said: "Ah! I did not know we had given you all these things. I see you have painted out our signs and substituted your own." He would not believe that the similar weapons which the Russians had used had been made in England and shipped to them with huge losses by our Arctic convoys. No wonder the Russians thought our contribution to the war was negligible! I really thought that he imagined himself to be at risk of being kidnapped or taken hostage.

There was little doubt that they regarded the rape of any female refugees as a price for being allowed to cross the frontier or as a form of justified revenge. The number of weeping women who poured out their stories to us on reaching safety made that quite plain. It did little to improve relations.

One day I got a message from the Bürgermeister, to say that he had received a complaint from a German refugee that one of the Poles from our camp had raped and robbed her. She was sure she could recognize him, because he had platinum blond hair and was very small and thin. I pointed out that the difficulty of finding the right man among 5,000 Poles was formidable, but agreed to take her back to the camp to see if Boadicea had any bright ideas. So I took the victim (who was so big and entirely without any sexual attractions that I would have thought her capable of laying out any thin, small Pole) back to the camp. She was still tearful and incoherent but, as we were driving past the main barracks, she suddenly plucked me by the sleeve and said "There he is". Indeed a small blond man was talking to a group of people by the roadside. I stopped the car, got out and beckoned to him to come. At once he recognized the German and started to run away. I pursued him, eventually catching him up, waving my revolver and marched him back to the car, where things were not looking good. The group with whom our blond Pole had been talking were trying to pull the German out of the car. I pointed my bulletless revolver at them, got in and drove her to the squadron quarters, leaving an angry crowd behind us. We were lucky. About the whole squadron was out on an exercise, except for Boadicea and a few remnants to whom we handed over the blond Pole and his victim. We looked out of the window and saw a crowd making for our temporary prison. There were a couple of armoured cars left, some of the cooks knew how to drive them. We got in, Boadicea beside me, and no ammunition. We drove over to the prison and Boadicea raised her hand. Exactly what she said I don't know: but she began by indicating that if anyone went within 10 yards of the prison door we would open fire. She then got them to be quiet and to listen and finally to agree to appoint two people to come to my office and tell us what their grievances were. Again Boadicea was superb. We reassured them that careful evidence would be taken and that they would be kept in touch and any punishment would be fair. She saved the day again.

By the time I was summoned back to Cambridge to complete my degree course, to be introduced to my first-born, Jennifer, and to return to a sane world, Mariental was at least reasonably fed and tolerably peaceful. But they remained an overcrowded and unhappy group. Return, to a country where their friends and relations had been murdered in their thousands by both Germans and Russians, was impossible, and the West seemed to be unable to find jobs for often totally unqualified refugees. For me it, together with the war, was the most valuable experience of my life. To be plunged into chaos, to be forced to make vital decisions quickly, and to come across every facet of human behaviour is something that, in retrospect, I would not have missed for the world. I had been in great need of a bit of maturity, and, although I was not entirely cured of doing silly things, I learned from them. It gave me an entirely different outlook on life and a different sense of proportion. Curiously enough, when I asked my brother Rab after the war why he took a small bottle of sand around with him, he replied: "It is a bit of desert sand from North Africa. I look at it and remember, and everything falls into proportion."

I also think that Mariental was a uniquely useful preparation for the job of Headmaster of a boarding school – far better than any teachers' training college. I remember a Headmaster saying to me years later: "The thing that astonished me was that, over the years, I've come across every kind of human aberration from schizophrenia and sadism to delusions of grandeur, murder and attempts to raise the Devil." That referred to the distinguished public school he looked after. I could have said the same about Mariental, except that they happened in weeks, not years. I quickly dismissed any idea of staying on with the regiment to become a peace time regular soldier, although I had come to like my colleagues and admire many of them. Most of them had private money. The Guards, when at home in England, lived a somewhat Ritzy life combined with spit and polish, which would be beyond my means. Anyway I had the firm prospect of a return to Cambridge which might open up other possibilities. When I left Germany in 1945 it seemed an appropriate time to try to resolve the question which had been bothering me for a long time.

Chapter Twenty Three

Germany Then and Now

How and why could a great country like Germany be induced to give fanatical support to a group of people with repulsive views and policies, which led to world-wide carnage?

It is important that everyone should have a clear answer to this question, because it is the most vivid example of History's repeated lesson: mankind has always been capable of extraordinarily savage behaviour when faced with certain circumstances. The whole purpose of History should be to understand these circumstances which lead men (and women) to burn or torture each other to death. Spain, Russia, Japan, America, France, Ancient Rome, Britain – nearly every nation has done it. Germany and Russia have shown us that modern civilization has not improved matters: indeed advanced scientific knowledge and religious extremism can make our inhumanity worse. We, in Britain, are quite capable of following suit, if we fail to identify the early signs.

My maternal grandmother was German, and I studied German language, literature, music and art at Cambridge. I loved Bach and Beethoven, Schumann and Mendelsohn (the most popular German Jew of his day!), and Goethe and Schiller and the romantic poets, and the gentle stories and poems of the poetic realists like Storm. If you have heard the great Fischer-Dieskau sing, you will know that there were still pillars of European civilization in Germany immediately after the Second World War.

But I heard Hitler speak at the Nüremberg rallies before the war, and I read "Mein Kampf" as a teenager. Even then I knew that something was going disastrously wrong.

I then fought against the Germans, perhaps against relations. I saw concentration camps, including Belsen, and became obsessed with the question: how and why did Hitler manage to turn around the nation, already exhausted by one horrible war and a grim financial crisis, and prepare the ground for vicious racism, violence and brutality, culminating in Auschwitz, Buchenwald, Belsen and Warsaw?

I saw the aftermath of the war with the army of occupation, had the unusual experience of becoming involved with Mariental 'Displaced persons' camp, and returned to Cambridge. There I re-read German literature with a more wary and observant eye, and discovered clear evidence of widespread Nazi type ideas up to 200, and is some cases, 2,000 years before Hitler. He was in no way an original thinker: all he did was to understand the complexes and resentments, which were rife in Germany after the First World War, and play upon them with skill, profound understanding and complete ruthlessness.

After Cambridge, I kept in touch with the swift changes in Germany. Jo and I had three successive German au pairs we returned to Germany on a cathedral and castle tour, to visit my brother (for a time our M.I.6 man in West Germany) and to fish the River Ahr. Later on my nephew James was our man in Bonn. Now my son Bede, after a spell looking after a French company's sales, is working for the Commerzbank, and my grandson went on a long back-packing trip round Germany with his Swedish girl friend. So I have had a good picture of the astonishing changes which have taken place.

Most Germans have become charming, hospitable, modest and have even developed a sense of humour, no longer mainly based on shoving children or witches into ovens. They are not only plainly top European nation, but they are not trumpeting the fact, and they manage to be on relatively good terms both with the French and with us. By now almost all the fanatical Nazis have gone. A few sons and daughters of the old gang still meet to talk nostalgically about the old dreams: but they have little influence and generally keep quiet. Anyone who wants to know what it was like to be Himmler's daughter during and after the war has only to read her fascinating account of the good husband and father, who took his family to the Alps and didn't discuss his office work with them.

One thing is quite clear to me. If I had been brought up between the wars in Germany instead of England, I would have joined the Hitlerjugend and the S.S. With my fair hair and blue eyes, my love of the outdoor life and sport and my enjoyment of singing patriotic and drinking songs and the intense Nazification of German education in the Thirties, I could not have avoided it. Before long I would have been ordered to do vicious things . . . What then? Would I have had the courage to question orders? For the whole of the Thirties every school was made to teach that obedience was the highest virtue together with eagerness to give one's life for the advancement of greater Germany and its Führer. Racism was systematically taught, and all Germany's ills conveniently blamed on the Jews. Any books or magazines publishing contrary views were confiscated and the authors punished.

The complexes on which Hitler played were simple. He spread the convenient myth of the 'stab in the back' at the end of World War I. German morale collapsed after their huge losses in their 1918 attacks and the arrival of fresh American troops. The allied blockade was working, and there were strikes in the docks and munition factories. The German forces were trained to believe that they could not be beaten, so they looked for an excuse, or for someone to blame. What could be more convenient than to put the blame on Russian-inspired communists and Jews? The strikes were actually caused by the military defeat rather than the other way round: but terminological inexactitudes never bothered Hitler.

The second complex which Hitler found useful was the universal resentment of the Treaty of Versailles. The Allies had presented Germany with an impossibly massive bill, forbidden them to rearm and drawn frontiers in the Saar, Sudetenland, Silesia and Alsace which left substantial German populations on the 'wrong' side. The large scale humiliation was felt by every class and political group in Germany.

The third was Germany's desire for a 'Place in the sun'. Throughout the 19th Century England, France and even Belgium and Holland and Spain had helped themselves to colonies which they exploited for their own prosperity. Germany, which had grown faster than any other major country, had come on the scene too late. The British command of the seas made a belated bid for more German colonial expansion impossible. Between 1830 and 1880 Germany's population rose from 30 million to 70 million. In 1830, 75% of Germany lived in the country or in villages of under 10,000. In 1880, 75% of Germans lived in towns of over 10,000. They had almost overtaken Britain in the production of iron, steel, coal and shipping by the end of the century. They felt 'all blown up with nowhere to go' and an acute sense of injustice.

The fourth was the longstanding feeling of encirclement. Germany was always afraid of potentially hostile alliances between the states surrounding it: Russia, France, Britain, Italy, the encroaching Ottoman Empire and the Slav states near Russia's borders.

Out of this grew the fifth: the 'Drang nach Osten'. They felt that expansion to the north was limited by the sea, that expansion to the south was barred by the Alps and Switzerland, that France's army was still redoutable in the west. But Silesia, the Sudetenland and, especially, Poland were much more tempting targets. Germans have an expression 'eine polnische Wirtschaft. Literally 'a Polish economy': it was used to describe a sluttish household. They felt that German farmers would make a much better job than the supposedly incompetent Poles of getting the fertile plains of Poland to produce the riches which they should yield. Furthermore that would help to keep the Russians further away. If Germany didn't act, the Russians would take over: it would really be doing the Poles a favour!

*

None of this represents new thinking. Read that most exciting of Old Testament stories: the Book of Esther. King (or more properly Emperor) Ahasuerus was in command of a huge empire, extending from Western India to almost all of the Middle East. His very successful military commander was a ruthless general called Haman. To celebrate his victories Ahasuerus decided to lay on a great party for all the kings and princes of his subordinate states: fountains of wine, displays of gold and jewellery, entertainments of every kind. At the height of the celebrations, he called upon his wife to perform a striptease to dazzle his V.I.P. guests. She bravely defied him: "Oh King live forever, I will not strip in front of your drunken friends."

King Ahasuerus was in a dilemma. He really was in love with his Queen, but, if she defied him in public, all the princes and monarchs of his realm would face a wave of feminism. He called for his half dozen wise men advisers and asked for their advice. "Oh King live forever, as you are reluctant to have her executed, you must at least banish her to a remote part of your Kingdom, where she can live in comfort, but not be seen as a feminist in court circles."

So Ahasuerus took this advice. He asked Haman what reward he should give a person who had done him the greatest service. Assuming that he must be the person, Haman replied that he should ride on a white charger through the streets preceded by trumpeters and followed by the best of his troops ... But, while he was with the King, there was one other matter on which he wanted advice. "There is a people who dwell in our land whose ways are not our ways and who do not follow our laws."

Guess who! Anyway Haman got permission from the King to dispose of the Jews at the earliest opportunity.

It so happened, however, that a cunning old Jew called Mordecai lived near the Palace gate. He had mortally offended Haman by not standing to attention when the General came in to the Palace. So much so that Haman decided that all the Jews should be massacred. Mordecai, however, had two great assets: a very beautiful daughter named Esther, and the fact that he had saved the King's life by keeping a sharp eye open and unmasking a plot to murder him. By this time the King was feeling lonely and missing his wife. He called again for his wise men, and asked them what he should do. "Oh King, live forever. You cannot forgive the Queen. Instead you should hold a beauty competition and replace her with someone even more beautiful."

Ahasuerus did as he was told. At the beauty competition he was so smitten with Esther that he decided at once, called her to him and pointed his sceptre at her saying: "Live forever. You have pleased me greatly: you have but to express a wish even up to half my kingdom and it shall be granted."

Esther gave it a quick thought, and came up with the idea that, as the new Queen, she would like the King to invite Haman to dinner.

The King duly obliged. In the meantime he had been informed of the great service Mordecai had done for him – and that he was a Jew.

Haman came to dinner. The conversation did not go as well as he hoped. The King left Esther and the general for a couple of minutes to attend to a message. Esther actually threatened Haman. The warrior went on his knees to implore her not to ruin his career – at which point the King returned, Esther screamed and accused Haman of trying to rape her.

The upshot was that Haman was hanged on the gallows 50 cubits high, which he had prepared for Mordecai, who was promoted to be a trusted adviser, Esther and Ahasuerus lived happily ever after – and the Jews were not massacred.

The reader will rightly understand that this is a somewhat free abbreviation of that great story – but it is, in its slapdash way, close to the Biblical text – and could well have happened at any time in history.

Anti-semitism is a very long standing disease. The Jews pay for the crime of being rich and intelligent, following their own customs and playing the violin better than anyone else. It is not surprising that extreme justification of anti-semitism was inspired by a French diplomat (Count Gobineau) and an English admiral's son (Houston Stewart Chamberlain). Chamberlain was particularly vicious, and he inspired the Kaiser in the pre war years to a wildly appreciative correspondence on the subject.

Anti-semitism was perhaps not so extreme and widespread in France and England, but it certainly existed throughout the last 200 or 2,000 years. Many of the French were as eager as the Nazis to send their Jews to concentration camps during the German occupation.

The doctrines that the nation was more important than the individual, that only ruthless militarism would bring the dream of a greater Germany into reality and that complete obedience to its leadership was essential were all much older than the 20th century.

One of the earliest events which affected German mentality was the Hermannschlacht, or as the Romans would say, the battle against Arminius. The Romans were getting tired of the lawless tribes in the northern plains, which had frequently been invaded by the savage Barbarians from the east. They sent an army under Germanicus to punish them. It resulted in a complete and humiliating defeat of the Roman legions. The barbarian troops hid in the forests of the Teutoburger Wald and took the Romans entirely by surprise. The two sides took an entirely different view of the battle and of its consequences, as is the way of History. The Roman view was that Arminius treacherously guaranteed them a safe passage, only to go back on his promise and stage a Glencoe like massacre. Thereafter the German tribes never experienced the civilized law and order of the Roman Empire, and have always lagged behind the rest of Europe ever since.

The German view was that the blue eyed, fair haired German outfought and outthought the inferior Mediterranean races, thus preserving the purity of the North German race against the corruption of southern blood. Tacitus, anxious to show the decadence of the Roman Empire at that time, partly agreed.

Later the Minnesänger went round German speaking courts from Rhineland to Austria celebrating mythical or semi-historical heroes from the battles of the Frankish or Western Germans against the successive hordes of invaders from the East. There were mixtures of several traditions: the lower Rhineland, the northern coasts, which incorporated elements of Scandinavian mythology, the Burgundian legends, and a version of the Arthurian legends. Siegfried and Brunnhilde were Rhineland figures, and the Nibelungenlied, from which Richard Wagner derived his inspiration, was the first major poetic written work, drawing on all these sources, more usually passed on by troubadours or by story telling. In the absence of reliable historical records, Germany felt the need for a heroic past to reinforce their conviction that they were a superior race forged by the hostility of their neighbours.

*

The dream of a Great Germany, disciplined, heroic and obedient, continued almost unabated through the centuries, reaching a new peak in the years after the French Revolution and the defeat of Napoleon.

Partly because the Germans had always had to fight ruthlessly for survival, they learned to be tough, and to value power above any consideration of international morality or Christian humility. Hitler so continually reminded them that they were superior to anyone else that eventually they nearly all were convinced that it was true – and his initial success reinforced that view. In the early 19th Century the Romantic poets, like Arnim and Arndt and Görres, so gentle and sentimental in their quieter moments, wrote the most bloody and nationalistic songs in praise of battles for the greater Germany. Historians like Treitschke (immensely popular and influential), and philosophers, like Herder and Fichte and Spengler confirmed that while France stood for the reign of Reason, the Germans believed in emotions, power, national supremacy and the subordination of the individual. As Nietzsche put it: "Ye say that a good cause will even sanctify war! I tell you, it is a good war that sanctifies every cause!" Wagner, whose political and racialist views are not entirely obvious in his operas, reveals himself as a typical anti-semitic nationalistic fanatic in his correspondence.

All the early myths, largely borrowed from mediaeval Minnesänger and stories about the Scandinavian gods, tended to end in bloody murder and wars. They were all waged to 'bring light to dark places': a vague association with a Christianity that had little to do with peace on earth or humility. The ruthless were the heroes, the spread of power their aim: the Barbarian values got results.

Of course the prevailing views were not universally accepted. Goethe and Schiller, Bach and Beethoven were not held back by the pressure to uniformity. But in high places there was little disagreement; the Prussian junkers and the

Kaisers were solidly united in their ultimate view of a greater Germany. Bismarck was cunning enough to avoid directly offending powerful opponents, but quite happy to drive the Danes out of Schleswig-Holstein. Even Frederick the Great, with his musical gifts and admiration for French culture, was equally clear about his priorities: Deutschland über alles. Exceptions prove the rule: Mendelsohn was a popular in spite of his Jewish background. Even Bismarck expressed admiration for Disraeli: "Ah, the old Jew! There's a man for you!"

Remember too that Marx was a German Jew and had a considerable following in some of the German states. One must never forget that until the war of 1870 Germany still consisted of a number of very different states, of which Bavaria and Baden Würtemberg held out against Prussian influence for a very long time. Some states were Bishoprics, or had Grand Dukes or Princes in charge, some were very Roman Catholic, some very Lutheran, some enlightened and cultured, like Weimar, some even fairly democratic. Yet, step by step, they saw that their bread was buttered on the Prussian side. The customs union, and then the defeat of the combined states by Prussia, and the success of the Franco-Prussian war united them as never before. It taught the southern states the advantages of being allied to Bismarckian ruthlessness.

As far back as the mediaeval times there were references to a greater Germany. The nationalist-romantics of the late 18th and early 19th Century generally agreed that this should ultimately include Alsace, the Saarland, Schleswig-Holstein, Poland, Austria, Sudentenland, most of Switzerland and bits of Holland.

*

Yet a marked difference persisted even after two World Wars in Hitler's time. Bavaria was much more liable to go through periods of unstable extremes. Prussia and Brandenburg in general and Bismarck in particular shared the long range aims, but they had a military discipline, which included a certain sense of honour and a thorough contempt for democracy. Although there was never any possibility of disobeying orders on grounds of individual principles, or of avoiding a good chance of a profitable invasion on moral grounds, they viewed the formation and the viciousness of the S.S. with a distaste, partly due to snobbishness. Munich was a fertile ground for support for Hitler's extreme plans – but also a centre of opposition, and of left wing ideas.

The story of Ernst Wiechert is very revealing. Wiechert was the most popular novelist of the Thirties and Forties. An ex-officer and holder of the Iron Cross, he had a considerable following among the youth of the country. His "Jerominkinder" gives a remarkably vivid and objective account of the sufferings of an East Prussian village throughout the first half of the 20th Century as they affected all kinds of different people. His outlook was tolerant, conservative, deeply attached to the country life: in no way a revolutionary. But he didn't hesitate to criticize the Nazis, and was duly sent to a concentration camp. Fortunately he had powerful friends. Goebbels sent for him and told him: "We know that you have considerable influence and have served our country well, and we are prepared to release you. But if you publish any criticism of our policies again you will return to the concentration camp and will never emerge again."

So Wiechert went home, went on writing and gave a full account of the horrors of the 'Totenwald' (forest of the dead), carefully buried in his extensive garden and published after the war. Most of the distinguished writers of that time, like Thomas Mann, left the country, or kept quiet until after the war.

There were serious, but ineffectual and disorganized attempts by liberal socialists and Marxists to gain power under the Weimar republic, but the great financial crisis called for a strong hand – and the time and circumstances gave Hitler the chance to unite the country in pursuit of old ideas.

The extreme policies which he was able to introduce later were entirely due to von Schirach's monopoly of ruthless control of education in the Thirties, which provided ready material for the S.S. and the Gestapo.

*

The post war change was astonishing. There was no sign of the expected resistance, resentment or sabotage. All the German energies were thrown behind the rebuilding of the country: new car parks, where there had been devastating bombs, slums making way for splendid housing. Jo and I watched builders working all night with the help of floodllighting, rebuilding Hamburg at an unbelievable speed. The almost universal feeling was one of relief. What had happened to the millions cheering at the Nüremberg rallies? Where were the thousands who had worked in the concentration camps and execution squads, or the hundreds of thousands who stood by, knowing what was going on?

Many were killed, a few of the worst were tried at Nüremberg and executed. Some escaped to South America. Most put aside their uniform and found respectable jobs, kept quiet and thanked God they hadn't ended up in the Russian Zone. The trials for war crimes were inevitable, but it was also inevitable that they should be trials of the vanquished by the victors. War is by its nature criminal and most of the horrific crimes are caused by fear. We were not free of guilt ourselves – but the concentration camps were different.

Yet senior German officers in prisoner of war camps in England were recorded reminiscing to each other quite openly and with no sign of repentance about the parts they had played in mass executions.

Now the generation which was brainwashed in the Thirties has gone. A few of their children, now old themselves, may occasionally meet and talk nostalgically of the dreams of their youth. But now a new generation has risen to the top, which has put the past aside, made friends with its former enemies and is working for a peaceful Europe. It is led by a woman: Hitler would have fainted with shock! They have achieved the position of top European nation by hard work and prudence, without stepping on the toes of France and England – although there is no open discussion of whether France or Germany is to be the ultimate leader. War is no longer a subject of enthusiasm.

There are still traces of anti-semitism and of fear of gypsies. There are still a few discontented youths who resurrect Nazi ideas when things go wrong. Let us hope that they don't, and try to keep our eyes open. I remember very vividly one of my au pairs watching a film about the concentration camps. She burst into tears, then asked me who all those brutally treated people were. I told her that most of them had been Jews.

Her reply was: "Oh, I see . . ."

It is, indeed, a strange world, and we are, I fear, just as strange as the Germans – and even the French!

*

I will conclude with one or two pre 1914 quotations to support my view that most of Hitler's ideas were by no means his invention.

The poet Arndt wrote in 1809: "What is your Fatherland? Prussia, Sweden, Rhineland, Baravia, Westphalia, Pommerania, Tyrol, Switzerland, Austria?"

"Oh no, no, no! "The Fatherland must greater grow . . . "Where every Frenchman is a foe."

Houston Stewart Chamberlain (the son of a British Admiral!) wrote in 1901, to the Kaiser: "Science, Philosophy and Religion can today take no onward step save in the German tongue . . . and because the German soul is indissolubly bound up with the German tongue, the higher development of mankind is bound up with Germany: a mighty Germany spreading far across the earth the sacred heritage of her language, affirming herself everywhere and imposing herself on others . . . God builds today on Germany alone!" The Kaiser was delighted. Chancellor Bülow addressing the German nation in 1914: "Our troops have occupied Luxemburg and are perhaps already on Belgian soil. Gentlemen, this is contrary to international law. It is true that the French government has declared that France is willing to respect the neutrality of Belgium, as long as her opponent respects it . . . France could wait, but we couldn't so we were compelled to override the just protest of the Luxemburg and Belgian governments. The wrong – I speak openly – that we are committing, we will endeavour to make good as soon as our military goal is reached." He said in another speech a little later: "I feel no embarrassment in saying here publicly that for Germany Right can never be a governing consideration."

In about 1906 the Pan German League published a map for greater Germany to be achieved by 1950. Alsace, Lorraine, Flemish Belgium, the Netherlands, Southern Denmark, German Switzerland, N.E. Italy and Trieste, Hungary, Bohemia, Slovakia, part of Lithuania and most of Poland. It was not very different to lists drawn up by the Romantic nationalists at the beginning of the 19th Century.

In 1899 an article in the press declared: "Germany will never win Germandom in the East March as long as there are Poles: this people whom fate had unfortunately given as the irreconcilable enemy at our side . . . the premise that there is equality of nationality in the East March must be given up."

And – so – on. Although Germany is by now largely cured, some of the complexes, which have for so long haunted it are still lurking and could be resurrected if it had to face disasters again.

Chapter Twenty Four

Return to Cambridge

There was a small grant towards members of the Forces returning to university, but it was not enough to enable Jo and me to live together throughout the university years – nor was the university able to cope with the large number of returning students who had become married. So poor Jo had to spend most of her time either with her parents or mine. With the best of intentions on all sides this was not an ideal set up. Money was short, rationing of food and clothes still in force. But she made a great go of it.

In England generally, and in Cambridge especially, the returning members of the Forces were startled to find how big a difference they felt between the civilians, who had never been away to war, and themselves. We thought the older generation were continually fussed about matters that seemed to us to be of no real importance. At Cambridge we had an arrogant contempt for the 'children' who came straight from school to university and studied Arts subjects – languages, English, History etc: – and wrote and talked about Death, Disease, Love, Hatred and Poverty without having experienced any of them. We felt the same way about the older Dons who had spent all the war years at university. Most of us were in our late twenties; some had been Majors, or Wing Commanders or Naval Captains. We played at obeying university rules – not being outside the college and not having ladies in our rooms after midnight. The college Porters were very understanding and helpful. To save them bother if we wanted to come back late we found it quite fun to climb in: St. John's was too widespread a college to be an impregnable fort.

Jo's parents had never had the experience of having a son; mine had never had a daughter and St. John's had done its best to keep all females outside the college walls – except the bedmakers, who, according to college statutes, had to be "horribile visu".

I felt a completely different person to when I had first been to Cambridge. Jo was beginning to open my eyes a little to the world to which I had been a complete stranger ... motherhood, a small baby, the world of feminine concerns, the love of beauty and elegance from a new angle, the deep preoccupation with truth about the spiritual dimensions and concern for other people's feelings. Much though the war had done for me it had done little to cure my selfishness; whereas Jo had an amazing ability, even after a very short acquaintance, to understand, sympathize and help with other peoples' fears, difficulties and problems. The big world of 'male chauvinist piggery' was even bigger in the 1940s, and I had never realized quite how unbalanced our excellent pre-war education had been. Jo, very sensitively and tactfully set about trying to cure me over the next half century or so.

Another change was that I was really motivated to work and deeply interested in reading more to find the answers to the German problem.

So with the help of Robin Robinson, now returned from bomber command with a D.F.C. and in adjoining rooms, I reorganized my work and enjoyed a profitable and successful year. I got a First in both French and German, a Wright Prize for Languages, and a Larmor Award for outstanding all-round contribution to the college. I was secretary to the May Ball, got my blue for Rugby, played for the University at squash and the Crusaders at cricket . . . it was a year in which St. John's won the 'cuppers' at rugby, and, I think, cricket, football and rowing.

I owe a lot to the 'Robinson system' of work. He advised me to go to only one or two outstanding lectures, once I had got a reading list for the year. He pointed out that most lecturers were bad speakers and had expressed what they had to say much better in books. Instead of reading widely and thinking for themselves about what they read, most undergraduates went to all the lectures and regurgitated the same views as were given to them by the lecturer. Lectures also wasted a huge amount of time. You would go to one at 9 a.m.–10 and another at 11–12. In between 10 and 11 you didn't have time to go back to your rooms and get down to serious work, so you went to the 'Whim' where all the prettiest student-hunting girls served coffee. When the second lecture finished at 12 there was no time to get down to work before lunch, so you went to the Baron of Beef, where a half pint of mild cost only two and a half old pennies. The afternoon was reserved for games and/or choir practice and another lecture, and after dinner you socialized, or had a tutorial, or wrote an essay as demanded by your supervisor. Three hours of work at most, and the greater part of it note taking and listening.

Instead of that Robin recommended going to the University library, getting the books on the reading list, or buying them in the cheap editions with which Cambridge abounds and working from nine to one every morning without fail, except for away matches. You would work either in the library or your rooms. In my case Robin and I shared a working room. We would put in another hour between games and 6 p.m., meet in the Hawks Club for a pint (where we would meet with Sandy Smith and sing Beethoven's 7th) and, after dinner in college, work from 8 to a variable bedtime, usually midnight. Every book we read we would briefly summarize, collect quotes and write down our own reactions. And we would always read a relevant book not recommended by the lecturers. Robin was a historian, and eventually recognized as being a great one. He became Professor of Modern History – starting as a left-wing critic, and ending by writing a book which gave credit to the British where credit was due. When it came to an overlap between our two courses – French and German History literature and culture – we would sometimes break for an exchange of views. Of working class origin, Robin, I suspect, felt he had a mission to make ex public schoolboys understand and sympathize with the lot of the workers.

> "It's the sime the 'ole world over
> It's the poor wot gets the blime.
> It's the rich wot lives in clover
> Innit all a bloody shime."

He certainly taught me how to work, although he had moved substantially to the centre politically by the end of our time. He was already mumbling about the importance of a third party by the time Roy Jenkins, Shirley Williams and co. brought one into political life. He also kept goal for the University football team. He became a popular Don working both at Cambridge and Oxford. I was sorry to lose touch with him, but it was inevitable after, in spite of having a bright young American wife of his own, he attempted unwelcome advances to Jo.

If Robin taught me to work, Sandy Smith taught me to play. He had that rare and wonderful capacity to bring cheer, kindliness and humour to every place and situation in which he found himself. In the invasion he had played a vital and heroic part, about which he was always absurdly modest. He was one of the select band chosen from the 6th Airborne to land in gliders on the night before D. Day, seize and hold the Pegasus Bridge over the canal which a German armoured Division would need to cross if it was going to attack the Allied beachheads. Sandy's part was described in a well known book devoted to that famous attack. He was wounded in the wrist and awarded an M.C. That wound probably cost him a place in the England cricket team after the war, though it didn't stop him driving 300 yards and scoring centuries in club cricket. At the time he was recorded as saying: "There goes my batting average!" [He had topped the batting averages and scoring rating for English schools in his last year at Tonbridge.] I was privileged, years later, to hear a much more vivid account of his war-time role from his platoon sergeant. He told me: "Sandy Smith was the greatest officer in the British army. However frightening the situation, he would turn it into a game that you were going to win. You somehow knew that you were safe with him." Sandy was only 22 at the time.

It was not long before he was promoted to Major and had more adventures near the German frontier.

The Germans had put concrete blocks in the field where any gliders would have to land. Sandy's glider hit one of them, and most of the crew including himself were badly shaken up. Sandy had a badly bruised thigh. It was very dark and some of the weapons, including anti tank piats were scattered and couldn't be found. The other two platoons had a rough landing too, and of the other two officers one had been killed and the other wounded. Sandy led his men across the bridge against sporadic fire from the Germans, who were just beginning to wake up in the pill boxes covering the bridge. A grenade splinter went through Sandy's wrist, but his platoon cleared the pill boxes. The one containing the officer in charge, provided a touch of comedy. The German officer, still in bed just wouldn't believe that Sandy was really a British officer; he thought it was an elaborate leg-pull or a trial run arranged by his superior officer to see how alert they were.

Once the Germans guarding the bridge had been killed or rounded up, the really grim problem was that the tanks would come and retake the bridge, in which case the operation would have failed.

Sandy turned to his Sergeant, 'Wagger' Thornton, and called his men together. He told them to expect a tank attack, and soon. They were all to remain hidden and not to move or fire, until he gave the signal. The small but extremely cool and brave sergeant was told to take the piat and its one and only missile – the others had been lost in the landing – get into the trench nearest to the end of the bridge and when the leading tank stopped, and the crew started to look for signs that it might be mined, he must fire and be sure not to miss. He apologized for not doing it himself, but his wounded wrist would make his aim unreliable.

Firing a piat, which lobs an armour piercing bomb not much further or more accurately than a cricketer throws a cricket ball, requires the firer to stand up. It was a hell of a responsibility. But the Sergeant carried out his orders with spectacular success. The leading tank, covered by the guns of the second one, lurking in the shadow of the trees 100 yards behind, halted just short of the end of the bridge.

Not only did he hit the tank, but set fire to the ammunition. There was a huge series of explosions: the tank blew up and there followed a firework display that could be seen miles away. This was the signal Sandy had hoped for. His platoon opened fire with everything they'd got. The second German tank didn't wait to see any more, but turned tail and fled. Afterwards it transpired that he had reported that the bridge was held in strength with powerful anti tank guns and that it would be impossible to attack until the next day ... By the next day reinforcements had arrived and the situation was saved.

I kept in touch with Sandy after the war. He joined Burmah and became Personnel Manager. He was sent to Pakistan, which he loved, because he had been brought up there by his parents. The Pakistanis chose him to go at the head of their troops sent to the Coronation of Elizabeth II and invited him to address their officers on modern warfare. He had the delightful knack of always saying what he thought without causing offence, always seeking the positive side of any situation, and laughing at any sign of pomposity. He returned to England to captain the Cotswold village cricket XI and to be the focus of the attention of nearly every twenty year old girl in Wiltshire. Eventually he settled down with Carole as a third and final wife and became a good paterfamilias. Sadly he developed a swift cancer before he was old. Age would not have suited him ... I think the Canadian nurse who helped to look after him in his characteristically gallant last days fell in love with him too.

It was a great privilege to know him. At Cambridge we used to fight most evenings at 6 o'clock, clearing the furniture to make room. Hitting the face or testicles was banned and, if intolerable pain was being inflicted, we tapped the ground three times. It lasted about 5–10 minutes, kept us fit and gave us a thirst quenched at the Hawks' Club.

On one occasion, when we were at Cambridge together, we had celebrated St. John's great success on the games field. We were in evening dress, black ties. Our way home took us along the river. There was a small stream about 20 feet across, a tributary of the Cam. A pipe crossed the stream, which would save us an extra quarter of a mile's walk. Sandy said: "I bet you £5 you can't walk across the stream using that pipe." It was about 4 inches wide. Naturally, being well primed with good wine, I could not refuse. I was successful, and Sandy followed suit. Before handing over a fiver, Sandy said: "That was a bit too easy: can you do it backwards?" Flushed with confidence, I said: "Of course". I managed it again, followed by Sandy. I should by then have been on my guard. This time he said: "Right, but if you were a real athlete, you'd be able to hop over on one leg". Like an ass I set off, slipped and fell in up to my armpits in filthy mud. Sandy roared with laughter, made no attempt to follow, and walked the long way round.

But he paid the cleaning bill + £5, saying that it was well worth it to see what an idiot I could be.

At the end of that very good Cambridge year, I had to make up my mind whether to turn my war-time degree (awarded to service men on two years' work) into a full peace time degree on three years' work by staying on an extra year. I was getting on in years (27) and was anxious to get started on a career and earning money and to see more of Jo. The college persuaded me to stay on. This was a pity in some ways, particularly because I failed (by a tiny margin) to repeat my First, getting a 2 (1), but I met some great people and represented the university at squash and rugby again.

I think it would be sensible at this point to give a brief account of what had happened to my parents and my three brothers during the war. Dad and Mum battled on in the face of all the war time difficulties and worries about their sons – not only to keep Sedbergh School going but to make its reputation for academic distinction, music and games flourish. With minimal domestic service and an elderly teaching staff, they made their four sons royally welcome on the few occasions they were in the country or got leave, and provided a refuge, not always without tensions for their daughters-in-law.

John, the eldest brother was the first to join the army. He gave up his job teaching at Rugby and became an intelligence officer, for which he showed such aptitude that he was soon put in charge of a course for intelligence officers in Oxford as a major, and was then taken on by MI.6: he was put in charge of the Italian campaign intelligence later with the rank of Brigadier. Married to Margaret Hone at the beginning of the war, by the end of hostilities he had two sons, but his prolonged absences abroad, even after the end of the war, resulted in his falling desperately in love with a girl in Paris. This caused a few years of acute strain on his marriage to Mar, who finally agreed to have him back, and to go with him to America where she found happiness again, and gave him a daughter, Sally, to add to James and Sandy. John was a great leader, equally at ease with Top People and the locals in the village pub: his charm consisted of a strange blend of self-deprecation and immense confidence. Except when they fell in love with him, women were either slightly afraid of him or resentful of his tendency to live in a world dominated by males. I think he was in reality shy with the fair sex, although extremely attractive; they often mistook this for a personal slight. I was a huge admirer of brother John: kind, generous, always fun to be with, good at everything – but must record the fact that, in a family who were mostly male chauvinist pigs, he was no exception. I remember on one of the rare occasions that he undertook to cook a meal, his voice coming from the kitchen. "What is a knob of butter?" And then a little later "I'm sorry about the cauliflower . . . I though the white sauce came out of it automatically when it was boiled." To be fair, he did his fair share when he and Margaret reached old age and retirement!

Rab too had just started on his teaching career at Harrow, got married to Priscilla Crump, to whom he wrote every day of his absence in the army. As we expected, he joined the gunners, specializing initially in Bofors anti-aircraft. After training on Salisbury Plain he went to Egypt with the Eighth Army, was promoted to Captain. When his Bofors unit was disbanded for the Italian Campaign, he got a job, with some help from John, in Intelligence and finished the war in Northern Italy, Bavaria and Austria. He made some firm friends in the army, great admirers of his personal standards in some fairly wild company, who met with him every year to dine and reminisce together. He returned to Harrow after the war, and we had a great couple of years together playing for London Scottish, but he soon left for a Housemastership at Appleby College in Canada, and then to New Zealand as Head of Wanganui, ending up as Head of Loretto.

Pad served his medical apprenticeship at Edinburgh and then Bath. He married Pat Seddall from Edinburgh and was sent as a member of the Army Medical Corps to India. This was a very prolonged parting at a young age, and I gather that there were faults on both sides. Pad ended up in charge of the military hospital in Poona. On return to Bath at the end of the war Paddy and Pat were reconciled. Pad was overworked as a registrar waiting for dead men's shoes, looking after more obstetrics and gynaecology cases than the consultants. Eventually he decided that he was likely to get his consultancy more quickly abroad, and he got a tempting offer from Canada through an admirer. They insisted on his retaking his consultants examinations, although they had to send them back to England to be assessed! Pat and he had three children, Michael, Simon, and Ferelyth, but soon after they left they found that Pat had a brain tumour. In spite of the highest level attention, it carried her away. He quickly married again, Eve Didychuck, a humorous and kindly Ukrainian. Not an easy time, but Pad's career in Canada was brilliant: largely the result of his phenomenal determination in his own troubles in his youth. He had 3 more children by Eve: Patrick, Tacey and Logie.

By strange coincidence mum's brother, Captain John Brougham R.N., who ended up in charge of the Dartmouth Naval College, also had four boys of almost exactly the same ages as us, all four in the navy as we had been in the army. The eldest, Micky, was gunnery officer on H.M.S. Hood, luckily transferred to another ship just before the Hood was sunk by the Bismarck. The second, Tim, was involved in the hunting of the Graf Spee on either H.M.S. Ajax or the Achilles and became a naval historian after the war. The third, Pat, was in the Fleet Air Arm and emigrated after the war to Australia. The youngest, James, was a submarine officer who lost his life when his boat was sunk on its maiden voyage with the loss of all hands.

Chapter Twenty Five
Rugby

On leaving Cambridge I joined the London Scottish Rugby Club. In those days it was a great side as well as tremendous fun. I was lucky to be able to come to an arrangement whereby I could coach Tonbridge School for the early part of the season and play for London Scottish for the rest of the season.

I played fly half, with Rab, Donald Sloan or Eric Ogilvy in the centre and two formidable wings: Dr. Doug Smith and T.G.H. Jackson. Tommy (later Sir Tommy) MacPherson, uncomplainingly took on the role of all rounder, playing at full back, stand off, centre or scrum half as required. All the three quarters played for Scotland at one time or another. The forwards could be quite formidable on their day, but it was a time when Scotland tended to be out-powered in the scrum. Bill MacPherson, (better known, later, as Sir William of the famous report exposing institutional racism among the police), was a doughty front row forward, and captained the team the year before I did. Howard Campbell too was capped for Scotland, and so was Doug Keller in the back row, although an Australian. Frank Coutts was a rugged forward who had had a gallant war and became President of the Scottish Rugby Union. Bill Young was later a missionary doctor to Africa, but his experience as a successful heavyweight boxer was of more immediate use to us. He used to specialize in catching kick-offs and handing off any intending tackler with unusually well directed vigour. Alan Todd and Charlie Lowe completed the pack: Charlie was a baker, and he used to turn up after working most of the previous night. Jock Hazell was a sprightly wing forward unlucky not to be capped.

They were a distinguished lot, but also a lot of fun. In those days Bill was better known for his ability to sing previously unknown verses of the 'Ball o' Kirriemuir' all the way from the Gare du Nord to the Gare de Lyon. Not the formidable wigged judge of later days.

Amateur Rugby was very different from the modern game. We loved to win, but it wasn't worth cheating for. There may have been the odd bit of punching in the scrum, but we didn't set about injuring key members of the opposition systematically. Considerations of health and safety have not made the game less violent; although some new rules are sensible, the general effect has been to make the scrums and line outs more complicated. Who was responsible for collapsing the scrum? Did the man who was tackled fail to release the ball and roll away? Was that a high tackle, or did the man tackled try to duck under a legitimate tackle?

Sadly these decisions decide the fate of matches more often than tries do. And it is exasperating for players and spectators to see a scrum being interminably reset until one side (usually the defending) is penalized over an offence which is largely a matter of opinion.

There is no doubt that the professional teams of today would beat any teams of yesterday's amateurs. Sheer size, speed and defensive tactics would make any such match unequal. The successful New Zealand side which toured Britain just before the war was considered big by the standards then prevailing. Their backs averaged only just 13 stone and their forwards 14½ stone. One forward was particularly feared as a giant. He was 6ft 3ins and 16 stone. Today he would scarcely be large enough to be considered for a second row place with a first class club.

Defences were not so highly organized. But for that very reason, individual backs had more opportunity to develop attacking skills. There were players whose side steps, swerves and dummies were devastating. Do you remember little Phil Bennet's three electrifying side steps which eluded the entire All Blacks pack near his own line to start That Try? Of course you do. And there were half a dozen, who could always, given 4 yards, be relied on to beat even the best defender. Cliff Morgan, Barry John, Gareth Edwards, Gerald Davies, Jacky Kyle, P.B. Jackson, Philippe Sella, D. Camberabero, Serge Blanco, Bleddyn Williams, David Campese, Andy Irvine, Ken Scotland, Grant Batty and one or two more. Any professional team would be glad to have someone with their skills.

The difference in sporting outlook started before professionalism. I remember two steps on the path downhill. The first time, at a Varsity match, when a wing forward appeared to deliberately kick a prostrate player on the head. Then, in a match between New Zealand and Wales, there was a line out near the Welsh line. A New Zealand forward fell out of the line out holding his jaw, pretending to have been punched by a Welsh forward. A penalty was awarded and converted.

The contrast in playing attitudes is most clearly seen in an incident in a match between France and Scotland immediately after the Second World War. Scotland's captain that day was Keith Geddes; a good full back and a great man. The match was evenly balanced, when the French centre put a clever kick behind the Scottish backs, which rolled towards the corner flag. The very fast French wing chased after it in a close race with Keith. It was one of those situations which nowadays would be referred to the television cameras. The referee had not quite caught up with the play (they often didn't in those days!), but felt that, in view of the uncertainty, the benefit of the doubt should go to the defending side, Scotland. He was actually in the process of signalling a drop out, when Keith stopped him and told him that the French wing had definitely beaten him to the touch down and that he must signal a try. The referee changed his mind and awarded the try to the French.

If that had happened in the 21st Century, Keith would have been shunned by his team and dropped by the selectors. But in 1947 Scotland preferred the truth . . . the match was lost 8–3.

The French team were so impressed that they got together to buy Keith a golden cigarette case inscribed: "To Mr. Keith Geddes who today showed us all an example of British sportsmanship at its best. From the entire French team".

That's not quite the end of the story. Keith himself told me that some official of the Scottish Rugby Union advised him that he should not accept the gift because it smacked of professionalism! None of it could happen now.

My move to London Scottish was a very happy one. They were extraordinarily kind in allowing me to move straight into the team in the second half of the season, and I think I repaid them by playing really well for the next 5 or 6 years. I had a real stroke of luck immediately after leaving Cambridge. I was picked for the Rest of Scotland against the first choice Scottish team in the final trial. My scrum half turned out to be Arthur Dorward, who had been my partner at Sedbergh, and whose brother Tom had played for Scotland with Rab. We knew each other's play well, which was very important in those days when international teams had no time allocated for training together. Later on I was only introduced to my scrum half on the afternoon before the match. Anyway, I played one of the best games of my life. We thrashed the first choice team, and Arthur and I were promoted to the Scotland side at half time, and we reversed the tide being largely responsible for 4 tries.

That led to my first 3 caps, against France, England and Wales. The first two were won and the third lost. For some strange reason I was picked with Arthur Dorward for only one match and although we both earned more caps it was never together.

Playing successfully for the London Scots in the south of England, we always felt that the Scots who were living in Scotland were at an advantage. The Scottish press didn't see us play except on occasional tours and the selectors only paid us occasional visits. And there were a lot of good players in the Borders, who felt that we were Sassenachs in disguise.

I have relegated a more detailed and conceited account of my rugby days to an appendix, with the intention of avoiding boring those uninterested in matches 60–70 years ago.

* * *

In the meantime Jo and I had to earn a living.

There was an opening at N.A.T.O. for interpreters, but a life interpreting other people's views didn't seem attractive. Finally, I applied for a post teaching modern languages and coaching games at Tonbridge School.

Jo and I were summoned to an interview at rather a difficult time. We were just returning from a very joyful and successful tour of France with a combined Oxford and Cambridge side, and, on the last night had danced through the whole night. We arrived at Tonbridge, distinctly the worse for wear, collecting our daughter, Jenny, on the way. The Headmaster was Eric Whitworth, who had been a Housemaster with my dad at Rugby and had known me as a small boy. We distinguished ourselves by oversleeping in the morning. While we were waiting to see the Headmaster, Mrs. Whitworth entertained Jo, me and Jenny to a cup of coffee and a chat. Jenny was aged about three and, unfortunately, decided to crawl into the dog basket. Mrs. W. had always been a doggy person. She said "Don't do that Jenny, dear, it's covered with dog hairs." Jenny gave her a sharp look and said, loud and clear: "Bugger!" It was almost the first word she had spoken, and was not the best prelude to an interview of her parents by a kindly, but distinctly old-fashioned Headmaster.

Nevertheless he must have been broad-minded, because he offered me the job, plus a number of things which were important to me. I would be allowed to play 1st class rugby after the end of the Michaelmas term, provided I coached the school for the rest of the year. I would also have a share in coaching cricket and squash. Jo and I would rent a flat on the edge of the school for £90 a year (quite expensive when the salary offered was the usual teacher's starting salary of £350 a year!). But it was a good school conveniently not too far from Richmond, where the London Scottish ground was situated, but also close to some attractive southern England countryside. Jo and I were very excited by the prospect.

I should perhaps explain this particular French rugby tour, because it had consequences later on. Relations between French and British rugby unions had become a little strained. During the war interpretations of the rules had grown apart. A well-known English club had gone over to play a Parisian side and had made such excessive use of their host's very generous hospitality that only half a dozen of them could manage to put in an appearance on the field of play the next day. They had to borrow half a dozen players from the opposition 2nd XI and were duly humiliated by a huge margin. This did a lot of harm to relations between the two countries, and the French came to use the word 'promeneurs' for the good-time Charlies we were sending over. The combined Oxford and Cambridge side were determined to put matters right. The only untoward incident was in the Hôtel de la Truffe Noire at Brive. Our international wing, Martin Turner, was leaning against some banisters protecting a mezzanine from where he was looking down at the diners, when they gave way beneath his considerable weight. He landed on the corner of a table, had to have six stitches in his massive chin – and scored 3 tries the next day.

Jo was desperately in need of a break after moving to Tonbridge, and I wrote to Serge Saulnier, the President of the French Rugby Union and asked if I could take her, as long as I paid for her share. Serge wrote back charmingly, saying that he would be delighted and that it would be a pleasure to have her on the tour, and he wouldn't dream of letting me pay. He was as good as his word. Jo was fêted everywhere we went. She was the only lady on the tour, and at every new place we went to – Paris, Clermont Ferrand, St. Cyprien, Brive, La Rochelle – there was a bouquet of flowers for her and a seat beside the President of the club. The mission was accomplished. In spite of their excessive hospitality, we won all our matches, never argued with the referee, made good friends and repaired relations. I don't know whether they thought Jo was comfort for the troops, but they treated her like a queen.

Chapter Twenty Six

Tonbridge

Back to Tonbridge. The good thing about our arrival was that we had the best of neighbours. Dry Hill House consisted of three flats. Ours was the middle one, between John Stanton and his wife Helen and Dick Bradley and his (first) wife Meryl. They were roughly the same age as us, John and Helen a little older and Dick and Meryl a little younger. We were all enthusiastic beginners. John was a scientist who frightened his wife by suddenly deciding to take holy orders. He later became Headmaster of Blundell's and a very good water colour painter of landscapes. Dick and Meryl had a rather up and down relationship. He was a useful rugby player (Blackheath) and an amusing wit. Later he was Head of Teddy's Oxford, and then, with his new wife, of Ridley College, Canada. They have all remained good friends who look back at our days of poverty and overwork with surprising pleasure. It was very cheering to have friends who shared our interests and ambition. I think we all hoped, rather conceitedly, that we might bring fresh interests and wider horizons to that very good, but, it seemed to us, a trifle suburban school. Rather like Winchester, a highly competent producer of excellent civil servants, but not of Prime Ministers.

I found that I loved teaching French and German and coaching games and the opportunities for informal contacts with the boys. But shortage of money was a real handicap, especially when it came to furnishing and equipping the house. We had no furniture. Any that could be spared by our parents had already gone to other siblings. Nor did either of us have any money in reserve. After the rent there was little to spare: barely enough to eat well or to dress reasonably smartly. We scraped and scrounged a table and chairs and, greatly daring, bought a sideboard for £25 – an 18th Century mahogany beauty. Thirty years later it was valued at £3,500, but, as is the way with fashion, would not make £1,000 today. No hoover, no fridge, no radio or T.V., no car, no wine except at Christmas and beer only on Saturday night. Life was punctuated by embarrassing visits to the bank manager. It must have been a great strain on our wives. It is greatly to Jo's credit that she never grumbled and was unfailingly cheerful and supportive.

In term time the work was in many ways rewarding, but was all round the clock. We started every morning at 8.45 with assembly or prayers. We then taught all morning, except for a twenty minute break and an occasional 'free period' we used to catch up on corrections. Then it was back home for lunch and to change for games coaching, followed by two more afternoon periods. On half holidays we usually had to look after visiting teams and their teachers. On Saturday afternoons if we were not accompanying our teams on away matches, we were entertaining visitors in the local pub . . . our weekly ration of beer. Saturday mornings were the same as all other days. Even on Sunday, we attended chapel and ran informal training sessions. To pay for our furniture and little extras we volunteered to take little groups of pupils into our homes to play games with them and get to know them and to try to make them feel part of the family. For this we got paid a little more. It usually involved us in two sessions a night: 6.30–7.30, and 8.30–9.30. This meant that I couldn't start reports marks or preparation of periods until the late evening. In those days and, to a slightly lesser extent, still now, the independent schools thought it their duty to report to parents regularly on how their children were doing. So we brought out a fortnightly order in each subject with a brief comment on whether they were working well or not, and how their prospects for the next examinations (O or A levels) were shaping. All work was to be corrected, marked and commented on within a maximum of three days.

I believe that this is the right system. It keeps up competitive pressure and watches the progress of every pupil without the strain imposed by external exams. Now so much time is spent taking exams and mock exams, even in the precious Lower 6th year, that there is not enough time to teach and to learn.

Jo and I were extremely lucky to have two delightful and kind friends outside the school circle: Bill and Betty Hooper. Bill was a charming and modest man, who always maintained that his considerable fortune was the result of luck and was in spite of what he described as his entire lack of brain. He had made his money in Covent Garden after the war by importing bananas of which we had long been deprived and which had suddenly become very popular. Betty was just the same: utterly free of snobbishness or slavery to fashion. They went far to relieving our rather poverty stricken existence by inviting us to their nearby mansion and treating us to champagne dinners every now and again, where we would meet some of the rich and the famous. It was good to glimpse another world.

Returning hospitality was a problem, but they seemed to enjoy our little flat, and Jo had a gift for finding unusual but not very expensive food and turning it into an exotic feast. We invited the new Head, Lawrence Waddy and his twenty year old wife. We had no wine glasses and couldn't tell a Claret from a Beaujolais, let alone what glasses were suited for either or both. However, we borrowed some elegant glasses and Jo arranged (for it was Christmas time) a beautiful crib and manger, complete with cotton wool snow, wise men, angels, donkey, Mary and Jesus. It was all going well until Lawrence leaned across the table to move the crib so that he could have a better look. In so doing he knocked over a candle which set fire to the cotton wool. In a gallant attempt to put out the fire he pushed two of the glasses off the table and shattered both of them ... We replaced the glasses, but hadn't realized that they were extremely expensive antiques. It took us a month of taking extra pupils to make good the loss.

The nicest thing about teaching is the pupils. They really seemed to enjoy the informal contacts we had with them, playing football with a tennis ball on the lawn, or playing card games, or talking about their home hobbies. The greatest reward of that ill-paid profession is that sixty years later you get wonderful letters of appreciation from ex-pupils in all kinds of distinguished jobs. It seems as though time draws a veil over one's failures and weaknesses, and they remember only legendary or imaginary successes and virtues. Old men do not lose their taste for flattery: it is cheering, and very kind of them to take the trouble.

Rhu was born during this time at Tonbridge. I had been in Germany when Jenny was born, so it was a new and vivid experience for me. For some strange reason Jo insisted on staying at home until the last moment. The waters broke, and she had to be half carried downstairs to a hastily summoned taxi. Luckily the hospital was close: Rhu arrived about five minutes after we had got her into a bed. I was asked by the Doctor to unscrew a gas cylinder, but it was too late. Rhu was a fine baby, except that his red hair extended to his back as a carotty fuzz ... hence his name: Rhu is the Gaelic for red.

The whole process is miraculous, but if there is to be another life for me, I hope I shall never be a woman. On the other hand, I shall never forget the look of sheer delight, pride and love in Jo's face.

Two children, a hungry husband and always worried about money. I don't know how Jo remained cheerful through it all. But we were young, and we felt we were doing something worth while and getting somewhere. I think the profession was held in more respect in those days than it is now. The Tonbridge bank manager grew more accommodating, he was a rugby fan and accustomed to dealing with impecunious teachers. In retrospect I think that the chronic worries about money were a valuable part of our education. No-one should be a director or manager unless he has some understanding of the impact of being poor, and many of today's young are brought up to get everything they want without earning it.

In the meantime the rugby, cricket and squash was an escape to pure joy, both as a player and a coach. I had been a little depressed at the standard when I first arrived. We were well beaten by Harrow, which was coached by my brother Rab, and were thrashed by Uppingham, which was in the middle of a great run of success. Their excellent coach was Smallwood: a fine teacher of three-quarters, but a somewhat insufferable opponent. They were the best of the great Midland schools at that time, and when we went to play them we were, I felt, deliberately treated as second class citizens. Instead of being offered hospitality in Smallwood's home I was told to go to the sanatorium for my overnight stay. To make matters worse his remarks on the touchline were extremely patronizing. He left me to my own devices after the match, until the very pleasant Headmaster took pity on me and entertained me to tea.

It was therefore hugely satisfactory when, a couple of years later, Tonbridge had an unbeaten season – including Uppingham. I was very lucky in having some real talent to work with. Colin Cowdrey, of cricketing fame, was also a most useful performer as fly half. Although not the most slender and swift of players, he had great hands, was a fine timer of a pass and could kick as required: short kicks ahead, 'Garry Owens', drop goals, kicks for the corner flag. Another with a great future was David Marques, who captained England a few years later. He was redoubtable as a schoolboy and, like Colin, would practise for a long time after most others had left the field. Several others made their mark as players after they left school: Peter Fuller, Derek Whiting and Alan Gardner. Many of them came to see me years afterwards. David Marques brought his wife and children the year before he died, still looking imposingly fit, although he must already have been beginning the cancer which was to carry him away so swiftly. He confessed to me that when he visited me every Sunday in the rugby season it was not entirely to get the benefit of my advice, but in the hopes that he would catch a glimpse of Jo, for whom he had developed a teenager's crush!

I kept in touch with Colin Cowdrey, too. I was pleased to have bowled him in the Masters' match and to play squash with him, which I was able to win: I could never have done that in the rackets court, where I was a beginner, and where mobility is less important than crisp hitting.

There were many interesting people on the staff. John Knott had guided the cricketers for more than one generation. A man of few, but well chosen words he was still a redoubtable batsman and an old-fashioned respected Housemaster. James McNeil and his wife Jean were wise and amusing. James Stredder and Kitty were good friends and had a daughter the same age as Jenny. He made a skilled job of coaching junior rugby especially as I don't think he had experience of the game himself. An affectionately caricaturable and mildly eccentric institution was 'Bathy', who took all the patter-song parts in Gilbert and Sullivan. In ordinary life he had a pronounced stammer: he must have taken up Gilbert and Sullivan as a cure. When he performed the "nightmare song", or "the very pattern of a modern Major General", or the "cheap and chippy chopper on a big black block" the stammer miraculously disappeared. I still know most of the G. and S. operas by heart.

The Headmaster for most of our time was Lawrence Waddy. He was appointed at a very young age and looked even younger, and his wife was only twenty. Lawrence was a gentle and profoundly Christian man, unfailingly kind. Sadly the stress of being in that very public and responsible position weighed very heavily on his wife, and I believe it was for her sake that he decided to go to the United States, where he made a success of writing religious plays, and was very influential in the educational world.

Another notable character on the Tonbridge staff was the Chaplain, Harry Gripper. A large, comfortable and comforting man, he was involved in a most unusual incident.

The sister in the school sanatorium, a nurse of the firm no-nonsense school, was worried about strange happenings in its, for the time being, empty wing. Beds were moved and banging noises heard, yet as soon as anyone approached it was clear that nobody was there. She didn't want to risk being made to look a fool, and she understood that boys are often clever at arranging pranks, but her assistant was frightened and had threatened to leave unless 'something was done'.

Lawrence listened in some dismay. This was just the kind of problem that a young and religious Headmaster should not get involved in. He wisely thought that Harry Gripper was a highly suitable delegate. Harry took all precautions. He ensured that all doors, windows, and even the chimney should be closed and taped, and he sat outside prepared to keep watch all night if necessary. To his astonishment the reported noises started up, loud and clear. He unlocked the door. There was no sign that any tapes had been interfered with, but beds had been moved and one or two pictures reversed.

He became convinced that this must be a genuine case of a Poltergeist, whose activities are supposedly caused by a disturbed teenager. Harry consulted the Bishop of Rochester, at that time, 'Peg Leg' Chevasse, V.C; Chevasse was totally unsurprised, recommended that he should bless some holy water and repeat certain prayers as he brushed or sprinkled it round the dormitory.

The last bit of the story is even stranger. A short account of it appeared in the press, and Lawrence in a routine masters' meeting said that he regretted the unexplained story, but could not say that it was inaccurate. Dick Bradley and John Stanton remember very much the same version. The Poltergeist (or the ingenious prankster) seems to have disappeared, and no old Tonbridgian has admitted involvement. Only Harry really knew what happened, and he is no longer with us.

Chapter Twenty Seven
A Shocking Sign of the Times?

At Tonbridge, in the early days of peace, there was an unusual incident of a different kind, which seemed to be a sign of the times.

One evening in December 1949, Jock lit a fart. It was a total surprise. Jock was, to all appearances, a typical English gentleman: an ex war-time officer aged about 30. He had recently married my wife's oldest friend, but it was almost the first time I had met him. Over 6 foot tall, elegantly turned out in a smart but conventional suit, nothing in our conversation had suggested the imminence of this unusual ploy. We had dined well, but soberly, at our home, and had been talking of the changes which had befallen us since the end of the war. I don't think that either Jo or Jock's wife, Pat, were the kind of girls that pre-war gentlemen would light a fart at.

It was new ground for me, although war brings out some very strange behaviour. I have no idea what percentage of our population have either lit a fart or seen a fart lit. I can imagine that it might not be rare among teenagers anxious to show off, but I don't know how most people would react if a 30 year old stranger were to perform the act without warning. Is it a purely British phenomenon? I cannot easily visualize a German or Frenchman doing it. Was it an expression of his utter boredom with our conversation? Or was it a bizarre compliment, intended to show that he was happy to be on intimate terms with us? Or, perhaps, an insult, assuming that Jo and I were the kind of people who would never be offended by any breach of good manners? Or was it his usual and highly practised way of breaking the ice?

My parents would have been genuinely and deeply shocked and disgusted. Three of my children would have laughed (as did Jo and I), and one would have been shocked. My grandchildren? I just don't know. Was I just lucky not to have come across this particular party trick in the armed forces? Perhaps in the Sixties it was a common pastime in universities?

Skilled it undoubtedly was. I'm sure that Jock must have devoted a lot of time to perfecting his performance. Nothing could be more certain to fall humiliatingly flat than a failure to ignite.

From a purely technical point of view it was a spectacular success. He took advantage of a pause in the conversation to lean back in his chair. He lifted his knees and clasped them to his chest with his left hand in which he had placed a box of matches. With his right hand he struck a single match, which he applied to his taut trousers with good judgement about an inch from the prospective source of methane. The timing was just right, and the result startling. There was no feeble flicker, like a Christmas pudding too scantily soaked in brandy to produce a lasting flame. A brilliant blue flame spread over an area at least a foot in diameter and lasted surprisingly long. How it failed to scorch the costly material of his suit remains a mystery. It was greeted by a bewildered silence – and then a roar of laughter.

Well . . . what do you think? Queen Victoria would not have been amused. Princess Margaret? At that time I was not a Headmaster . . . Would he have done it, or would I have laughed ten years later? Or is it only funny when done in the presence of pomposity? It would not be in the least amusing, if widely practised among teenagers as part of binge-drinking vulgarity.

How does it rank among the sins? It hardly ranks among the deadly. Nowadays the sins against social conventions and notions of decent behaviour are not thought to be as serious as the new Great Sins: unkindness, intolerance, snobbishness or racism.

Farting is inconsiderate, rude and antisocial: the very essence of uncontrolled decadence. But, as a once in a lifetime surprise in the presence of slightly pompous friends, it can be highly amusing. If it became widespread, it would cease to be funny.

I suspect that much depends on the period of history. Unforgivable in the 1930s it would have been unsurprising in the Sixties. I guess it would be common in the 16th or 17th Centuries, but rare in the 21st Century.

And always to be avoided by Headmasters.

Chapter Twenty Eight

Gresham's

In about 1953 Jo and I found ourselves again in difficulty about money. I began to think about moving to a better paid job – reluctantly, because I loved teaching at Tonbridge. I had a premature shot at the Headmastership of Scotch College, Adelaide. I was only just over 30, and I was understandably rejected. The example of brother Rab in New Zealand, where he and Pip were blissfully happy, may have had something to do with it. Many Bruce-Lockharts and MacGregors had left Scotland for the Antipodes. I thought again of MI6, but the shadow of brother John loomed too large. A lifetime in the organisation where he was close to the top would be embarrassing for both of us. Besides I've always been disorganized where bits of paper are concerned. I would undoubtedly have left top secret documents on the seat of a train. I went up and passed the language tests, but decided against. Then the offer of a quite large salary, if I would look after Harrods' recreation centre. That might have been fun for a while, but I couldn't see it leading anywhere.

We were getting desperate, when I saw that Gresham's School was looking for a new Headmaster. It sounded a most attractive proposition. In the first 40 years of the century it had, under the Headmastership of the remarkable Howson and his successor Eccles, acquired a reputation being a fairly small school, with high standards, a liberal outlook and a producer of remarkable men. It was in a beautiful part of North Norfolk, famous for its bird reserves and even with the possibility of trout fishing. During the war it had been exiled to Newquay, because of fears that Norfolk might be a target for a German invasion. It must have been a difficult time for the school, whose entire campus had been taken over by the military. On their return to Norfolk there had been a stormy period leading to the departure of the Headmaster – Martin Olivier. The press was not kind about the affair, so it was likely that the governors would look for a peaceful solution. Jo and I went up to be interviewed by the Governors at Fishmongers' Hall, more in hope than expectation. I was surprised when they gave me the job: still very young at 34 and rather cocky.

I'll never forget being told by Jo that we had been chosen. She had taken the telephone call and was even more delighted and surprised than me. Of the many kind letters of congratulations I received I treasure the slightly scurrilous verse from my good friend and next door neighbour at Tonbridge: Richard Bradley, later Headmaster of 'Teddy's' at Oxford and Ridley College, Canada:

> 'Oh sing praises, sing praises unto the Lockhart: he has gone up with a merry noise.
> Play to him upon the well-worn symbol: oh sing unto him with a Harpy's melody.
> The vales shall be exalted, and the little hills shall sneer like rams.
> His enemies have emptied an iron tank before him, but are fallen into the midst of it themselves.
> No longer is his handle upon the door, for he has passed into the chamber of Headmastery.
> He, who has dwelt on mushrooms and other fungi, shall eat shrimps and honey in his brightness.
> He shall sip the Ovaltine of Righteousness, who has drunk the waters of Lebeknott.
> A Rose and Crown shall embellish him, and he shall wear a Garter and a Star for ever.
> Oh sing praises, sing praises unto the Lockhart: may he and his kin dwell out of the courts for ever.'

By way of explanation: the 'iron tank' is the bank, much visited by us both when begging for an overdraft. 'Lebeknott' is a reference to John Knott, famous Housemaster at Tonbridge and cricketer, who held court at the two pubs mentioned after matches on Saturday night.

In the next weeks, before going up to be shown round the school, we were invited once or twice to go and meet the Chairman of the Governors, Weston Backhouse. He put us at ease, reassured me that it was Jo's new £18 hat that had done the trick (was it he who had leaked that bit of gossip to the press?) and told us all we needed to know. He was to prove a great Chairman. He had the all important gift of being able to tell you if you were making a mistake so tactfully and gently that you couldn't possibly be upset – and, likewise, to praise you without doing so directly. A fountain of knowledge, he was Chairman of Twining's Tea; before the war he had been the only Briton to beat Amar Bey the great Egyptian squash player, and had had a trial for Ireland at Rugby. A much feared bridge player, he combined a great sense of humour with a razor sharp mind, which he hid carefully behind a somewhat bumbling, self-deprecating manner. A chairman's contribution to speech days is normally confined to an announcement that the fees are going to be increased.

But everyone looked forward to Weston's speeches, which always had a story, which teetered on the brink of doubtful taste, yet never quite overstepped the mark, and had his audience in fits of laughter.

He arranged for Jo and me to go on an introductory trip before we took over. A sunny day in the summer term. The countryside was beautiful. We were met by Bruce Douglas, the second master, fairly small, bespectacled and wise looking. We found out later that he was nicknamed the owl. His alarmingly elegant wife entertained us to tea, and they told me all that they thought a new Head should be told. I was introduced to those members of the staff they thought presentable and got a glimpse of the large boarding house, of which the private side was destined to be our home. It emerged from the conversation that we were expected to run a boarding house as well as the school and that Jo would be responsible for the feeding of boys and guests and finding domestic staff. The private side was large enough for our family and for school guests: the downside was that we would have to pay for almost all the furniture for that very capacious house.

Weston Backhouse told us that the governors would guarantee an overdraft, repayable over the years, which would cover furniture and the purchase of a car, which was a new and exciting departure for us. The salary was £1,800 a year, which was about average for public schools in those days and seemed to us to be undreamed of riches. It was enough for us to live comfortably, but we were not out of the red for about 15 years.

"Callooh! Callay! Oh frabjous day!" No more serious games, though coaching rugby, cricket and squash was still a joy. I found time to become Norfolk's veteran squash champion for six successive years, until my opponent hit me in the eye with the ball, and I had to retire with double vision that lasted a fortnight. The same year my nephew Kim, who had been Scotland's no. 1 squash player for many years, died in a squash court playing someone not in the same class, after only two or three points. I decided that to go on trying to beat players half my age was unwise and gave up at 50. I played an occasional game of cricket with my rustic batting and erratic, but sometimes puzzling leg breaks and googlies. I got 8 wickets for 10 runs against the School 1st XI in one match, when the ball was going more or less where I intended. It included one 6 hit by Crow Goodley, who later played for Norfolk and became the Coroner in Norwich.

Had all that games playing been a waste of time? I sometimes regretted not having spent more of my youth pursuing art, music and writing – all of which I now love. I was always a little frightened of becoming a typical public school games bore. Yet there is no sphere in which one makes so many good friends as the world of rugby, and it is a game which seems to produce people of distinction in a number of ungamesy directions in after life. Being trampled into the mud by an opponent seems to result in a long and close bond.

There is something about the sheer joy of sending an opponent the wrong way, or of timing a side step right, or of flicking a drop shot an inch above the board and into the 'nick', which, even if unrepeatable in old age, gives an exhilaration, which can never be quite replaced by any of the much more worthwhile successes of riper years. Writing a best seller or painting a Highland landscape would be nice, but it could hardly equal an eagle at St. Andrews by an 18 handicap golfer! I learned much of my squash from Brian Phillips at Tonbridge, who was more than once runner-up in the amateur championship, and brought real excitement to the game.

Gresham's in 1955 was celebrating its quatercentenary. In his capacity as a Fishmonger, Prince Phillip paid one of his periodic visits to the school within three weeks of our arrival. Three days before he arrived no carpet had come for the drawing room. It had been a hectic start. Everybody in Norfolk wanted to see the new incumbents. Jo and I were invited almost every day and sometimes twice a day. With all the work for a new Head combined with my own total disorganisation I dropped one or two bricks by failing to turn up to V.I.P. invitations, because I'd duplicated invitations, or just forgotten. I quite enjoyed the Duke's visit ... the first of three or four occasions on which I've met him. We had a long conversation about the relative educational value of team games and of individual sports: particularly athletics. The Duke was a great admirer of Kurt Hahn at Gordonstoun, although his son didn't enjoy his school days there. Like Hahn the Duke preferred individual sports to team games, explaining that to struggle to raise one's own standards was of more benefit to most people than to be caught up in competition with boys of a superior size and physique. I did not entirely agree. The experience of working with a group of people with different gifts seemed to me to be of considerable importance in later life. I could hardly say to the Duke that Hahn had gained his popularity with the press by cultivating V.I.P.s whose sons were not bright enough for Eton or Winchester. Because they wouldn't excel at academic work or games, Hahn tried, quite sensibly, to give them a sense of public service, by his lifeboat and fire service training, and a certain moral atmosphere – which did not always preclude the usual boarding school weaknesses: bullying or snobbishness. My dear nephew Kim went to Salem, where Hahn had taught previously, and, to be fair, had bravely opposed Nazi ideas. His influence was still strong: partly genius, partly mountebank. A powerful character, who attracted disciples, but with a certain lack of humour. Kim said that little moral slogans were posted over their beds: "We must remember to be kind to the little ones."

Salem was a baroque castle converted to a school. As it was one of the first schools to be co-educational, the powers that be decided that the girls should inhabit one wing, and the boys the other. Both had little bed-sitting rooms. They were allowed to visit each other (I hope that this is true, for I only have

Kim's word for it) only on condition that the bed should be trundled out into the corridor. I suppose that, if it is true, it must have been done with the idea that, should anything untoward take place, it would at least be in the maximum discomfort. At least that would be in the best British tradition! Joking apart, a little mockery was justified by his tendency to take himself very seriously, Kurt Hahn was a powerful personality and a valuable innovator, if you took him with a pinch of salt.

I like to think that Gresham's had something of the better side of Gordonstoun about it. Howson, at the beginning of the century had reacted against some of the games and classics-centred traditions of the great public schools of the 19th century, like Arnold's Rugby and Thring's Uppingham. Howson served his apprenticeship with Thring, and admired him, but disagreed with him over some of his policies.

He was convinced that the future of good education lay in something different. It was important that they should learn to do things, instead of just discussing the ideas of the long dead. He wanted his pupils to have the time to learn to work on their own. An atmosphere of trust was created, which encouraged them to work in pursuit of their own interests even if these were outside the normal curriculum. Yet Howson was no woolly idealist who thought that boys should do as they pleased; in some respects he was a bit of a puritan and certainly a disciplinarian. A gifted schoolmaster, his powerful personality was accompanied by a kindly and genuine concern for the successful development of each boy: he would take some of them on dry fly trout fishing in the North of England during the holidays. Most of his pupils admired him, and he ran a school which prided itself on being more adult, more liberal than and morally superior to its contemporary rivals. Certainly he was successful in attracting bright parents and their high-minded children.

He was more widely known for his 'Honour system'. Every pupil was, on arrival, asked to promise:

> Always to avoid impurity,
> Always to confess the truth to the Headmaster,
> Always to refrain from smoking.

This was a mixed blessing. By impurity, he meant dirty talk or masturbation. As a middle-aged bachelor, he viewed sex in all its forms as the great sin. For many intelligent boys this was not easily reconciled with telling the truth to the Head. It is now recognized that nearly all healthy teenage boys masturbate. I have spoken about the impact of the honour system to a number of men who had been in the school under Howson. A few rejected it as an impracticable dream, but many took it very seriously and some agonized over whether they should confess. John Reith (of the B.B.C.) told me that it upset his relations with women for years afterwards. Eric Berthoud, later a distinguished ambassador, told me that he had been beaten in front of the whole school, for what Howson had regarded as a breach of trust and honour. Which was strange, because Howson was widely thought to be against corporal punishment. Few would deny that he achieved a school with a happy atmosphere, conscious of being a forward looking, somewhat superior place. But perhaps there was a whiff of priggishness. For some time they didn't play matches against other schools, partly to avoid vulgar competitiveness and an exaggerated regard for sporting success, partly to avoid contamination by the impurity of other schools. Nevertheless they played against adult teams to enable those who had natural ability to hone their skills.

Howson died soon after the war, heartbroken at the loss of so many of his most promising pupils. His successor Eccles was a different kind of man. Not an innovator, he nevertheless admired Howson's ideas. A powerful personality and a stern disciplinarian he was a very efficient and effective Headmaster, perhaps lacking enough warmth to be as remarkable as Howson. That the school continued to flourish until the Second World War can be seen by the exceptional number of brilliant men it produced. Eric Berthoud (ambassador to Poland); Sir Owen Wansborough-Jones (scientific adviser to the government); David Keith-Lucas (the inventor of the jump jet); Sir Jocelyn Simon (the solicitor-general); Lord John Reith, Sir Cecil Green and John Tusa (the creator, the Director General and the Managing Director respectively of the B.B.C.); Alastair Hetherington (Editor of the Guardian); Harry Hodson (Editor of The Sunday Times); Alan Hodgkin (President of the Royal Society and Nobel Prize for Medicine); the poets Stephen Spender, W.H. Auden and J. Pudney; Ben Nicholson (the artist); Spencer-Jones (the Astronomer Royal); an archbishop and three bishops; Christopher Cockerell (the inventor of the Hovercraft); Benjamin Britten and Lennox Berkeley (the musicians); Peter Brooke (the director); Erskine Childers (the President of the Irish Republic); Tom Bourdillon and Percy Wyn-Harris (Everest climbers and explorers); Sir Robert Wray (Deputy Supreme Commander of European Allied Command); David Lack (the world's leading ornithologist) and countless more, eminent in a wide variety of fields.

There were also a few who some would consider notorious. Donald MacLean, traitor and spy, but also a scholar and top of the batting averages. Several of his contemporaries were prominent members of the Communist Party Tom Wintringham commanded the English battalion of the International Brigade, though he left the Party later. James Klugman became joint leader of the University of Cambridge Communist Party and Secretary of the World Student Association; Cedric Belfrage worked as a wartime Russian agent.

For a small school to produce all these was indeed remarkable. The communist ideas of intellectuals in the inter-war periods were very widespread: liberals who had witnessed the effects of the depression crisis and unemployment at the beginning of the Thirties felt that radical reform was needed and that the cause would be furthered by the Spanish Civil War. They were completely deceived by Stalin (who called them "my useful idiots"), and they imagined Russia to be Utopia. There was no evidence of extreme indoctrination at Gresham's, but some of the liberalisers must have been touched by 'useful idiocy'. It can in no way detract from the astonishingly high proportion who achieved eminence in such a profusion. The pupils were taught to pursue their own enthusiams, and encouraged to think – which is rare and wonderfully effective, but sometimes dangerous.

Not all were happy at school: men of genius seldom are. If a school finds that it has one, the best it can do is to give him time to pursue his speciality, to find help for him, and to keep his feet firmly on the ground of ordinary human decency. This, at least, was something that Gresham's managed to do. The left wing influence was not entirely surprising. It was a time when a large part of the intelligensia in England were keenly aware of the Spanish Civil War as a cause worth dying for, and they believed misguidedly in the Russian Utopia, which they fondly believed was being guided by the benign hand of 'Uncle' Joe Stalin. The fact that two or three prominent members of the communist party emerged from Gresham's is possibly due to the influence of one master in the Thirties, but the extent of his extremism probably went unnoticed because of the prevailing political confusion.

The outbreak of the Second World War hit Gresham's particularly hard. The government decided that Norfolk was a likely target for the threatened German invasion. Gresham's was exiled to far-off Cornwall, and its campus and buildings were given for the duration of the war to the military. The school did a remarkable job under Newall in the south-west, taking over two hotels, as well as having to cope with the usual war-time difficulty of shortage of young staff and domestic help. Their return was not easy either. Valuable Norfolk connections had lapsed and the campus had to be demilitarised and returned to its intended purposes. They also had to cope with a change of Headmaster: Martin Olivier took over. There were disagreements over some of his policies, and complaints were made by boys and staff to the Governors. Max Parsons, an effective and some would say inspiring Housemaster, added to the divisions in the staff by unashamedly running his House as a superior establishment: almost the new Greeks among the Barbarians. He would run some better event – lecture or concert – when Olivier had arranged something for the whole school. It can be a temptation for any Housemaster, and it is not necessarily a bad thing for boys to think that they are better than others; but it was overdone, and I grew to be able to recognize some former pupils of his by their conspicuous failure to acquire the graceful gift of modesty, even after 20 or 30 years.

I do not intend to take sides by entering into details of Martin Olivier's resignation. Knowing the governors of that time as I do, I think they acted for the best. I only met Martin once, and got the impression of a nice, but emotional man. He is supposed to have said of himself and Lawrence: "I ought to have been the actor and he the Headmaster." Let's leave it to him; he ought to know!

Chapter Twenty Nine

Choosing Staff

When Jo and I arrived, we were delighted to find that there were lots of good things to work on. Whatever the prevailing theories and whatever the prevailing condition of equipment and building, there is one thing that matters above all else: the quality of the staff.

Great schoolmasters, those who can inspire moderately talented pupils to a new level of living and learning, will always be rare. Most of us can remember one or two at primary or secondary level, or at university. If a school has three or four of these, it is indeed lucky. It will be a great school, whatever the other circumstances. Such teachers are often mildly eccentric: laws unto themselves who don't necessarily follow the syllabus meticulously. The next group are just good schoolmasters, whole-hearted, hard working and with high aims. Then there are those who, often through no obvious fault, are ineffective: usually because of a mysterious inability to keep order in class. The last group consists of the charlatans and villains, of whom nearly every school will have occasional experiences. At the secondary level false references are not uncommon; at boarding prep school the great danger is from predatory homosexuals. I have been a governor of three prep schools. All three had to deal with members of the staff who had seduced numbers of underage pupils. The saddest and most difficult task is dealing with another group, those who started as whole hearted schoolmasters, but are beginning to lose their grip through sheer exhaustion, money difficulties leading to marital troubles, and disappointment because they have been passed over for Housemasterships or Headmastership. By about the age of 45 they are finding it ever harder to summon up the energy to spread good cheer or inspiration. It is difficult to help them or to find alternative employment for them, although different schools in different settings with different pupils can sometimes spark a surprising recovery.

Ah! That ability to hold your pupils' attention and keep order effortlessly! One gets better at recognizing it at interview, but I don't think there is any infallible way to identify it. A hearty, self confident rugby blue may forfeit all respect and be mercilessly ragged. An Oxford physicist with a First can be incapable of commanding any interest. Teenagers have a shrewd and quick eye for any weaknesses in a newcomer. At some public schools the pupils set about putting young teachers to the test in their very first lesson. Rugby used to specialize in this, with some unusual results. The newly appointed Rev. Waddy had heard about this and decided to take the initiative. He took his place at the rostrum. "Please sit down ... I hear that it is the custom at Rugby School to allow every pupil one warning before he is beaten for any offence – You are all warned."

Others were less lucky. One was tired of being asked frivolous questions by a particular member of his first class. "Oh, do shut up, Robinson", he said. "If you think you can explain things better than me, come up here, put on my gown and take over the class for a minute or two. We'll soon see how clever you are."

Robinson went up, put on the gown, leaned forward and smiled at the expectant class. "You'll be glad to hear, gentlemen, that I've decided to celebrate my promotion by giving you all a free period. You may leave the room." The whole class obeyed him at speed, and had dispersed to their various houses before the novice could stop them.

It was at Rugby yet again that a class carefully set up an amusing little trap for a beginner. The head of the class arranged for every pupil to have a hymn book on his desk. When the master came in everybody stood up politely, and the head of the class handed him an open hymn book and said: "At Rugby, Sir, it is a longstanding tradition that we start the term with a hymn: 'Dear Lord and Father of mankind, forgive our foolish ways.' Unfortunately we have no piano, so you just sing the first line, and we join in." A little embarrassed, because he had no musical training, the newcomer nevertheless did as he was told; at the end of the first line the whole class closed their hymn books, applauded and sat down.

Not really vicious or unkind, even faintly civilized, but the newcomer's reaction might be instrumental in deciding how easy or difficult he might find his relations with that class.

How should a Headmaster decide whether a candidate is likely to teach his pupils with ease and confidence? Adolescent boys tend to like a touch of eccentricity or originality beyond the ordinary run of the mill competence ... some distinction or enthusiasm in a non-school context, or experience of a wider kind. Immediately after the war those who had seen active service found it easier than those who came directly from school and university, and the division persisted for some years afterwards. Over the years I improved at selecting. To begin with it was important to know how to evaluate references. I was astonished to learn how untruthful many of my Headmaster colleagues were. The better the school giving the reference was, the more likely it was to be critical, but also truthful and reliable. Bad schools usually try to make out that all their geese are swans. Given a list of qualities to be graded one to ten, they will tick every quality as grade one for very moderate candidates. My service with officer selection boards, for all three services, provided spectacular proof of the unreliability of such grading. You watch a group of candidates go through all manner of tests, and you find that the one graded as lowest by the board is rated as top grade in all the qualities by his Head.

References for applicants for the post of Chaplain, or assistant Chaplain, were equally unreliable. Bishops, in their well meant efforts to be kind to curates who have found it impossible to cope with tough big town parishes, tend to write: "His keen scholastic mind and academic interests make him deserving of the kind of atmosphere a good school such as yours will provide." Apart from the gratuitous flattery, the implication is quite clear. He has made a mess of his job in the slums and may find public schoolboys easier to deal with. The odds are that they may be just as difficult: teenagers are much the same, but the brighter they are the more tricky they may be. Yet big city comprehensives can be formidably difficult, and I've known teachers who couldn't keep order, to the extent that their lives were becoming a misery, who found it easy in our environment.

Then what about the interview itself? How to get at the truth? You look at the candidate's application. He has made a list of his special interests. All too often Art, Rugby and Mountaineering would turn out to be one visit to the Louvre with a rich aunt who lived in Paris; the rugby would consist of two trips to Twickenham; the mountaineering, the ascent of Snowdon by its mountain railway. So I became more reliant on applicants backed by people I knew I could trust. That may, of course, lead to a kind of nepotism or 'Old Boy Net', but I could never see the harm of that when qualifications appear to be equal or better. In fact I suspect that nepotism is the secret of success in many businesses. In France twice as many follow their parents' profession as in England: that is why their family-run hotels offer so much better value and so much better service than most of our not-family-run hotels with their grumbling on about staff. And it is why the Swiss watch makers, who have passed their trade on from father to son for centuries are so excellent. As for the Old Boy Net, Oxford and Cambridge exert nothing like as much of a monopoly of High Office as the "Grandes Écoles" of France, even under the socialist governments of that supposedly egalitarian country.

The unreliability of references got worse over my 27 years as a Head. After about 1970 open testimonials became increasingly useless. Confidentiality was no longer safe – I've had my confidential report on a Cambridge candidate read aloud to his parents. Reformers became increasingly nervous of saying anything critical or suggesting weaknesses. They were reluctant to do anything more than vary the intensity of their praise. I learned that it was wiser to telephone referees of good reputation and to ask them a few direct questions.

More recently still a tendency has grown, instead of submitting a brief and factual curriculum vitae and leaving it to others to sing their praises, to encourage candidates to submit a gushing account of their own qualities and ambitions. Although this may be distasteful to the old school of managers, it at least gives the candidate an opportunity to betray themselves. I well remember an application which started: "I am 6 foot 2 inches with fair hair and blue eyes and very fond of boys." At least one knew where one was.

Homosexuality between consenting adults has rightly ceased to be regarded as an offence, but sexual relations between staff and pupils are a different matter and are an abuse of trust. Everyone would agree that a master of a boarding school who seduces half a dozen 8–12 year olds is breaking the law and must be punished by the law. But lines are becoming blurred. A 17 year old girl pupil and a 23 year old young master? Often a very strong temptation, but I know that most parents would be very angry and would press for his dismissal. What about the reputedly homosexual master who writes suggestive letters to a pupil – opened by the pupil's father, but does not break the law because the boy is a Sixth Former?

I used to warn all teachers I appointed that, although their sexual orientation was no concern of mine, in a boarding school any suggestion of seduction of pupils would not be tolerated. It is increasingly difficult. On the one hand accusations can be laid against an innocent teacher by pupils with a grudge or whose advances have been rejected. The mere fact that a complaint has been made can ruin a teacher's career. Suspended while the case is examined even if they are cleared, it will be a burden of which they may never be able to rid themselves entirely.

On the other hand if the Head looks the other way and takes no action, the parents and the law may do so, and it will be he who suffers as much as the culprits. Even to give a warning about the impression a teacher is giving might be interpreted nowadays as politically incorrect. I am not sure that we are nearer a solution to these problems.

Back to the all important business of selecting good staff and avoiding blunders. I would hold a brief interview in my office after looking at the manner of his or her arrival: method of transport, dress, how he related to the pupils from whom he asked the way etc. I would check his application, asking about his special interests and hobbies and asking him about any unusual experiences. Then I would leave him with my secretary while I attended to other matters, telling him to ask her any questions about the everyday routine of the school. Then I found a senior boy to show him round the school, while I fixed an appointment for him to see his prospective Head of Department, to be grilled about his strengths and weaknesses in his specialized subject. Then I asked him or her home to meet my wife, children and dogs; Jo and I would make a point of leaving him alone with the dogs and children for a spell.

Finally, before and after dinner I would ply him generously with drink, believing that "in vino veritas".

Selecting teaching staff took a very long time, but it is the most important thing a Head has to do. Sometimes I resented it, when one glance at a candidate was enough to know that the time would be wasted. Later on I had to modify my methods slightly when selecting lady teachers who would help over the introduction of co-education.

At any rate it seemed to work. If I achieved anything at Gresham's, it was because of my early appointments. Richard Copas, who had been Head Boy at Epsom, had not got brilliant degrees or a blue, but he became a good teacher, a useful rugby coach, a very good batsman, an excellent runner of the corps involved in all outward bound activities, a natural disciplinarian liked and trusted by the boys, an unstinting worker who took on the difficult tasks. He was an excellent House Tutor and then Housemaster, and, in due course, Second Master to four different Heads. Above all he was a good man of unwavering standards, always anxious to help those in difficulties – as was recognized when he was encouraged to put in for the Headmastership of Gresham's. He refused, perhaps rightly; it is not easy for anybody to become Head of a school where he has served for most of his life. If he is worth anything, he will have made friends and enemies, which is a bad start. Also he will not have experience of other schools with fresh ideas. I'm sure he would have done a good job, but he felt that he did not want the extra responsibility which might not leave him time for the part of the job he loved. His wife Sandra was a rock of common sense who helped him do the best thing that any family can do: raise three successful and loyal children.

On retirement Dick did marvels for the parish of Holt and founded, ran and financed a boys' club to help the unemployed and impecunious young of the area, as well as helping with the organization of the church. I owe him a big debt of gratitude, and so do the Parish of Holt and the youth of North Norfolk.

Oh dear! I must be careful. I can't do justice to each one of my overworked, underpaid and loyal staff. It might turn this part of the book into a series of recommendations for an O.B.E.

But I must pay tribute to the other early appointment I made: Steve Benson. Built like a buffalo and with formidable eyebrows, he was capable of being angry and frightening. Those who got to know him well discovered a kind and even soft heart beneath his alarming manner. He was a good Housemaster, and a great all rounder who gave a real boost to my ambition to have a school where there would be teachers to help with every kind of hobby and skill outside the classroom as well as in. A fine hockey player, a good wicket-keeper/batsman, a useful rugby forward, he was above all a good singer, with a rich bass-baritone voice, which, when it was not shouting at a boy the other side of the parade ground to go back and change his dirty shirt, enabled him to take the lead in all kinds of musical events from 'The Messiah' to Schubert's 'Lieder' and anthems. His house's victories in the music competitions I introduced were regrettably more common than mine. He also found time to produce plays and to act, and his role in improving school music and drama was crucial. His wife Peta, apart from exercising with exceptional tact the gently deflationary role, which every good House or Headmaster's wife has to play by pricking the inevitable balloon of her husband's potential pomposity, is an accomplished artist. She is so modest that I only recently discovered it. Steve and Peta got the Headmastership of Bishop's Stortford, where they served for several years before retiring to a house next door to Gresham's. He still enlivens local churches with his better than ever solos and local drama groups, and is involved in providing remedial education for young first offenders.

At this point I should call a temporary halt and mention instead some of the teachers I found on arrival. Although the troubles of my predecessor, Olivier, had to some extent split the staff, they responded positively to my inexpert efforts to mend fences and to ignore past events. In this my second master Bruce Douglas (alias, the owl) was a help. Shortly before he retired he confided to me that he had thought it would be his main duty to apply the brakes to any over-enthusiastic reforms threatened by the incoming young Headmaster. Small, shrewd and precise, he was an excellent maths teacher, which provided a base for the school's continuing success in the sciences. He had a gift for keeping my feet on the ground when one of my enthusiastic schemes seemed a bit stratospheric. I had always thought him somewhat conservative, but saw him in a new light when he gave a party on his retirement. He offered us as 'nibbles' bumble bees in aspic, ants in chocolate and fried grasshoppers. I enjoyed two of these, but drew the line at the third? Which would you avoid?

Dick Bagnall-Oakeley was a very different kettle of fish. I have written a short biography of that remarkable and unusual man. A great number of former pupils have written to me to say what a tremendous influence he had had on their lives. Dashing, good-looking, a great story teller he excelled in everything he touched. Officially he was just a geography master, but his broad interests made him seem omniscient. He could tell a story about a Polynesian tribe and draw a precise map with contours, rivers, mountains and population figure of the island they inhabited with hardly a glance at the board. He had a passion for vintage fast cars, and would take boys out on bird watching expeditions, driving at forbidden speeds down the narrow Norfolk roads, and buying them a pint of beer to soothe their nerves before delivering them to their housemasters. He combined his teaching with work for Anglia Television, was one of the first to be concerned about the disappearance of the coast and a pioneer of bird photography away from the nest. He was not one to confine himself to the syllabus. I remember on one of the school inspections, the Geography inspector saying to me: "I don't know what his lessons have to do with the

A level syllabus, but I'd gladly give up my job to sit at the back of his class for a year or two".

Not renowned for punctuality, he would arrive having stopped to pick up a peregrine falcon or a coypu which had been knocked over on the road and pull it out of a bag and hold forth about it entertainingly for half the lesson. He introduced some boys to falconry and others to the complex mysteries of how migrants find their way: he also opened up the techniques of advanced photography and film work. He was bilingual in Norfolk and English and specialized in Norfolk humour. An asset to any establishment provided he didn't crash a car full of pupils. I used to listen to his tales told to guest speakers with whom I would ask him to dinner and periodically tried to catch him out in some exaggeration. It was difficult, but not impossible and one or two boys succeeded in doing so. His brother had been a long jump champion and Dick was a gifted hockey player. His eyesight was phenomenal. There is a story that he went to the Norfolk and Norwich for a health check, including an eyesight test. After reading every line with each eye he read the small print at the bottom. The Doctor was astonished and asked him if he could read the number plate of a car on the furthest corner of the car park. Dick peered out of the window and spelled it out easily – what he didn't say was that it happened to be his own car.

Sadly Dick died quite young, leaving stacks of notes and drawings for books he had hoped to publish later. He died of a sudden heart attack at the side of the road, when driving up to give a lecture in the north. Strange to say, he had come to see me three weeks earlier, when my son Bede had a bad nose bleed. Dick said: "Oh, you need not worry about that, I can do it at will!" He had then produced an alarming nose bleed just by blowing that handsome organ. I wonder if there was any connection.

Hoult Taylor was another influential master. He was in charge of the mostly Shakespearean plays in the open air theatre, was a fine pianist and a broadly cultured person: a magnet for the brighter pupils. Unfortunately he was already nearing retirement when I was appointed, but he left a very good platform on which John Coleridge was to build a little later. Another who was only with us for a short time was Hubert Hales, an old Etonian composer and organist of some distinction. Hubert was a kindly, gentle soul, at his best with boys who had talent, rather than a populariser of classical music. He died in action: falling across the organ in the middle of a voluntary in Cromer church. His daughter Penny was a family friend going to the Royal College of Music with Jenny and later editing the Oxford Music magazine.

John Coleridge was appointed shortly before I came. He was a great choice. As a teacher of 6th form English he gave many pupils a real appreciation of poetry and plays. They learned to have confidence in their own reactions instead of saying what they felt they ought to say. Some of his own verse – particularly what he wrote in retirement when fighting cancer – was really good; but I found his novel about the women in his life quite beyond me. His production of a wide range of plays were enjoyed by actors and audiences alike. He was an ideal choice for the Housemastership of Tallis, the new bed-sitter house, and also served a spell as Second Master and, for a brief interregnum, Headmaster. He did not have an easy life. His mother had suffered from a depressive illness, and he occasionally had to struggle with the same trouble. His first wife died too young. His second wife was a tower of strength in the long, brave battle that they fought against his cancer soon after he retired. Long after he should, according to normal medical prognosis, have been dead, he continued to play good golf, to take a lead in Norfolk poetry groups and to be cheerful company. To add to his troubles, his son Andrew died in a car accident soon after he had a brilliant report from the American school to which he had had an exchange scholarship. A truly brave man.

One appointment by my predecessor was notably unsuccessful. Let me tell you the true, though almost incredible story of Peters the Parson. Peters was appointed to teach History and Divinity, and to be assistant Chaplain. He claimed to have had a First at Keble College, Oxford, before taking holy orders. It was not long before he began to arouse some suspicions. Dick Bagnall-Oakeley had been at Keble at the same time as Peters claimed to have been there. Peters appeared to know little about the college or any of the prominent people associated with it. Later that year a member of the staff complained to the Head that he had made unwelcome and improper advances to his daughter. Before the Head could take action, Peters disappeared, only to surface again at frequent intervals. First it was rumoured that he had extorted a couple of thousand pounds from two old ladies in a fishing hotel in the Highlands, then he committed bigamy (apparently he was married before coming to Gresham's). This was found out and he was sent to prison. It turned out that his references were forged. He had never been to Keble or been ordained. He had failed to get a degree at Lampeter.

Undaunted by this he decided to embark on an academic or ecclesiastic career a littler further afield. He managed to persuade the Bishop, who was the Visitor of his prison, of his repentance and was taken on as a personal assistant for a while. The Bishop liked to have his mail brought in to him for signature. Somehow or other Peters managed to slip in a splendid reference for himself, which the Bishop signed without looking at it. He took advantage of this to get jobs in Scotch College, Adelaide, and in Toronto University, which he held for quite a time. When he felt that people might be beginning to make enquiries, he returned to Britain and held a post in Glasgow for a while. He thought, however, that he deserved better. Trevor-Roper was looking for an assistant at Oxford. Peters applied for and got the job. Not only that, but he found another girl willing to marry him: reception in the senior common room and all.

Nevertheless it wasn't long before Trevor-Roper began to smell a rat. He wrote to me and asked me if I could tell him anything about Peters. Just to be sure I got confirmation from Owen Chadwick, the vice-chancellor, and via him from the Church: not ordained, and no degree. Previous wives still alive. At this point Peters rang Jo and asked her to tell her husband that if he continued to harass him and stand in the way of his career, he would take legal action against him. He had expiated his sins by his imprisonment. I rang him and referred him to the Archbishop or the Vice Chancellor, and heard no more from him.

But his career was far from finished. The next time I heard of him, he must have been in his fifties. A mother superior of a group of 'Old Catholics' came, unannounced, into my office one day and said: "Headmaster, I've been wrestling for the soul of a rather unusual man who wants to join our order. I'm puzzled about him and was told that you might know something about him." I put her in the picture, and Peters did not become an Old Catholic. I managed to scotch his application to a neighbouring girls' school, but he turned up again when a Norfolk clergyman told me his daughter was in danger of becoming entangled with an elderly man, of whom he did not like the appearance. It was Peters again.

Hereabouts the story gets even more bizarre. Peters was evidently tired of the deception game and he made up his mind to get a genuine degree. He persuaded Sheffield University to offer him a place to read (I think) Theology. He studied for the proper period. When it came to taking the Finals, he persuaded the National Health Service to support his application for an 'aegrotat'. He made out that he was suffering from a depressive illness, and that he could not face the strain of the exam. He must have excelled himself in the art of persuasion, because he was duly awarded a degree.

So he finished his last years before retirement as an honest man. The Headmaster of a good school, to whom I related the facts, gave him a temporary job after telling him he knew all about his past, and he finished his days, giving private tuition to Cambridge undergraduates. He may have been a rogue, but he was clearly no fool. A wonderful case for a psychiatrist!

My own appointments never quite equalled the Peters saga, but were certainly not free from mistakes. For instance I appointed a man who turned out to have lied about his previous career. He claimed to have played rugby for Cardiff. I should have spotted that this was untrue, because I had played against Cardiff myself and was about the same age as him. It gradually dawned on me that he didn't know any of their great players. By that time I had also discovered that he was unduly fond of the bottle. He played the piano very well, but could not be entrusted with the care of the young.

Rural boarding schools find it difficult to find a good supply of music teachers for the less common instruments. I was therefore delighted when an east German turned up who could scrape or blow almost any instrument needed. He was moreover quite a good teacher, but a touch eccentric. After a while one or two people became concerned about the origin of some of the instruments which he produced for his pupils. When I started to make enquiries, he disappeared, leaving a message to the effect his wife had reappeared on the other side of the Iron Curtain, and that he was rejoining her.

Art masters, too, can be hard to find: artistic talent does not always go with discipline and efficiency. My father, usually a good selector, was hugely impressed by a candidate called Fison-Bates, whose portfolio showed he could draw like Rembrandt. Dad should have guessed all was not well, when Fison-Bates rang up, late for his appointment, to ask if he might come later in the day: "I'm feeling a little bent". Within three weeks he was renamed Siphon Bates by his pupils. It was not long before he avoided dismissal by running away with a colleague's wife, whose strikingly elegant figure decorated the book cover of a popular thriller in the station bookshops, to our amusement, but not surprise.

Chapter Thirty

Some Peculiarities among Teenagers

Headmastering is a wonderful job when things go right, but something is nearly always going wrong. If you have responsibility for over 400 adolescents, there are few disasters that will not come your way in the course of time. My father, my brother Rab and I had over 60 years experience between us, and we came across every form of human aberration from madness and suicide to delusions of grandeur. A distinguished psychologist/psychiatrist told me that some 35% of teenagers aged between 14 and 17 go through a form of depressive illness arising from imbalance during growth: emotions, mind body and hormones get out of synchronisation. Teachers and parents too often blame it on faults of character or temperament. In many cases they would benefit from treatment; for instance a shortage of copper in the system is a frequent and easily remedied factor – much more effective than arguments at home or punishments at school.

It also appears to be a fact that some teenagers in a disturbed state of mind can radiate energy or brain waves, which seem to affect the balance of mind of others. I know several Headmasters who have become convinced that a boy in this state has been the centre of psychic phenomena. A Headmaster's instinct must usually be to regard such things with extreme caution as nobody wants to be caught out by an elaborate prank. But the Church of England takes them so seriously that every diocese has an exorcist, officially appointed to investigate and heal any psychic manifestations.

I will quote a few cases without finding myself able either to accept them as complete truth or able to reject them as fraud.

One evening in the late Sixties I was doing some marking in my study, when the Head Boy of the House [who later became a Housemaster at Repton] knocked at my door: "Sir, something rather tricky's happened, could you come and have a look?" It transpired that one of the senior boys had been reading a book on hypnosis and had decided to experiment with a friend. The experiment had been all too successful. The boy who had volunteered to be the subject had been "put away" and was slumped over his desk, looking distinctly pale and breathing slowly and heavily. Unfortunately they hadn't found any instructions as to how he should be restored to normality.

I carried him upstairs to a warm and comfortable room and rang the school Doctor, an old friend and a good man to have in an emergency. It was after 10 o'clock in the evening, and he was out. What next? Should I breathe into his ear in hypnotic tones: "I am going to count from ten to one, at the end of which you will return to full consciousness?" I decided against further experiments and, fortunately, he came round gradually. His recovery, however, was somewhat alarming: to begin with he made little sense, he seemed to be struggling his way out of a nightmare, in which he was evidently haunted by a vision of a friend involved in a motor cycle accident and dripping blood ... No after effects, except that the amateur hypnotist got a science scholarship to Cambridge, while his victim was ordained into the Church of England.

In the evening I often went round the individual studies to have a chat with the boys. On one such occasion I was surprised to see a 6th Former, who, amongst other things was studying art, but was not as yet a particularly accomplished painter, standing in front of his easel, on which there was a freshly painted portrait of a striking and distinctly spooky Chinaman. "That's amazingly good and very unusual", I said. "It's not at all like your usual style."

He explained that he just stood in front of the easel and "sort of got into a trance." It was, he added, the spiritual guide of the spiritualist group he attended with his parents. He was as surprised as everybody else at "how well the pictures have come off." He didn't think that he could do it in an art class. The spirit painter became a well-known architect – and when I heard from him fifteen years later, was still a convinced spiritualist.

Of all the remarkable accounts of psychic phenomena associated with teenagers Matthew Manning's are the most exhaustively investigated: David Frost was bewildered by him; Professor Owen of Trinity College, Cambridge; the Nobel prize winner and Regius Professor of Physics at Cambridge Professor Brian Josephsen; and countless interviews and experiments on the television revealed all kinds of strange occurrences, over which he had intermittent control, but which sometimes took unexpected turns.

Manning's strange powers became evident when he was at Oakham, a public school very much like Gresham's, with a Headmaster very unlikely to believe in ghosts. Matthew found himself at the centre of powerful poltergeist activities: beds were moved, objects dislodged from shelves – not by any conscious or controlled intention. Boys were upset and frightened, and Matthew became something of an outcast.

For the next few years the forces surrounding him were at their peak: psychokinesis, metal bending, telepathy, automatic writing, often in languages of which he had no knowledge, or from historical figures or from 'Thomas Penn' a diagnostic expert from the long past. I saw him draw a Dürer hare while apparently in a trance, with extraordinary speed and accuracy . . . in front of an audience of about 100. But his most often tested and unusual power was his ability to produce a quasi-electrical force that could interfere with machinery, especially electrical machinery. It could apparently also, when he was at the peak of his powers, occasionally kill cancer cells and stimulate plant growth.

For about 7 years he was famous. I think it is fair to say that he was never caught out in any trickery. Eventually he tired of ceaseless investigations and public demonstrations and devoted his time to healing. If you want to find out more, his two books 'The Link' and 'Matthew Manning' give his own account. His more spectacular powers gradually faded or became more intermittent.

After a talk with his Headmaster, I decided to invite him to talk to the Gresham's 6th Formers and enjoyed having him as a guest. He was a good looking youngster, distinctly 'with it' in dress. He talked frankly about the unusual forces which had always surrounded him. He drew the Dürer hare, and invited boys to stand up, and he would give a picture of their background and any health problems. I remember one of these particularly. A boy whom I knew well had spent years in another country, where he had been ill. Manning was so accurate in his assessment that I wondered if he had read my mind. This he denied, merely saying that as with most of the apparently supernatural phenomena that accompanied him, they were preceded by a change in the level of his consciousness, over which he had imperfect control.

More astonishing stories are less clearly confirmed. His automatic writing produced messages from Sir Stafford Cripps or Bertrand Russell – in their handwriting. He shared a house with a spirit from another century with whom he exchanged gifts. When so much is verifiable, it seems uncharitable to turn sceptic – but one must draw a line somewhere! He produced automatic writing in foreign languages unfamiliar to him, translated, as he wrote, by a professor of the relevant language. Matthew Manning was not a believer, and he could offer no explanation for many of the things that happened, except that some powerful energy came to him, which sometimes could feed on the energy of an audience or even of an electrical machine and could certainly extinguish bulbs or bring lifts to a halt.

Twenty-seven years of Headmastering can bring nasty shocks. At Sedbergh there were two accidental deaths. One boy was killed on a toboggan run in winter. It was a fast run on a nearby fell. In the middle of the course there was a gap in the stone wall enclosing the field. He missed the fairly large gap and was killed outright. Another was drowned falling off a bridge over the river Rawthey in flood.

At Gresham's I was woken by an early morning phone call to be told that there was a corpse in the swimming bath. The indoor bath was just being repaired. I found that it was one of the workers who had been finishing the job.

He had for some reason returned late at night to have a dip. He had hit his head on the side and drowned ...

Another late night call (2 a.m.) informed me that some rifles and machine guns had been stolen from the school armoury. The caller appeared to be a foreigner and a long way away, and I couldn't get any clearer information. He was implying that it might be the I.R.A. It turned out to be entirely untrue ... the armoury in question wasn't mine. However, it did not increase my liking for late night phone calls.

One last incident is worth telling in detail because it confirms the unusual power of adolescent minds (I exclude the apparently successful attempt by boys at another well-known public school to raise the Devil!). It was on the first day of term. A boy had been invited to tea, because he was an early arrival, by one of the masters and his wife. The wife felt unwell and collapsed, much to the alarm of her husband and the pupil. It turned out that she had polio. I asked the school doctor for his advice as to the right measures to take. It was an officially notifiable disease. The wife was taken to an Isolation hospital, and made a fairly good recovery. He recommended that the boy should be kept in isolation in the school sanatorium, well fed, cheered up by television, and he would keep an eye on him daily in case he should show any symptoms. Initially all went well, but just at the most dangerous time, the boy called out, desperately frightened. He had pains in the neck, and was quite unable to move. The Doctor was sent for and started to examine him. Suddenly the patient sat up and tried to punch him in the face. The Doctor was puzzled by the bizarre recovery, and carried out a number of tests, trying to reassure the poor boy that it was very unlikely that he had polio.

It eventually emerged that he had flu, which had, as it apparently occasionally does, led to encephalitis. The boy had understandably been so alarmed at the unusual feelings that this can cause that he had developed some of the symptoms of polio and had temporarily lost the balance of his mind.

I have been concentrating on some of the eccentricities of our pupils: it may seem fair, as they are sharp in their own observation of their teachers' peculiar habits. The great majority of schoolboys are not psychologically peculiar, but just interesting and often very likeable human beings in the process of ripening. If you treat a 15 year old pupil as a responsible adult he will respond in like manner. You must remember that he or she may turn out to be brighter than you. Yet an ill-judged or casual remark of yours may make a lasting impression, as may a timely observation. A Headmaster is in a china shop and must tread carefully.

Eccentricity is not confined to teachers and their pupils. I soon learned that Headmasters are liable to visits from people with strong and often peculiar views. They feel that, if they can convert the Head, they may be able to spread their ideas throughout the school.

One evening in term time, I answered a knock at my door. A most unusual looking man was standing on the threshold. A little smaller than me, he was wearing the kind of raincoat one associates with spies as portrayed in not very realistic films. The two most remarkable things about him were his wide-brimmed sombrero type hat and his penetrating eyes. He was probably in his mid forties.

He spoke first. "I know you must be a busy man, but I would just ask you for ten minutes of your valuable time to discuss an important matter". I asked him in. He then said: "I have just one unusual request: I would like to have our interview back to back!" This was too good to miss. I led him into my study, where he proceeded to arrange two chairs back to back. We took our seats. I heard a click and glanced over my shoulder. He had removed his hat and snapped back the brim to reveal an arrangement of mirrors. "I have come all the way from America, seeing the world upside down and backwards. You may wonder why?" I grunted non-committally. "It is of supreme importance to break habits if we are not to become automatons. Can you please, Headmaster, put that apple on the corner of your desk?" I obeyed him. He suddenly waved his arm, and a strange device like a hinged and elongated fork shot out from the depths of his capacious raincoat sleeve like the first stage of a Tommy Cooper magic turn. He speared the apple quite skilfully, conveyed it to his mouth and took a bite. "You see, Headmaster, one must never do things in the same way day after day. I would like you to introduce new ways of starting the day to your school, giving them new challenges at breakfast time every day".

By now the ten minutes was up, and he was as good as his word, leaving me politely and pocketing the apple with the words "Food for thought, isn't it, Headmaster?"

I made some enquiries and found that he had just been released from psychiatric care, and was reckoned to be harmless. There was a tiny amount of genius in his madness, but I didn't invest in hinged forks.

Another surprise visitor made an even more startling first impression. He chose the beginning of the holidays for his approach. 9 p.m. It was a strange figure that greeted me when I answered the door. A long-haired blond, about 30 years old, in Lederhosen like a Bavarian boy scout. In his right hand he carried a banner with a picture of the Virgin Mary. I asked him what I could do for him and where he came from. "I come from God." he replied unhesitatingly, "and I would be grateful if you could put me up for the night." I asked him why he had chosen me, and where, more recently and geographically, he had come from. "Doctor Slater told me that you might be interested in my mission." I find it hard to resist 'unusual' cases, and asked him in – to the drawing room and not the study this time. Jo and a couple of my children were there, and Jo raised an eyebrow at the strange apparition but greeted him politely.

He plunged in at the deep end at once. "I am on a one-man mission to convert as many people as possible to the true faith." He went on to ask if he might invite us and our children to join in prayers. I glanced at Jo, who accepted the challenge. After a short sermon-like harangue, we offered him a bed for the night. He still hadn't got up when I left for the office in the morning. At about 11 I got a phone call from Jo. "I think you had better come home. He has just offered to give me a kiss of holiness, and he has left a frightful mess in the spare room."

I hurried back and told him he must leave at once as I had another guest coming at midday. He duly packed and left. As he went he said: "You two dear people have been so kind that I would like you to read a special book I recommend to all my friends . . . But it costs £5 and I haven't got the money; can you possibly lend me that small sum."

I replied that I was Scottish and not prone to act as a money lender. He appeared to be in no way put out, and waved a cheerful goodbye.

The sequel was that the police called and enquired whether I had been bothered by him. It appeared that he had been visiting big houses all round Norfolk, usually getting bed and breakfast and an evening meal, and that this was his way of making a living.

The unexpected last word was that he sent us the book a few days later – at his or someone else's expense.

The teaching staff are by far the most important factor in a school's success, but I realize that to pay a brief tribute to all the main contributors who I found on arrival would hardly be of interest to those readers who have no connection with the school and so I have placed them in an appendix.

Chapter Thirty One
Education after the War

Education in the post war era can roughly be divided into four periods: 1946–1966; 1967–1972 (the student revolutionary period); 1972–82; 1983–present day (the period of the internet).

In the first period, after Rab Butler's recommendations, the Labour government was trying to make opportunities more equal, by ending selection by the 11+, introducing Comprehensives and reducing the number of Grammar Schools. Although they made some faintly alarming noises they didn't take any active measures against the independent schools. I have never been in favour of the 11+. An intelligence test held on a particular date, of a kind which was liable to change in accordance with fashionable views of what constitutes intelligence, is too inflexible to decide at much too early an age that children are destined to be either intellectual sheep or goats – and, like sheep and goats, one can't always be sure which are the goodies. Gresham's took many children who had failed the 11+ and went on to get good Oxbridge degrees.

The demise of the Grammar Schools and the rush to comprehensives was not destined to improve standards, nor did it provide a more effective ladder to the top for those at the bottom of the pile. The idea that all pupils should be taught in the same class and in the same way, and that the minority of very bright pupils would inspire the slower majority was only going to succeed with an exceptional teacher in an exceptional school. What happened more often was that the majority held back the minority, behaved badly and made life difficult for the teachers. You can bring about a kind of equality by levelling down, but to bring it about by levelling up is a Utopian dream which can only rarely be achieved.

Anyway, it is a case of all change when it comes to puberty. Another factor is the period of maximum growth. Boys, and especially if they are destined to be very tall, sometimes grow 6 inches in a year. Their emotions, physique and mental processes get out of sync and, for a couple of years (often affecting their G.C.S.E.S), they are incapable of doing themselves justice. By the time they reach A level they are recovering. At university, or even later, they reach their peak. Those are genuine late developers, and there are many of them. It has long been known that girls mature earlier than boys. There are also examples of pupils, who are precociously brilliant (I remember one with: 10 G.C.S.E's at 11; 3 Arts A grades at A level, when he was 13; and a science scholarship to Cambridge at 16), but who gradually fizzle out in their twenties.

So, if you add to these factors the impact of a first love affair, the after effects of glandular fever, for some girls the timing of their sexual cycle, and (very important) changes of school, it is vital that exams should never be regarded as infallibly accurate guides.

But they are important hints about progress at a certain stage, and, as such, must play an important part in school life – so long as employers take them with a pinch of salt. They also give guidance and motivation to teachers and pupils, provided they are not worshipped as all-important.

People ask me sometimes what the difficulties were that we discussed at the Headmasters' Conferences in the Fifties and early Sixties. It is a strange comment on the speed of change within the education system that in my last year as Head we were still discussing the same issues: what use to make of the Lower 6th Year; whether to have a subsidiary A level or to follow the example of the Scottish Higher; how to enable scientists to take an arts subject at A level, and Arts pupils to take a science subject; whether S levels should be widely taken. And they are still discussing closely related issues now: whether we should adopt the International Baccalaureat; whether we should have a more taxing exam, along the lines of the old S Levels.

Looking backwards, with the benefit of hindsight, we should have been discussing the effects of the Bomb, the Pill, the collapse of Empire, Women's Lib, drugs and new factors like television, computing etc. And, as always, the two great failures of British education: failing to spend money on good education for the bottom 10%–20% and failing to provide first rate technological schooling with highly regarded degrees. We never seemed to look to the excellent examples to be found abroad: Scandinavia, Germany and now South Korea. Sweden has small classes for this bottom group, excellent and well paid staff, a special curriculum which can light enthusiasm for children of low IQ and is shaped in consultation with employers who can offer good jobs to unacademic youngsters. They also have special careers advisers.

It costs money. But the result is the virtual absence of an underclass, which saves incalculable sums. Our best brains are already well looked after, and teaching them is in any case a much less demanding task than teaching the unacademic or difficult. Does our Department of Education and Science never ask itself how Sweden has nearly 90% of pupils taking two languages and three sciences – and still punches well above its weight in golf, athletics, winter sports and even beats us more often than not at our national game of football? Its population is somewhat smaller than that of Greater London.

Chapter Thirty Two

The Student Revolution

As the late '60s drew nearer some of us realized that we had been making bad mistakes. In our desire to recover stability after the war, we had become stuck in old ways. We hadn't faced up to the fact that huge changes were taking place. We should have been quicker to help our pupils to find their way through this new world: the eradication (some hope!) of snobbery and class consciousness; the sexual freedom brought about by the Pill; the tolerance of homosexuality; women's lib; the new attitudes to racialism; the widespread criticism of the Establishment, Parliament, Oxbridge, the Church, the Civil Service; and, ultimately, anyone rich or successful (bar, as always, footballers and pop stars). And the spread of drugs.

We should have started to deal with these matters as soon as they arose. The young were much quicker to see those changes and to react to them. The result was the explosion of the universal student revolution in 1967–72. As is the way with revolutions, they initially went too far, so that the changes brought more chaos than improvement.

The impact on schools and universities was sudden and remarkable. One term the pupils crowded into my drawing room, shoes polished, neatly brushed short hair, and dressed in clean school uniform to relax for a while before afternoon school by listening to the great works of Bach, Mozart, Beethoven and Schubert. A term later they had become scruffy and long-haired, and they disappeared into their own studies to stomp to rock music with the volume turned up high enough to make the walls shake. Parents and school teachers wondered if they had lost their grip.

The 'Little Red School Book' was distributed to nearly every school in the country. It was written by Danish students: it was an attempt to spread methods of obtaining pupil power by Trotskyite methods and with Trotskyite aims. It taught pupils how to get rid of unpopular subjects and unpopular old fashioned teachers; how to put an end to prayers and hymns in assemblies or chapels; how to arrange classrooms' desks in a circle instead of facing the blackboard; how to make punishment impossible; how to use solidarity and strikes and underground magazines; how to use the support and experience of adult left wing organizations; how to recognize discipline as a method of imposing bourgeois values.

The 'Little Red School Book' was not all bad. It advised against drugs "because they will limit your personal freedom". It advised against becoming addicted to pornography "because it bears little relationship to reality." It recommended everyone to take a radio into class with them, so that "there might be something interesting to do!"

I am not sure to what extent it really had any practical influence, and how accurately it reflected the European spirit of that time. In most of the independent schools, there were sufficient teachers with good relationships with their pupils to make any serious attempts at pupil power unlikely.

Some, especially in Scotland, determined to stand like rocks against the winds and the tides. Some bent with the wind like reeds and sought a reputation for progressive liberalism. Most, with a typical British gift for compromise, made up their minds to hold fast to what they felt was of fundamental importance, while accepting changes for which a real case could be made. Many created School Councils, in which pupils at all ages and levels could put forward suggestions for improvements. At first, those brought about some liberalising of silly restrictive rules. Then the pupils asked for more access to the opposite sex, dances, beer, cigarettes, television and radio. When those matters had been decided, usually with small concessions, such as allowing beer to pupils of legal age under controlled and limited conditions, the school councils began to tire of hoping for more 'cakes and ale'. They started to ask for more homework on Friday nights, and access to educational programmes on the television in a room set aside for that purpose. By the late '70's unemployment and the need for hard work had gone far to restoring an industrious atmosphere.

In some state schools the revolution caused lasting harm. This was probably caused by the undermining of successive Departments of Education and Science by 'progressive' ideas which did nothing to help good order, without which no educational programme can work. Various slogans became bases for policy. "All life styles are equally valid" was an excuse for all kinds of excesses. New crimes were invented. "Authoritarianism", "Paternalism". "Child centred education" became "Do what each child wants, and not what is of benefit to him." "Don't impose bourgeois standards" meant "Let him be rude and use bad language". "Never forget his human rights" became "Don't talk of any duties towards society, but only of society's duties towards him."

Competition became a dirty word: in the new Utopia there would be no losers. Gradually all this seeped into the consciousness of the whole nation, until success was always suspect and hard work a dangerous aberration. Our sensible determination to keep a vigilant eye on the abuse of power by the Establishment became an assumption that those who got to the top were corrupt. Our rightful longing for equality of opportunity began to assume the appearance of a determination to achieve equality by penalizing success.

Yet the rich became richer and the poor poorer.

The revolution, however, brought about many real improvements.

We learned to listen to and even learn from our pupils, while ensuring that they learned from us.

We learned: "We hear and we forget, we look and we learn; we do and we remember;" and added "we think, and we find a short cut to the answer."

We adapted to the increasingly sophisticated new machinery.

Hypocrisy became less common – though we must not forget that it is the tribute paid by vice to virtue.

Snobbery became a little less disgusting, although it is so much a part of human nature that it has reappeared in new forms.

We have become tolerant of unmarried mothers and homosexuals instead of condemning them to lifelong disgrace.

We acquired a great N.H.S., even if criticizing it has become a favourite national pastime. Racialism is a dwindling problem, although to have made it illegal may be counterproductive.

Class barriers are becoming a little less rigid. Women's Lib has freed a lot of women from slavery, although much remains to be done (Can it ever achieve a truly satisfactory balance?).

Arrogant nationalism has generally failed, perhaps being replaced by a too ready willingness to think the worst of ourselves and to undervalue our best traditions. All great nations have taken it in turn to believe that they are Top Nation: Britain, for longer than most; the Dutch, more quickly; the United States, until China brought a tiny element of doubt; Germany a couple of times, until it had caused millions of deaths; Russia, now and again; Italy in the Renaissance; Spain once upon a time; France always, even when manifestly not; Japan, until the bomb; China soon, India before long; North Korea frighteningly.

On balance, and when its excesses had blown themselves out, the student revolution brought more good than bad – but the loss of discipline and good relations in the classroom did almost irreparable damage to all but the best state schools. And the loss of belief in orthodox Christianity has not been adequately replaced.

We were fairly lucky at Gresham's in that the student revolution didn't interfere with our plans for improvement and enlargement. Big town schools had more trouble than rural ones. We may even have benefited from the fact that many parents felt that their children would avoid the drug culture if they were sent to a remote school in beautiful countryside.

It was interesting to see what impact the changing times had on my own family. John ploughed on at the top of M.I.6., being in charge in Italy, France,

Germany, Africa, the U.S. and the Middle East, and ultimately became the number two. The impact he felt was through his children. Sally, sent to Benenden, was a bright child of the revolution in revolt against a school she felt was utterly out of touch with the times. James was entirely pre-revolutionary, scholarly, excelling at classical music and languages and painting. Sandy was a law unto himself: a poacher turned gamekeeper – Cirencester Agricultural College was more prone to pranks than to demonstrations. He was given £100 to go round the world in his gap year and an address in each continent to refer to if he got into trouble or difficulty. He made great use of it. Meeting the girl he was eventually to marry at the beginning of the year, he persuaded her to accompany him round the world. They washed up in France; climbed Kilimanjaro and farmed in Africa; farmed again, sheared sheep and shot kangaroos in the Australian outback; explored South America and tried living together on a desert island. This must have been the perfect start to a career, starting as a Kent apple, dairy and sheep farmer, county councillor, and eventually Head of the Local Government organization with a Knighthood and then a peerage. He became more and more distinguished looking but never lost the ability to laugh at himself. He ended up in charge of English Heritage, but got cancer soon afterwards and died within a few weeks.

My own children reacted very differently: Jenny was a strange blend of being very square (admiration for the Monarchy, fondness for tradition and etiquette), as befits a pre-revolutionary child, and extreme sensitivity. She had a strange dislike or distrust of the horsey, county, sub-aristocracy she found in Norfolk, perhaps most of all in Runton Hill, the girls' school to which I sent her initially. At the age of 16 I sent her to Gresham's, which was a mistake. My own experience should have been a warning. To be sent to one's father's school is never ideal. To be the only girl in a still all-male school, and beautiful and 17 was a situation which was really tricky, and my stupid decision was responsible for some of her difficulties during the next few years. She was determined to 'be good' and not to let me down, whereas Pony and Bede, who went when the school was already co-ed, managed the situation with apparent ease, because 'being good' was not something that held them back! Jenny had genuine difficulty in adjusting from Runton Hill's curriculum to A levels at Gresham's. She wanted to be top, but if she found it hard, would give up and stop working. However, she did fairly well in English and very well in music, gaining acceptance at the Royal College, left behind her a string of admirers, and took with her personal ideals which have distinguished her life ever since.

Bede was post revolutionary. His remarkable success at games together with his cheerful fondness for adventurous pranks made him increasingly popular. He seemed to have a peculiar IQ. Very low on the mathematical side (less than 20%) and over 90% on verbal aptitude. I suspect that both he and the maths staff were too willing to accept the superstition that "B-L's don't do maths".

I notice that he is quite quick now with £.s.d. and percentages! He broke the discus record, was a good sprinter, shot putter and long jumper, a good member of an outstanding squash team, a useful fast bowler and an outstanding centre at rugby, playing for the English schoolboys. He surprised us all by getting 3 A levels, after doing very little work – including an A grade in Divinity. This earned him a place at Durham, where he thrived in all manner of ways. In middle age he has turned out to be right-wing, square and very successful. We got the news of his 3 A levels in France. He had run to the post office (4 miles) to be sure to get any news before Jo and me. We drove down a little later to meet him on the way back. I'll never forget the three jumps he performed in the middle of the road with three fingers raised on both hands: sheer joy!

Pony was, in early days, the wildest. As is almost a universal law, she has become the most matriarchal and responsible ... though never orthodoxly square. At Holt Primary School, at the age of 8, she was late back and, questioned as to where she had been, admitted that she had been with Willie Beaton on the disused railway line. By way of explanation or excuse she added "We have every right to our love." She was prone to temperamental spells, and also sudden illnesses which gave us frights. But she was a great 'bouncer back', had an uproarious sense of fun and showed real promise in English. She got a 2(1) at Bangor, and a P.C.G.E. as well as a good husband and a start on a teaching career, in which she brought poetry and literature into the lives of hundreds of pupils – recognized as an outstanding teacher by the National Poetry Society – and became Head of English. She ran the drama too at Wellingborough Prep School, involving her in hours of late evening work, but also very rewarding. She played squash for county and university and shot for school and country.

Rhu. I still wonder whether I was right to send him away to prep school at Taverham, under the worthy Peel and the very able Robin Wilson. I now believe that 8 is too young for boarding. But to do him justice Rhu flourished from the start. He was always independent and more mathematically gifted than the others. He had a great voice as a treble, and I often feel that he could have done more with music. But he became good with money, good at languages, good at business, outwitting lawyers and accountants in their own field – so I can't complain.

Funnily enough this most responsible and hard-working man was, because of his age and his tastes, the most clearly a late Sixties man. His idea of bliss is still a Rolling Stones concert, his humour is entirely Spike, Pete and Dud, and he went through a long-haired period. A passion for travel not only saved me money, because he paid his own way through St. Andrew's by taking bus loads of tourists round Europe in the holidays, but gave him a wide knowledge of the world and its ways, especially the museums, restaurants and history of Florence, Venice, Prague, St. Petersburg, Budapest, Paris, Rome, Cairo and Istanbul.

He also ventured further afield, spending time with a remote tribe in New Guinea, who had hardly ever seen a white man previously, India and Thailand and a comprehensive tour of the United States. Always a leader, he excelled in his chosen field of travel, and was never happier than in an aeroplane or boat (he also gained a Master's certificate). His great generosity earned him many friends, especially at St. Andrew's where half-a-dozen have kept in touch over half a century and have all done remarkably well. Of his achievements in Holt I shall write later.

In general those who were at school after the revolution are far more tolerant, much less punctual and punctilious, more broad minded, more relaxed about sex, less liable to be racist. Those at school before the revolution are more punctual and punctilious, always write thank-you letters, always turn up on time, tend to wear suits and ties when going out, are more likely to be faintly racist and to prefer classical music to pop. But there are exceptions, and a surprisingly high proportion of hippy, pot smoking demonstrators of 1970 react by becoming ultra square when their children seem likely to go through a similar stage. And a wild youth is often the precursor of a distinguished middle age.

It is a peculiarity of mine that I have never made many close friends. I like people: there are very few that I dislike. There are male friends whose company I enjoy and who I admire, there are female friends who I find attractive and whose conversation and presence is a joy. But my family are always slightly puzzled that there are no 'best friends' to whom I should confide my innermost thoughts and feelings and to whom I would to turn to repeatedly in times of trouble and perplexity.

I can see that it is true. 27 years as a Headmaster are partly responsible. I was surrounded from morning until night by my staff, to whom it was vitally important that I should show no favouritism. Hundreds of guests: but they were chosen for the benefit of the school and were not my personal choice. Among them there were wise and charming people, but they were usually either governors, other Head teachers, or outstanding members of staff or birds of passage, who I consulted once or twice but with whom I never could have a real relationship.

Old rugby friends always remain fairly close even if you don't see them more than once in five years or less. And people like my neighbours at Tonbridge – John Stanton and Richard Bradley, both Headmasters – however geographically distant, have stayed good friends.

The real cause is that my love for my wife and family have been so intense and all-consuming that I have not felt the need for great friendships outside the clan. I was brought up by my parents to put family first and I have found that advice infinitely rewarding. I do not imply that I have never cast a roving eye elswhere, but never with a view to an all-consuming commitment.

I am vaguely aware that some people find this intense clan consciousness rather intimidating. It extends beyond parents, brothers and sisters, nephews and nieces to the third or fourth generations in far off lands. Shared interests, a similar sense of humour, the same kind of standards, hopes and ambitions. I understand that it can seem like a mafia – which outsiders either like or dislike.

The clan is at its strongest in my relationship with my grown-up children. I've always loved babies and even teenagers, but when they turn into delightful, mannerly, infinitely kind adults, that is the best possible kind of relationship.

Even, perhaps, better than dogs!

There is, however, one reservation. Although I love teaching all ages, and believe I can be quite good at it, I have never been good at teaching my own children. I wonder if this is widespread or a weakness confined to me? Some attempts culminated in tears.

An example of my ineptitude was my attempt to get my children to lose their fear of animal or insect life, even with due respect, scorpions, spiders, wasps and rats. The theory was that, if you stand still and show no fear, you need not be frightened of any animal. Remember David Attenborough and the gorillas or James Bond and the tarantula creeping over his chest.

I took two of my children for a walk in the country. It so happened that a rat came out of the edge of the wood. My daughter squeaked with disgust or alarm. "Nothing to worry about," said I: "Stand still and it will do you no harm." We all stood still. The rat trotted around, minding its own business. Suddenly it changed direction, coming towards me. It climbed slowly onto my shoe, peered up my trousers and decided to go up to have a closer look. I had to undo my belt to let it get out of the top of my trousers.

Fortunately it bit nothing on the way, but my children roared with laughter at my discomfiture and loss of dignity!

Flight is sometimes justified. Later on I was fishing near Sedbergh on a lovely day in May. Everything was perfect: a bag full of trout, spring sunshine, a brilliant buttercup meadow and an idyllic landscape. Walking to the next pool I was vaguely aware of a large bull on the far side of the meadow, quietly cropping the grass. While I was wondering whether it was a Hereford, I suddenly realized that it was no longer minding its own business. It was pawing the ground, lowering its head and coming towards me, trotting at first, but accelerating fast. For a moment I considered folding my arms, staring at it and extending my arm in the style of Crocodile Dundee. Just in time, I changed my mind. I raced towards the typical Cumbrian loose stone wall, threw my rod, net and bag over it (I was 30 at the time) and vaulted over the wall. Two or three seconds later the bull's horns smashed into the wall, knocking several stones off the top.

There are exceptions to the rule "stand still!"

* * *

Before leaving the pre-revolutionary years at Gresham's I should return to Jo and myself. In term time we led hectic lives, never being alone with each other except in bed at night – and not always then. There are worse places to meet, but to meet in daylight would have been nice. I went back to our 'private' side at lunch time, to deal with a queue of boys. I would then go to the drawing room for five minutes with Jo – and the matron, the chef, the house tutor, the au pair and any teacher who had not been able to catch me during the 11 o'clock tea break. It was the same in the evening. In a desperate attempt to get at least one evening a week, when we could do something together, we arranged for pottery classes. Somewhat typically Jo did a Virgin and Child, while my soaring imagination could only produce a duck. On the second occasion a boy was sent to find me to come and deal with some crisis and we gave up. Instead we developed the habit of playing 'racing demon' every day either at lunch time or at night. Fiercely competitive, it got rid of all our hidden complexes, often leading to uproarious laughter or furious shouting. We became unbeatable by any third person who dared to challenge us.

In those busy and demanding days, although the work was fascinating and rewarding, Jo and I both felt deprived of opportunities to have fun together away from the observant eyes of pupils, staff, ex-pupils and their parents. It was barely possible to go to a pub, a cinema or a restaurant within 50 miles without finding ourselves in the close company of people connected with the school. We took what chances we could to escape and enjoy some privacy once or twice per term. We much enjoyed dancing together at secret venues. Jo, of course, was a wonderful mover with a great sense of rhythm, excelling in her former professional spheres of tap and ballet. While I was not in that class, I had won the Highland dancing prize at Cargilfield, where the art was taken seriously and professionally taught. Training for foursome and eightsome reels had been combined with solo dances like the hornpipe, which had given me some nimbleness of foot. Anyway the combination seemed to work surprisingly well when we tackled the Twist and Rock together.

In our last years at Gresham's, it was consequently sad that Jo began to suffer from bad arthritis. She put off having a replacement operation until my retirement. Dancing was becoming very painful. By a stroke of luck the consultant allocated to her by the N.H.S. turned out to be Hugh Phillips. He was a a brilliant pioneer of hip surgery, who was later to become President of the Royal College of Surgeons. He undertook, with Jo's brave consent, to replace both hip joints in one operation: a procedure which was almost unique in those days. It proved a remarkable success. In three weeks Jo was walking: in three months she was dancing again. In three years she was nearly back to her best.

Over 20 years later she returned to Norwich for a check-up. Hugh Phillips was in charge. He put her through some demanding tests and commented: 'That seems to have been a wonderful job . . . I wonder who did it?'

We're still not sure whether he had forgotten, or whether he was expressing delighted self-satisfaction.

In either case, both hips lasted for the rest of her life.

Jo was kept busy ordering the food, entertaining the guests – every Saturday and Sunday – organizing the cleaning, the cooking and the flowers (for chapel, for entertainments and the dinner table). She tried to make time for the children at bath and bed time but had to have an au pair to help. Some were very good, some not so good and one dreadful. Tony was the daughter of Mum's pre-war German lawyer, not much older than Jenny, but was a great success. Monicke fell in love with Bede aged three, and we kept in touch with her too until she married a German called Wolf and disappeared. Amrei was the daughter of a Wehrmacht Colonel, who was a prisoner of war of the Russians. On return he did well as a lawyer. She married John Harrison a bright young master who wooed her with Shakespearean verse. They went to Oundle where John did most of the play productions. They live not far from Holt in retirement – always fun to be with and looking younger than they are.

Jo struggled on for some time with 'the work'. It was she who was the first in the family to find the teachings of Ouspensky, Nicol, Orage and, above all, Gurdjeff. There were groups in every major country following their method of acquiring a higher level of consciousness through elaborate movements harnessing the joint energies of body, emotions and mind. Jo introduced Jenny to the London group, and tried to get down to work with them periodically, later transferring to a smaller group in Norwich. While she was unable to devote her whole life to it, as Jenny did, she remained a great admirer of their ideas, and continued to meditate in the way recommended by them. They both made gentle attempts to get me interested, even seeking to make Basil Tilly (the head of the Norwich group) and me special friends. He was quite an impressive man, and I liked him well enough, and I read all of the books written by and about the high ups in the work; but I could not follow a man who says that you must work hard for many years before you understand where you are going. Nor do I like those who are convinced that they are uniquely right. But I did realize that Jo and Jenny were onto something of real value that could be of help to them.

It was in 1960 that something happened which changed our lives. Kirsty was our third child, born in 1953. She was a busy, happy child, at that most entrancing stage when she was suddenly bursting out with new interests and indications of the personality to come. She accompanied me on mushroom hunting expeditions, and (for she went to a school where there was a very religious influence) would tell me off if she thought I was behaving badly. I remember once she was with me when I was dressing to go out. A collar stud was being difficult and sprang to the ground and under the bed. I used the word 'bloody' in my irritation. She told me to stand to attention and sing "Holy, holy, holy" three times. I couldn't possibly refuse.

It is a long time since my little daughter was killed in a road accident. Time is a great healer. I can laugh, forget and even be happy. But there is something like a lump of cold metal at the back of your brain and in the pit of your stomach and little incidents remind you, and tears return.

Chapter Thirty Three

The Death of Kirsty

Ours had always been a cheerful family. We had occasional shocks. Jenny had swallowed a dollar, the only dollar we've ever had in the house, and got it stuck in her windpipe. Jo seized her by the legs and shook her like a recalcitrant money-box until it shot out, just in time. And Jenny had somehow manoeuvred a pea so far up her nose that it had become inextricable until the Doctor found a barbed pea remover. Jo had to deal with two miscarriages, which were grim disappointments. But this was so unexpected. Kirsty was so alive that Death seemed impossible.

She was seven. She had been given a wonderful end of term report and was so excited and eager to show it to us, that she got off one stop earlier than usual and ran across the road, impatient at the slowness of the bus, straight in the path of an oncoming car.

The two elder children were away at school. Jo was out shopping, taking the baby Pony with her. I was alone when the phone rang. A neighbour's voice said, in a low and unnatural tone: "Your little girl has been hit by a car and she's quite badly hurt. They've brought her to my house. You'd better come quickly." At first I didn't grasp what he meant. I suddenly felt ill, then life mercifully changed gear, so that reality became a dream. Everything I did or said was purely automatic; I seemed to be someone else.

I arrived just after the Doctor, an old family friend. When I saw Kirsty on the sofa I at first felt relieved. Here was none of the blood and mess I'd feared. Perhaps she wasn't too badly hurt. One leg was hanging over the edge a little awkwardly. Was it broken? If that was all . . .

There was a bruise over her eye and signs of a nasty bang on her head. She was lying on her back, pale, beautiful and unconscious, but breathing rather noisily and uneasily, sometimes taking a deeper breath as if she were about to come round. I had just time to take her in my arms, when Doctor Elliott said: "I don't quite like the look of her reflexes in that eye . . . there could be some brain damage. We must get her to hospital at once."

I went in the ambulance with her and the Doctor followed in his car after ringing the hospital to prepare them for action as soon as we arrived. The ambulance attendant, whom I knew well, looked dazed and worried. I was still trying to tell myself that she had nothing more than concussion and a broken leg, and that she would come round at any moment and recognize me. I held her hand, kissed her and mumbled little nonsenses of consolation to her; for 25 long miles I desperately prayed and hoped the power of love would prevail. She grew quieter and still, and I thought I felt her squeeze my hand. Now, surely, she would come round.

"I think she's changed colour", said the ambulance man. "We'd better stop and let the Doctor have a look at her."

The Doctor had a quick look and gave her an injection. It was only a minute or two before we reached the hospital. A stretcher was waiting. As she was gently lifted out of the ambulance she still looked little marked or damaged, but her eyes were open and looked glazed. I noticed a speck of dust against their bright blue. She didn't blink. My world swam round and went out of focus.

She was hustled away and I was shown into some kind of waiting room. The world seemed distant and my sensation of being in a trance deepened. One or two figures bustled, and time passed. It could have been seconds or hours. A Doctor finally came in.

"I'm terribly sorry, there was nothing we could do; she was dead from injuries to her brain when she got here. Everything possible was done. If she had recovered it might in any case have affected her all her life."

I stared at him quite unable to cry or to react. I had known for some time . . . since I had seen that speck of dust. I heard a voice say: "Thank you for trying", and realized that it was me.

I turned to Doc Elliott and said something like: "I don't feel very much on the ball, can you please take charge? What am I supposed to do now?"

"You'd better contact Jo."

Mercifully the trance persisted. It was barely me that went through the awful motions of ringing home. Dreadfully Jo's voice answered.

"I've been told about her being hit", she said. "Is it very bad?"

"Very bad."

"She's dead, isn't she?" asked the voice.

God knows why, but I hesitated a second before saying: "Yes." I said some other things, but there was nothing else to say.

I went home. From the nightmare of the next few days there are flashes which I remember vividly. The face of the au pair returning from an afternoon off. She had been told, and she looked at me with shock and horror as if I had been a being from outer space. There came relief of a kind as Jo and I talked about it in our bedroom and shared our floods of tears at last.

Then there was the surprise and joy when we discovered that Kirsty had, before going to school that morning, written on the wall of our bathroom: "I love you, Mummy and Daddy." We were sentimental enough to frame it, and to feel that it must have been some premonition or message of consolation.

Then there was the usual rigmarole of dealing with the practical mummery surrounding Death. Choosing the coffin, persuading the Rector to let us have a corner of the overcrowded churchyard. The last sight of her in the Chapel of Rest, beautiful and fresh as the spring, but cold to my farewell kiss and with the bruise on her head now spread over forehead, temple and cheek, sinister and purple. We shared a frenzied, unreasonable belief that love, faith and prayer would somehow work a unique miracle. At the funeral service we prayed as we had never, alas, prayed before that an exception could be made for us. Love and faith is supposed to move mountains, if strong enough, and nothing, we felt, could be stronger than ours.

But, no. I remember the strange continuation of the ordinary, very public duties of my profession. People would look pityingly at me or admire my 'courage', which was still nothing but the indifference of a trance condition. My mind and body went on functioning on automatic pilot, but I was in a sense dead, beyond the fear that anything worse could happen. Part of me had died, the optimistic, joyful, hopeful and strong part seemed to have gone for ever.

Death of the old, however beloved, brings a sense of mission accomplished and inevitability. Death at the age of 7 is an abrupt and intolerable outrage.

At the inquest I peered curiously at the driver of the car which killed her. I managed to say a few words to him to let him know that I didn't blame him in any way for what had happened. He looked so desperately upset. He may or may not have been travelling too fast. I felt only pity for him in his obvious horror and bewilderment.

But now at last I can look back and see things which were invisible for many years. How, for instance, it brought Jo and me even closer. We had always had a good and happy marriage, but in the early and ambitious days of my career I had let myself get swallowed up in my profession. I seldom got back before half-past seven, and, after that, there were interruptions and more work to do. Like many people over-keen on success, I had not left enough time for the things that really matter; having a happy home, being with the children, sharing outside interests with my wife. Now we were made to share something no-one else could understand: the wilderness of grief, the bitterness, the impotence, the fury, the futility of unanswered prayers. In an extraordinary way the sharing of it all brought us closer and ultimately calmed the resentment. We agreed to have another child.

It was no accident that Bede was born 18 months after Kirsty's death. His birth (a somewhat dramatic one) seemed to bring us back to life. His healing power was everything we had hoped for: very like her, a happy and marvellous child. He has retained throughout his life a wonderful ability to bring cheer and light in a place of gloom and dark. Jo and I were always unreasonably fond of him, and I only hope the others understand why. At the age of 91 I get a phone call from him almost every day, and I hope he has an inkling of how much it means to me. I still laugh and love life: it is largely due to him.

Jo was 40 when she gave birth to Bede, but looked as though she was in her twenties. As had happened with the birth of Rhu, she was reluctant to go to hospital until the last minute. The result was not only that the waters broke, but, much more alarming, the cord appeared. We called the long suffering Doctor Elliott, who put the Norfolk and Norwich Hospital in the picture. The three of us got into the ambulance. For 26 miles the Doctor ensured that the cord would not be pinched, and Jo was rushed in followed by both of us. The Doctor on duty in declared that he couldn't hear the baby's pulse. Doctor Elliott took over. He decided that he must do a Caesarian: he was certain that the pulse was still going. Jo, in the meantime, had an almost fatal reaction to the anaesthetic. Amazingly the operation was successful, and Jo was able to look on radiantly, while I gave the large and vigorous, but blood covered baby its first bath.

There is no doubt that Bede's arrival was a turning point for us. We stopped being sorry for ourselves. In my first years at Gresham's I had been enthusiastic, but also rather harsh and self-centred. It made me more understanding and sympathetic, but also brought back the zest and excitement of life. It brought Jo and me even closer, as shared suffering so often does. I increasingly realized how precious was her ability to turn troubles to positive sympathy and even good cheer.

There was plenty to do. The school was growing fast. When I arrived the Senior school numbered about 250 and the Junior school 70. When I left the numbers were 430 and 170. There is no special merit in numbers. I have always felt that if a school had more than about 450 pupils it was in danger of becoming less human. Certainly it becomes impossible for the Headmaster to know his pupils. Another advantage for a school of under that number is that boys and girls of moderate ability can get the top coaching in art, music and sport and compete against bigger schools successfully. A promising and talented rugby player going to a school with a thousand boys may not get into the top stream and may never experience the 1st team competition which would fully develop his skills.

But, in times when rising fees present a real problem, size makes finances easier. If a school is too small, it cannot offer the width of choice that is essential for a good education. In the case of Gresham's on its return from Cornwall, it was too small to offer that width of choice. Moreover the buildings were inadequate: to increase numbers we had to provide more buildings, and update many of the ones we had. Expansion would also give us the chance to bring in some first rate new staff to help us strengthen those subjects which were not doing well.

These things need cash. Over my 27 years I had to launch appeals every seven years to enable us to offer the best. Seven years because tax-free covenants ran for seven years. The Fishmonger's Company were a tremendous help, generally subscribing pound for pound for a large part of the sum required. To start with we engaged professional fund raisers (although I felt that Hooker and Rich were not promising names!). They provided us with valuable advice and a charming, tweedy gentleman skilled in the art of raising money. Nevertheless the professionals required me to travel up and down the country to speak to gatherings of potential donors: a part of the job which did not appeal to me very much. And to write to all the richest of them, preferably in my own hand.

For the last couple of appeals John Purdy, the Bursar and I undertook the task without professional help – and did just as well.

The Junior school was well below par in its buildings. We got the help of Bains, a talented northern architect, to design a completely new boarding house, which enabled it to expand and to have much better facilities. New biology labs, improved science laboratories and a new chemistry lecture theatre followed, and then a new music school with individual practice rooms. Then we became one of the first schools to build a new senior boarding house, in which the majority of boys would have individual bed-sitting rooms. I had long felt that the absence of privacy was a handicap for most public schools and that it was essential for them to have somewhere to work and to develop individual hobbies on their own.

We then updated some of the other houses along those lines, and built a big central dining and administrative block, designed by Bernard Fielden, who also reshaped the American White House. A lovely man to deal with, who, when the governors met in my house, would sneak back to the dining room after tea, because he was unable to resist Jo's cream cakes. Before the new block the boys all dined in their houses, under the organization of the Housemasters' wives, the masters all met in a small classroom, and my office was in a small attic on the top floor of the main school building. The new block had a dining room and modern kitchen, a sanatorium, a comfortable common room and a bar and further rooms for second master, careers master, secretaries, Headmaster's offices – and lavatories, which seemed to be rare facilities before the war. The Housemasters were sad to lose the chance, which they had under the old system, to have their pupils under their own roof in the middle of the day, but their wives were relieved, and the financial saving of central feeding was becoming essential.

Moving the sanatorium into the new building enabled us to adapt the old sanatorium as a girls' waiting house, while we planned the new girls' boarding house: Edinburgh House.

In the meantime we built a new indoor swimming bath, a CCF centre and a sports hall, big enough to double as a theatre or concert hall. The task was a never ending one. In my last year we were examining the possibility of a new centre for art, design and technology which my successor completed – and a new house for my successor, so that he would not have to run a boarding house like I did or buy a house of his own. Jo and I planned it on a site with its back to the woods, looking down towards the Chapel. The governors called it Lockhart House, a nice compliment, I suppose, but we never had the chance to live in it! Of the other little improvements we tackled I should perhaps mention the Chapel organ. It had either to be replaced or rebuilt. I'm not sure we made the right choice, but we set about rebuilding it. It was a difficult and costly job, but its main value was in the way a number of boys got fascinated by the challenge and dealt with all kinds of mathematical, musical and practical problems, under the guidance of Martin Renshaw and, ultimately, professionals. Most importantly, I believe that the staff and the pupils for the most part developed a truly happy and fruitful relationship.

Chapter Thirty Four

A Great Man

At this point I should pause to pay tribute to my right-hand man in all these undertakings: John Purdy, the Bursar. John was a great man, whose previous job had been the District Officer in Northern Nigeria, keeping, at the risk of his own life, Christian tribes and Muslim tribes from burning each other to death in rubber tyres, and advising the government. He told me after 10 years of amusing and profitable working together: "You know, Logie, my job hasn't changed much. I still look after an eccentric Emir's lavatories, surrounded by turbulent natives and periodically confused by directions from an out of touch government in a distant capital."

Apologies to the governors who in reality made such efforts to keep us on the rails and to help smooth away the inevitable differences between a Head, whose main aim is to get as much money as he can to further his ambitions for the school, and his Bursar, whose main aim is to restrain his expenditure and balance the budget. To be fair to John, he always did balance the budget, and at the same time managed to squirrel away secret sums, which, when he saw that I was dead set on some scheme, he would eventually produce with a flourish . . . I presume that is the nature of all big concerns from the Prime Minister and the Chancellor of the Exchequer downwards.

On a somewhat smaller scale we had some amusing little spheres of disagreement. The first concerned the date on which the central heating was switched on in classrooms and boarding houses. I favoured the beginning of the Michaelmas term, he wanted it to be a month later. After producing graphs and consulting weather forecasts, we always came to a compromise – thousands of pounds were at stake.

The other was when we were looking for possible economies in funding the school. He suggested margarine for butter. Having just moved from war time margarine to peace time butter, I was reluctant to go into reverse. He repeated that modern margarine was not only much better for you, but it was completely undistinguishable from butter in taste. I thereupon bet him that he could have his way IF I failed to tell five samples apart: wholly butter, two parts butter one part margarine, 50:50, two parts margarine and one part butter, and pure margarine. To my surprise as well as his, I got all five right. The school continued to have butter. Whether it still does so, I don't know. Medical science has come down firmly on John's side!

When John Purdy and I were both retired, Jo and I went to see him and Elizabeth from time to time. He was suffering from cancer, but faced up to it with his usual courage. Sitting up in bed he would cheer us all up by producing the best wines from his excellent cellar and laughing over the old days.

Just before he died he received a letter from the old Emir's son, who had now taken over in Northern Nigeria. As near as I can remember it said:

"Dear Mr. Purdy,

"Some friends have told us that you have been very unwell lately. I was sad to hear it, and would not like to miss the chance to tell you how much my father and I and your many friends over here appreciated your invariably wise and kindly advice and unstinting hard work on behalf of our country. You are remembered with admiration and affection for your steadfastness and courage in the cause of peace and prosperity. With best wishes."

Perhaps our Colonial Administrators were not all racialists and stuck up Blimps ... nor all countries ungrateful. It was said that John, apart from personally releasing an intended victim from a burning tyre, managed to send two hostile spear shaking tribal armies home by walking between them, addressing them and waving a stick at them.

He made enemies, as strong personalities must do, and I admit that we had rows in the early days. Some members of the staff, and especially their wives, occasionally complained that they were treated like errant tribesmen. However, the better you knew him, the better you liked him. I dare say that one or two of the ladies were not very different from errant tribesfolk.

Chapter Thirty Five
Co-education

The most important issue for the school in the Seventies was whether to go co-educational or not. If we did, how would we start? 6th Form to start with, and then, if it went well, all the way?

There were several reasons why we started to think about it. Parents who had children of both sexes found it inconvenient to visit schools which were far apart. Our own staff found it unfair that those who had sons could educate them free, while those who had daughters were obliged to meet the high fees charged elsewhere. A little research showed us that there was considerable demand, so that we would be able to choose the best. We knew that the main weakness of all-male boarding schools was bullying – from which the single sex girls' schools were not exempt either. It is a danger even in the best of single sex schools: as I have already explained. The experience of mixed sex schools in other countries was that where both sexes were taught alongside each other these difficulties did not arise. Boys in single sex schools tended to overvalue games and undervalue the arts. Theatre, art, dancing and music benefited greatly from the cooperation of both sexes.

We had an arrangement with the nearest girls' school, Runton Hill, that we would take their Sixth Form scientists to save them the expense of setting up laboratories. It seemed wasteful of time and money to make them travel between the schools every day . . . eventually, I am ashamed to say, as a Governor of Runton Hill, we were largely instrumental in taking their custom and bringing about their demise.

Not all of the staff at Gresham's were keen on the idea. Above all they feared the fact that most of us had little experience of dealing with girls' problems outside the classroom. They dreaded the possibility that boy-girl affairs would not only interfere with work, but 'lower the tone' and, worst of all, might lead to unwanted pregnancies and scandals which would be meat and drink for the press. How were we to deal with this? Was it to be barbed wire and machine guns, or prayer and the Pill?

Before deciding, I thought it would be wise to consult an experienced Headmistress on what mistakes we should avoid and what measures we should take. I took the unprecedented and brave step of inviting Miss Manners, in the chair of the Girls' Eastern Division at that time, to address the Eastern Division of the H.M.C. (all independent schools from the Channel Islands to Norfolk and Cambridge) at their London meeting. It was the first time that a Headmistress had been asked to talk to this all-male gathering. The formidable Miss Manners revelled in the chance to let us have it with all guns blazing.

We were stealing their brightest girls without proper notice, and we were condemning them to be corrupted by our coarse rugby playing louts. Pretty 6th Form girls would pull the wool over young masters' eyes and get away with murder by skilful use of tears. We were hopelessly inexperienced. Teenage girls needed seclusion from male distraction and guidance from women who understood their problems. Evidence showed that they performed less well, becoming easily intimidated in class, especially if they were in a minority. We would need to take on a large number of female teachers. Even then they would not give of their best.

The Headmasters listened. Some were shell shocked. They heeded some of her warnings and kept some of their disagreements under cover. I resisted the temptation to point out that the 'special understanding of girls' of one of her colleagues had led to an affair between one of her star pupils and the school gardener. Her evidence for the adverse effect of co-education on girls could only come from the two or three progressive schools which had already embraced co-ed for an appreciable time. They had already gained a reputation for trusting too much to Prayer and the Pill. There were stories of parties which got out of hand, as they continued their tradition of letting the students make their own rules and periodically pushing their teachers into the swimming bath.

If we wished to prove Miss Manners wrong, we would be wise to take her advice in some directions.

It was always the first year or two which were going to be the most difficult, while the girls were in a small minority. It was very stupid of me in retrospect to make my daughter Jenny one of the very first. Difficult enough to be the Headmaster's daughter: to be beautiful and exceptionally sensitive to what other people thought and to feel that everything you said and did was being observed and criticized by all the staff and pupils put her under a strain to which I, or all people, should not have exposed her.

Otherwise the start went surprisingly well. The first intake of nineteen 6th Form girls produced eighteen university places, six of them to Oxbridge. Once we had a complete girls' house, our fears were laid to rest. Perhaps one in ten felt isolated and unloved, but she would have felt the same in any school. Perhaps one in twenty had her head turned by male attention, but the majority were happy competing with the boys and successfully forming friendships within the girls' house and amongst the boys. The real delight was the improvement in the music, the drama, the art and in the generally more adult and pleasant behaviour. No more embarrassment as 13 year old boys with pimples, size 10 shoes and clumsy gestures wrestled unhappily with the roles of glamorous females. The choir under Angela Dugdale's experienced direction became really popular until eventually under Mark Jones it can claim to be the best in Britain outside the specialist music schools, in demand for services as far afield as Venice, St. Petersburg, Florence, Vienna, Paris, Nice and St. Peter's, Rome.

Admittedly it is sometimes difficult to tell the 6th Form girls from their lady teachers. It must cause some difficulty too to the younger male teachers. But the atmosphere of cheerful business and good relationships is all I hoped for – and the rugby has benefited too!

We owe a lot to the pioneering housemasters and their wives, very much in partnership. John and Jenny Rayner, both teachers, Richard and Julia Peaver, John and Sue Smart. A little bit of Prayer and a tiny bit of Pill – and a machine gun and slightly barbed wire in the attic under dust covers in case of need. Although no-one, where he and she are close together in their late teens, can dare to assert that troubles were unknown, they were more rare and discreet than most of us had feared. That is largely due to the thoughtful and tactful start made by those brave swimmers in new waters: a good start soon becomes a great tradition. It is interesting that Sue and John Smart, John and Jenny Rayner and Richard Peaver have all become deeply involved in liaison with the Old Greshamians.

Chapter Thirty Six
Family Holidays

Substantial holidays are one of the many blessings of a teacher's life. Although a Headmaster's holidays don't start until a week after the end of term and end about a week before the beginning of term, the pressure is off and the remainder of the holidays are still longer than they are in most other professions. But week ends are not free, and neither are most evenings. So the holidays are vital for family bonding.

When at Tonbridge our holidays were nearly always spent with my parents: first at Sedbergh, then at Drum Mhor. Drum Mhor was discovered thanks to the gratitude of Dawyk Haig, the Field Marshall's son. It was a simple, but capacious cottage looking out past Bemersyde (the Haigs' baronial castle) to that wonderful view of the Eildon hills on the other side of the Tweed Valley. The picture adorns a million beer mats in Scottish pubs. Dawyk was a charming, artistic and gentle man, unhappy in his childhood, because of the unfair criticisms of his father. My mother took an interest in him at Cargilfield, and he was always grateful. He gave Dad and his family the right to fish his beautiful stretch of the Tweed for as long as they were there. For that he shall be eternally blessed. It provided me with prime trout fishing in April for years.

Holidays at Sedbergh were in the post war years when I was teaching at Tonbridge. Jenny and Rhu were still very small. They enjoyed those because my mum was so good at entertaining the very young. She was rather less skilled at managing the daughters-in-law: she expected them not to go to the pub, to drink or wear trousers, and to do what they were told. None of them took to this kindly, though I think Pip was better at it than the rest of us. I got a lot of pleasure fishing the Lune, the Rawthey and the Dee or Lilymere – where I even persuaded Jo to fish, and where she caught one almost with her first cast, when I'd been fishing for an hour without rising a single trout. At that time our Uncle Captain John Brougham R.N. had just retired from being in charge of the Naval College at Dartmouth and was living near his sister (Mum). He sympathized with the daughters-in-law, who were banished every evening to the drawing room while the brethren were given cocktails in the study, and he made a point of asking them down to the White Hart for a drink. He had huge eyebrows and a delightful sense of humour.

Post-war Christmas at Sedbergh before dad's retirement were memorable clan gatherings: plenty of space for our increasing numbers. All four brothers and their wives. Aunt Freda, always a centre of bright conversation in her wheel chair. Broxton, dad's House Tutor at Rugby, was an honorary Godfather, performing simple conjuring tricks. Rhu and Jenny, Sandy and James, Karen – my children, John's and Rab's – all got to know each other and to play a great variety of games together: some recognized ones, some invented. It was a major part in the creation of clan closeness, an echo of pre-war get togethers at Rugby and Cargilfield, and a foreshadowing of ones where Jo and I were the hosts at Gresham's.

Dad's retirement took place just before my appointment to Gresham's and Paddy's departure for Canada. We enjoyed Drum Mhor even more than Sedbergh because Dad and Mum had time to devote to us and to our children, and because there was no school attached to make them feel that we should all be setting an example in our standards of dress and proper behaviour. The sad thing about it was that Dad's health began to degenerate quickly (he was only in his early 60's, but had always smoked far too much). He would have enjoyed a long retirement so much, with freedom to paint and fish and to enjoy the company of his sons. His last year or two at Sedbergh were darkened by the reaction to the appointment of his successor Michael Thornely. Michael was his young house tutor, married to the delightful but even younger Jennifer. Michael was a great schoolmaster: a wonderful sense of humour, a first class pianist and a gifted speaker. But the promotion of a junior master from within a school is always a dangerous move. There were senior masters who felt that, if an internal appointment was made, they should have had a better claim than this young beginner. It was assumed that it was Dad's appointment.

Dad said that all he had done was to act as a referee when Michael had put in an application for the job. It was a Governors' appointment, and he didn't even have a vote. Be that as it may, there was a lot of fuss. It was held to be nepotism, and there were resignations. I think that even the family thought that it was surprising that Dad had been so naïve as to be utterly taken aback by this reaction. It made Michael's first year or two very difficult and saddened Dad's retirement . . . he was really hurt.

Michael turned out to be a very good Headmaster; of the 4 B-L's who went to Sedbergh during his reign, one didn't get on with him, two liked and admired him, and one thought him outstanding. He is certainly now regarded as a man who continued to improve academic artistic and musical standards at a difficult time.

But Dad did not live to see his protégé justify his expectations – or to get the best out of his retirement to Tweedside. He developed a cancerous form of leukemia and died quickly. I felt guilty that I had not spent more time with him in those difficult years ... They coincided with the busiest time of Jo's and my lives, as such things always seem to do.

Mum continued to live at Drum Mhor. We had the family to stay at Gresham's in the Christmas holidays ... Aunt Freda in her wheelchair distributing good cheer, such of my brothers and of their children as were available while Sid and Jo presided.

Sid was the lovely 6′ 3″ chef from the Ukraine whom Jo appointed on spec and who turned out to be the most loyal and hard working honorary member of the family. He cooked for the boys and for us and our guests. Although he was liable to overdo the fatty sauces, he was a good cook and revelled in special occasions. When Lord Reith turned up, even taller than himself, he glowed with enthusiasm. "Ah! There's a proper Scottish Lord for you," he said. When smaller and less impressive peers came, he showed clear signs of disappointment.

He had been involved in 'Death marches' as a prisoner first of Stalin, then of Hitler and escaped from both. From time to time he would see one of our children watching a programme praising Russia under Stalin. He would ask me to tell them that it was all nonsense: our country didn't seem to understand the extent of his evil.

When we changed to central feeding, I got him the job of principal chef; but he never felt it was quite the same. He died suddenly of a heart attack in the kitchen, never having complained of any illness. A fine man. I remember his appointment clearly. We had lost our cook, and Jo had to take over. Sid answered the advert. Jo was somewhat alarmed by his size, his confidence and his absence of any strictly cooking references, or, indeed, any references. She sent him away and said she would think it over. Without waiting to see if he had a second summons, he came back the next day. "You make mistake, lady, if you not take me. We will get along together very well. I will be loyal and hard-working. You are worried because I have no references. I have only escaped to England a short time, and Hitler and Stalin don't give references. I like the English and I think they will like me."

Jo didn't hesitate this time, and the towering Ukrainian became a valued part of the family.

In the holidays we saw little of John and Mar apart from Christmas, but I went down to Rye to play for the rugby internationals against Rye Golf Club, of which John was the President at that time. He and Mar lived on the edge of that beautiful old town. Rab also played for the rugby internationals, so we enjoyed a family threesome. At that time I was an erratic 18 handicap man, Rab and John a shade better. It is a testing course for bad golfers: strong winds and nasty rough; one year Paddy was able to join us and we had a memorable match: Pad and I won on the last green when Rab missed a 6 foot putt for a half. Pad took a wonderful photo of John standing on the edge of the green. His back was turned on Rab while he shaped up for the stroke on which everything depended, and his head was bowed in prayer. But God was not on their side.

I enjoy an occasional game of golf. For about 15 years I played three or four times a year. It is fun to play a game which you don't take desperately seriously. I am good enough to enjoy an occasional birdie and bad enough not to be upset by the frequent double bogies. I used to find that if I hadn't played for 6 months my first 9 holes were often surprisingly good. Then I would start to think and to get ambitious and go to pieces.

It was much the same with my brothers, though Rab and John played a little more often and sometimes a little better. In the next generation Pad's son Patrick is of professional standard, and Bede hits the ball a mile and can be good when his putting doesn't let him down. Rhu seems to have improved since he got Parkinson's Disease ... Perhaps it prevents him from overhitting. John made oldest brothermanship pay. On one occasion he hesitated over the choice of club to take for the short eleventh hole at Sheringham. From the back tee it was about 160 yards, with a stiff breeze against. "Looks about a number 7 today," he said, and played a perfect shot to the middle of the green, holding his follow through as if for the press photographers. Luckily I knew my brother, and I looked at the club, still clearly identifiable. As I thought: a number 4!

Gradually we started to take holidays on our own – Jo and I and our children. It started with camping in the Highlands, and then caravanning: to begin with we borrowed my mum's caravan, and then bought one from Pam and Paul, when we had burnt Mum's by leaving an unguarded light in it at Drum Mhor. Not our brightest effort, though the blaze was spectacular!

We found camping and caravanning fun, even in Highland rain. In those days there were hardly any official caravan sites. You could park or pitch your tent in any roadside quarry or beside any wild moorland path. Nowadays the splendid road through Glencoe often has heavy traffic, and any roadside quarries are likely to have pipers in full Highland dress and trays of twee mementos. The Old Road was a rough surfaced track, and cars few and far between. But even now Glencoe is a wonderful introduction to the remote Highlands: Buchaille Etive Mhor looms over the entrance, nearly always wrapped in a mantle of cloud. It seems to feel it has a duty to remind travellers that it is the site of the hideous betrayal and massacre of the MacDonalds by the Campbells: "Abandon hope all ye who enter here." Then, a little further, there is a view over the Rannoch Moor, 40 or 50 miles of treacherous bogs and small lochs entirely uninhabited, reaching into the heart of the Grampians towards Loch Rannoch with its huge cannibal trout. Then, on the other side, the spectacular scenery of Glen Etive and the arrival at Ballachulish ferry. Then a few miles more to another ferry to Ardgour, or a long drive round via Fort William.

By this time you were in a far off land. The natives spoke a different language: some couldn't speak English. Ardnamurchan was almost uninhabited except for the village of Strontian and the two or three crofts at the most beautiful white beach of Sanna. It was not frightening country like Glencoe. It was a heavenly peninsula, with birch wooded hills, lochs and mountains. A single track road with grass or heather growing in the middle wound its way along a marvellously varied shore. Round one corner, sheer rock, round the next, machair: the short grass which makes Hebridean shores so unique; then a cove with white sand framed in birch trees. There would be herons or cormorants in the shallows awaiting the arrival of the sea trout. Overhead buzzards were always circling, and every cliff had its pair of ravens. Every now and again a seal would peer at us curiously and then dive, at which point the herons and cormorants would move expectantly towards it; the sea trout had arrived.

From Sanna, Scotland's most spectacular sight comes into view. In the middle of the day the pure transparent sea changes from light green to turquoise and then purple, as the bottom changes from sand to granite and then bladder wrack. As the September sunset grows in intensity the sea and sky become indistinguishable in a blaze of vermillion, scarlet, mauve and turquoise. No-one could paint it, not even Turner, because it is unbelievable and constantly shifting – and floating between sea and sky are the extraordinary shapes, at first dark blue and then black, of Eigg, Muck, Rhum and, a little farther away the jagged outline of the Cuillins of Skye. I have never seen anything so dazzling: every detail is clear in my mind's eye – a lifelong treasure.

Particular holidays stand out. A generous governor, John Scott, 6′ 6″ of imposing Scottish aristocracy, had to travel abroad and wanted someone to look after his lovely, but somewhat spooky house Eredine, half way up the southern shore of Loch Awe. For a fortnight Jo and I and our eldest son Rhu (then about 8) moved in and played the part of the Laird. It didn't get off to a promising start. We were met by Mrs. Campbell, the cook. There was a heavy storm, thunder and lightening. The lights went out, and by the flickering light of a paraffin lamp Mrs. Campbell set about telling us about her teenage life. Her father had cursed her for marrying a Roman Catholic, though it also had something to do with clan enmity. Not everyone loves a Campbell. He prophesied that none of her children would survive past the age of 21. Sadly Mrs. Campbell had a large number of children. She felt it necessary to pour out her account of how some had died in infancy, one had fallen into the loch and drowned, one killed in a traffic accident. Tears were rolling down her cheeks.

In the meantime poor Rhu had developed a nasty attack of flu, had a high temperature and was thoroughly scared. When we were putting him to bed he started to have delusions. He was sure a hand had emerged from behind the curtain. Later he was convinced that a small man had been crouching on top of the cistern in the loo. By that time Jo and I were not sure he wasn't right.

The next day the sun shone, Rhu had recovered, there was a great view over the loch and the trout were rising . . . but it was still a spooky place.

On the Sabbath I was told that it was my duty to play host to the minister from the other side of the loch. He would row over in time for a 12 o'clock service. There would be Mrs. Campbell, a gamekeeper and a ghillie and their wives and the landlord and one or two guests from the Portsonachan Hotel further down the loch. I might or might not have to play the small organ in the gun room. I was to wear my Sunday best, and Jo and Mrs. Campbell would sort out a light lunch.

It all went off quite happily. The minister, appropriately, preached on the subject of the miraculous haul of fishes, and Mrs. Campbell provided a splendid lunch. Our subsequent haul of fishes was not quite miraculous, but we had fun on the hill lochs.

Loch Awe itself is very variable. It is overfished or overpoached (rumours of night lines set up by gangs from Glasgow) but it still has more big fish than anywhere else in Britain. A guest at the Portsonachan Hotel with an 8ft. trout rod and 3x gut landed a 53 lb salmon, after over 3 hours of being towed round the loch, and it is still in glass case to encourage us. Loch Awe also holds the record for the British Isles' largest trout: 38½ pounds, and the River Awe, where it runs through the Pass of Brander, yields big salmon every year. But they are hard to find: the loch needs knowing.

The spooky side of Eredine was confirmed by two stories from Mrs. Scott. The first concerned the strange experience of John Scott and Sir Edward Neville, also a Governor of Gresham's and a colonel in a Guards regiment. They went for a stroll down to the lochside together one evening to admire the sunset. They saw, moving up slowly from behind the hills opposite, what appeared to be a large luminous rocket – candle shaped with a skirt of light. They watched it move gradually up into the sky until it was out of sight.

They rang Fort William and Fort George to find out if there were any experiments scheduled for that evening, or if anyone had reported seeing anything of that kind. No. A complete blank.

The other tale was that Mrs. Scott had been preparing a picnic for the fishermen by the side of the Loch. She suddenly looked up, feeling that she was being watched. She saw a little grey man about 2 foot tall sitting on the top of a rock about 30 yards away. She had no feeling that he was hostile, just curious. As she looked at him he faded away and disappeared.

Ah well! Descartes had a theory that people once had a third eye which enabled them to have 'second sight'. While the modern inhabitants of sunny countries like France have lost this gift, the Celtic fringe inhabiting the misty lands of the north have retained it . . .

Another memorable holiday was on the shores of Loch Sunart where the river empties into the Loch. There Bede was introduced to the delights of fly fishing for mackerel and sea trout. Every morning I would peer out of the window watching the water for seals and cormorants following the sea trout making for the mouth of the river. I would grab my shorts and my rod and landing net and wade out into the sea loch. It was dangerous work: the rocks were covered with seaweed and very slippery, and the sea trout were only just in reach, if you were up to your chest in water and cast a long line. The trout weren't shy, but playing them without falling in, or without the leader getting stuck in the weed, was a challenge.

There was a farm at the head of the loch, whose owner we placated with gifts of mackerel and sea trout. On this particular holiday, our last for a long time in the Highlands, our beloved labrador accompanied us. She loved it, and was generally as good as gold. One day she got unnaturally excited by a sheep, and we thought she was going to kill it as she was barking hysterically. We smacked her: she wouldn't speak to us for days.

A little later a sheep, possibly the same one, got stuck on a tiny island when the tide was coming in. It was obviously terrified and baa-ing at the top of its voice. When the water started to lap round its feet, I could bear it no more. I cast off my clothes and swam out to the disappearing island. When I was two or three yards away and still out of my depth, I began to realize I hadn't thought through my rescue very clearly. Was I to try a fireman's lift? I hadn't realized how big and heavy the sheep was. Should I seize it (it, I saw, was a ram) by the horns and swim on my back towing it? As I trod water trying to pluck up courage for method 2, the ram took fright and solved our mutual problem by swimming effortlessly and twice as fast as me ashore, its fleece floating out to either side like an ingenious form of lifebelt. I've seldom been made to look so foolish, and my family were not backward in mocking my distinctly unheroic return.

That was not the best of our Highland holidays for poor Jo. We had one or two when we caught the elusive Highland spring-summer. That late August – or early September it poured with rain, the caravan stank of fish, and when it stopped raining the midges came out in clouds. Oh those midges! The Carmargue has nasty mosquitos; Canada has the black fly; Provence has soft-footed treacherous, green eyed clegs, which you cannot feel landing until they've already landed and sucked your blood; the Amazon rain forest has giant soldier ants; but the Highland midge is in a class of its own for sheer intrusive, persistent irresistible torture. What do they eat when we're not there? I've seen Highland ghillies with tough weatherbeaten faces, so well preserved in whisky that you wouldn't think a hornet could penetrate their skin, drop their rods and plunge their heads under water, before running for what shelter their car could provide.

At the end of this unfortunate trip, the sun came out after the rain. Jo and I went for a walk. On return we saw a Highland bull standing mournfully by the side of our tent with a large section of the roof dangling from its mouth. He brought with him a huge cloud of midges, which attracted by the smell of fish were pouring into caravan and tent.

I was quite rightly sentenced to 20 years of holidays in France, which will provide a later chapter!

*

Chapter Thirty Seven
Fishing

At this point I will explain why I have been a lifelong addict of fishing. It has given me as much pleasure at the age of 90 as it did at seven, when I caught my first trout and almost died of excitement. It has provided thrills when celebrating with my sons or nephews, a consolation in times of grief, a joy which can banish depression, a refuge from fear, worry and trouble – and an abiding interest which spreads to all kinds of other skills and studies. It is the great healer.

I fell in love with the sport, when I was allowed to go on my own at the age of 8 with a light metal 8 foot fly rod to fish the burn connecting Loch Mudle with the sea in Ardnamurchan. To be alone in that marvellous countryside was a privilege. It was a gin clear mountain stream, its banks lined with birches, heather and rocks. Rapids alternated with deep pools. You had the certainty of meeting no other human being. Nothing except dippers, grey wagtails, buzzards and an occasional red deer coming down for a drink. The thrilling song of the curlews or the haunting wail of the divers ensured that I was never without good company.

There, fishing as my father had taught me with wet flies cast upstream, I caught a few small trout and learned the unique excitement of stalking a rising fish and watching it moving towards the fly and timing the strike.

But this was just the learning process. One memorable day I learned what fishing was all about.

There had been a shower, and the burn had become a little deeper. There was a light touch of colour in the water, always a hopeful sign. In the biggest pool, I cast under the far bank. As my flies were swept into the main stream the water swirled and boiled as I'd never seen before. A huge fish seized my tail fly (a mallard and silver) and tore out my line irresistably. I nearly fainted with excitement. It set off downstream, and I stumbled down the bank in pursuit. Every now and again I had to get into the burn to avoid the trees on the bank, getting soaked to my armpits in the process. It took me over two small waterfalls: how it didn't break me, I still don't know.

Beginner's luck! It didn't snap the leader on a rock or get the line entangled in an overhanging branch. At last we came to a big treeless pool. The heather was growing over the edges, which made it more difficult, but the fish was tiring and I was able to recover some line and get a good view of it – a large salmon. I was too inexperienced to guess its weight with any accuracy, but, allowing for the growth of such memories over the years, I think it must have been between 9 and 12 lbs. I managed to pull it in near enough to have a dab with the net, but it dived away deep and took out more line each time. I began to despair, but, a fourth time, it seemed to give up, and lay as exhausted as I was, immediately below me.

My net was not designed for salmon; I pushed it through the heather and under the fish, until it was half inside. I attempted, rashly, to lift it over the heather and onto the bank. It was an impossible balancing act. It gave a great flap, fell out of the net and snapped the leader, just above the tail fly. For a few seconds it lay exhausted on its side. At once I flung down my rod and net and jumped into 5 feet of water, grabbing the salmon in my arms. It gave a powerful wriggle, slipped out of my grip and steamed off downstream to make good its escape.

Never shall I forget that moment. I spluttered and choked my way out of the pool and onto the bank, where I sat paralysed by frustration and grief – and wept. For years afterwards that moment haunted me. I have since then lost many good fish and have learned to be philosophical about it, but the agony and the ecstasy of that first battle has scarcely faded with the passage of time.

* * *

When Jo and I transferred our holidays to the continent I began to look for a place where there was enough sunshine and bathing to satisfy Jo and enough trout to satisfy me. I was growing to recognize that more than two days a week fishing was selfish, but I found it hard to spend more than two days a week lying on a beach packed with middle-aged tourists smelling of Ambre Solaire.

I suspect that the best compromise would have been the River Doubs, somewhere in Auvergne, or the Upper Allier, or the Lot or the Tarn, a tributary of the Dordogne at the foothills of the Pyrenees. My uncle B used to swear by the Slovakian rivers.

We explored all the areas except the last. Provence had so much else going for it that we settled there and never regretted it. But great fishing it was not. There were lots of trout. Unfortunately the locals went out at the beginning of the season and caught most of them by every kind of means, legal or not. Netting, grenades or worms or grasshoppers. By the time we arrived the temperature had risen and the trout had retreated to the mountains and looked for shade and swift torrents. I found some in the upper Verdon and one or two other streams in the sub Alps, but it was mighty hard work among the woods well populated and defended by horse flies, hornets, snakes and prickly undergrowth. A charming President of the fishing association of the Var gave vivid advice and the gas cylinder merchant at Bargemon turned out to be truly knowledgeable.

If you wanted to get easy fishing there were several trout farms attached to restaurants where you could catch your dinner with a bit of bread as bait and collect as many fat trout as you had time for – but it was not the sport as we understand it.

Fortunately for our marriage I fell in love with Provence for other reasons, which we could share, and lived happily ever afterwards on one fishing expedition a month. We had a three week holiday in Germany to find out whether there was any money left attached to a house in which Mum had part ownership before the war. We found the lawyer concerned, and his daughter became our au pair for a year or two. She was a great girl not much older than Jenny. We saw a castle every morning and a church every afternoon, except for one weekend when we were put up by the managing director of Coca Cola, Germany. A little, round and charming man. He owned a stretch of the Upper Ruhr, usually associated with heavy industry, but in fact a lovely little rural valley with a stream about the size of the Derbyshire Dove, full of trout. He took me out for a day's fishing. It was beautiful, peaceful, and I caught lots of fish – but decided to put them all back, as they were nearly all 5″ or 6″ long. At the end of the day we met. He patted a bag full of trout. I had kept two of about 6 oz. We took them back. His bag full was swollen with tiny trout. His wife was delighted. She didn't clean them, but put them straight into boiling oil. They emerged like crisp whitebait and were soaked in lemon . . . I've never tasted better. My two were surreptitiously set aside as being too big for the treatment!

In a lifetime of fishing I had never caught a salmon of over 12 lbs. I was to beat that particular duck in a spectacular way when I was much older.

Harris at the age of 8 was the ultimate paradise which determined my lifelong lunacy. Fishing Loch Langhabhat with my brothers, I was tending the rods at the back of the boat, trawling a long line and sunken flies, when a large ferox seized hold and tore out the line. The reel handle caught in my jacket and the cast leader broke as the great fish jumped. I'm not sure I've ever been forgiven, but I'll never forget the excitement. At night I peered out of the cottage windows as my Dad steered the little boat out into the moonlit mill pool. I saw him hook and land 3 good sea trout and had enough sweet dreams to last me many nights.

The River Torridon. In brilliant sunshine and low water, I'd given up hope. Nothing but salmon parr in the shallows. I was 12 years old. Suddenly a big splash: a 1½ pound sea trout. I carried the glorious silver fish to a grass patch among a mass of gorse bushes in full bloom. I still remember the sweet intoxicating smell of the grass and the feeling of triumph.

There were other places almost equally magical. Ballina, and the Caragh River in Kerry, where the sea trout followed our lures tantalizingly and took them rarely, and where I saw a large salmon rise to the orange peel discarded by a boy leaning over the bridge. An angler went up and borrowed more peel – and caught the salmon. The Spey Valley, with its long association with our family. Lochindorb with lots of trout and the nest of the last osprey before they died out in Britain, only to return in strength recently.

For the sake of readers who are (incomprehensibly) bored by fishing, I have relegated further explanations of its magical attractions to an appendix.

The rest of the family enjoyed those Highland holidays in other ways. Pony slept the longest. Bede and I would fold up the tent round her. We got it to a fine art: about 20 seconds to the tune of 'Colonel Bogey' and the words of World War II:

> 'Hitler only had one ball;
> 'Goering had two, but very small.
> 'Himmler had something similar,
> 'But poor old Goebbels had no balls at all!'

In case it should be thought that I was bringing up my children to sing rude songs, I should mention that Rhu, at the age of 8, sang it as he bravely stepped into a cold river – and I am sure he hadn't heard it from me!

Pony took advantage of every moment to read. Aged 11 or 12 she devoured Mervyn Peake's 'Gormenghast' and Tolkien's 'Lord of the Rings'. Once she'd started she would plough straight through to the end. Her very successful career as a teacher of English Lit was founded on her reading at that age and stage ... and perhaps on her granny's imaginative story telling, and a good foundation of Grimm's fairy tales.

Jenny's camping was divided sharply between the pre Sanna era and the post Sanna era. I took her to Sanna's world's most beautiful beach when she was 13, hoping that she would enjoy swimming in the turquoise water. I should have realized that the gulf stream was not doing its stuff and that it was extremely cold. Our unkind mockery of her reluctance to go in above her knees, upset her deeply, and it proved a sharp dividing line in her life. Before Sanna she was a bouncy, physically exuberant girl, loving to dash about in bare feet and doing cartwheels. Afterwards she became 'frileuse' – the French word for a very French condition: a person who, like a highly bred cat, loves warmth and fears draughts, disliking violent physical exercise perhaps in reaction to the males of the family who were excessively addicted to it. Poor Jen had one great disadvantage for a camper. She had fair hair and blue eyes and a fine complexion, exceptionally sensitive to insect bites, but also almost magically attractive to every form of insect. Mosquitos, even if there were only one or two, were anathema to her, and they would make her face swell up. To add to that scorpions and bush crickets would make for the bottom of her bed roll, not unnaturally provoking her to give sudden yells.

Rhu was a born camper ... a good traveller of every kind. A good map reader, a good linguist, above all Head Cook. Stew à la Rhu became the evening central event; the rest of us were just kitchen maids. Apart from the main tent we had a small bivvy for overflow – to which Rhu resorted when he couldn't endure my snoring – or to which I resorted when I couldn't stand Rhu's. It all depends whose memory you trust.

Bede treated the camping as a basis for his curiosity or sense of adventure. If there was water he had to go into it, if there was a cliff he had to climb it. On one occasion he got stuck about 25 feet up a cliff unable to move up or down. It took me about a quarter of an hour with a landing net as an aid to get him down without a nasty fall.

I must make an exception to my portrait of Jenny as the delicate 'frileuse'. The worst night we ever had – in Provence a bit later – a huge semi-tropical storm hit us. 5″ in a night. No tent could have kept the hail and rain out. She produced her guitar and sang songs to cheer us up before we were rescued early the next day!

Chapter Thirty Eight
Birds and Mushrooms

It is very difficult to be an angler without becoming interested in other aspects of country life. I exclude shooting, because I love birds and animals, and from the first time I shot a pigeon and saw it fluttering, and after accompanying my brothers on a rabbit-coshing expedition, when we drove across a moor armed with torches and golf clubs, dazzled the bunnies and despatched them with blows from niblicks or mashies, I made up my mind not to shoot warm-blooded animals or birds.

I first got interested in birds, when Mum drove me to different parts of the country between the ages of 7 and 12. We visited the great gothic cathedrals and the famous country houses and carefully chosen beauty spots. She bought me a pair of binoculars, which opened up a new world to me. When we came to a lake, a reed bed, or heath or a crag, she would stop, and with a book on British birds in one hand, I would search for birds and learn to identify them by their calls, behaviour, size and plumage. I took art lessons at school and tried my hand at birds . . . not great! But Dad thought my enthusiasm worth encouraging. So at the age of 7 he sent me on a fortnight's holiday with the Rugby art master: Talbot Kelly. I don't think either Dad or I realised what a significant signpost he was in the history of bird painting, but he was one of the first great artists to paint birds as we see them: landing, feeding, soaring, hovering, taking off, behaving as no other species behaves. Bird books must of necessity provide accurate maps of birds, so that the colour and shape of every feather is clear, and the shape, colour and size of legs, beak and eyes are accurately recorded. That too is art of a kind. But we never see birds like that. They are moving living creatures, each in its own characteristic environment, probably half in sunshine and half in shadow and partly concealed by long grass or leaves or muddy water.

Kelly knew exactly whether a bird had twelve primary feathers or fourteen. But he never felt the need to record every detail. When we look at a bird we may or may not be able to see these things: certainly we never see every detail. Kelly's birds pulsate with movement and character and life. If any part of them is done in detail it is wonderfully accurate, but big expanses of breasts or wings are done with a few bold masterly strokes.

Thorburn was good, his birds are illustrations showing detail, but not always capturing movement. Audubon is a master of pattern. Tunnicliffe paints great pictures, because the composition is his main interest and the colour patterns of the plumage. But Kelly, although he might study details of beaks, feet and legs from museums, always did rapid sketches in the field to catch different movements. He was also influenced by Chinese paintings and, especially, Egyptian. I watched his speed and courage, and the way he took care to put each bird in the right environment, and did my best to do the same. Unfortunately I gave up painting, although I never stopped studying birds, because schoolmastering and family life left so little time. In retirement, however, I once more had time, and, in Provence, outstanding chances to try to paint exciting birds. As Winston Churchill said: "When I put up my easel, it is a screen against the relentless advance of surly decrepitude." When you reach the age of eighty, there is hardly anything you can hope to do better tomorrow than yesterday: painting is the one joy that can accompany you to the end, or near the end of the road. I still hope to get nearer the skills of Talbot Kelly, to whom I give thanks for one of the great joys of life.

Another countryside hobby was the collecting, painting and eating of edible fungi. I was started on that hobby by Marie de Moutoussé, engaged by Dad as an au pair. When on holiday in Drumfriesshire, and the weather was not good for fishing, Marie would take me to the well treed banks of the Palnure or the Penkiln burns. There we would find all kinds of mushrooms or toadstools and learn how to identify the dangerous ones. There were plenty of death caps (responsible for 95% of all British deaths from fungus poisoning), and fly agarics – big, red-capped with white warts. But also lots of delicious species, which she would show us how best to cook. chanterelles, boleti (ceps), the blusher, blewits and wood blewits, fairy ring mushrooms, the 'Prince', giant puff balls, sparassis like waxy cauliflowers, parasol mushrooms eighteen inches high, and ink caps good when young, luscious 'grisettes' and beef steak fungus, and St. George's mushroom.

They have formed a substantial part of my diet ever since. I used to have fry ups with a few senior boys at Gresham's which is very well off for unusual fungi ... I claim to have eaten 28 different species from their woods and playing fields alone – without losing a pupil!

*

As the school was steadily growing in numbers I was able to appoint more staff of the kind who would contribute to education outside the classroom as well as increase the choice within the curriculum. One of the best things I ever did for Gresham's was to appoint Graham Smithers to look after the Maths. He was a brilliant scholar: Leicester University said he was the best they'd ever had. In some ways he was an unusual man to inspire so many pupils, but it soon became known that if you could get into one of his classes, you would get an A grade A level in Maths. Unusual because he was in some ways shy, drank very little, was reluctant to go to parties and lived on his own with three or four Alsatians, a donkey and a peacock or two. But he had a wonderful clear mind – not only in Maths. He gave a memorial speech about John Rowley, who was a colleague and friend. It was in Chapel (Graham was a quiet atheist who lived a Christian life); it was funny, touching, altogether memorable, and delivered without a note. It was rumoured that he ran a small syndicate of people who gambled on the horses, and that it invariably won money for the participants, because it was strictly run on mathematical lines. He was so successful at teaching that I never dared to go against his wishes. It was no good my hoping that he would favour a candidate for his department who was a great portrait painter, had a cricket blue or even a First in Maths. He made them all explain to him their thinking in answering an Oxbridge scholarship paper. This was his own method and the secret of his success. He would put a problem up on the board, and when he saw a pupil being stuck, he went up to him and asked him a couple of questions – and brought light into dark places. It was the same when I asked him to rearrange the timetable so that people would be able to take a combination of Arts and Sciences A levels – and, of course, he was an excellent bridge player. On retirement he used to set 'teasers': complicated little puzzles for the 'Sunday Times'. A charming and good looking man. He presided over years of success and taught his colleagues to do almost equally well – people like John Rowley, who specialized in helping non-mathematicians, as well as turning out to be a brilliant shooting coach, or Alan Ponder. I must have had an influence on Graham when it came to Alan, because he turned out to be a very good cricketer and a useful squash coach.

Squash coach? Inevitably any Greshamian's mind will turn to Malcolm Willstrop. In fact any squash player the world over is likely to know the name. When he left us, he became a nationally acclaimed coach. He helped (sometimes over-zealously) my aim to make Gresham's a school that realized that if you wanted to succeed and to compete in the modern world, you could not always avoid uncomfortable effort, but his crowning achievement came after he left Gresham's, and his son James became the world number one.

When he came for interview I questioned him about his squash. He said (modesty was not always his greatest virtue!) "If you appoint me, I can promise you that Gresham's will be the best squash school in the country." I wondered if this conceited fellow might actually be any good and took him to the squash court. I was defeated, and appointed him. Malcolm was as good as his word.

Within a few years Gresham's won the national squash competition and went on doing so for years and years. He introduced many pupils to serious training and practice. "No pain, no gain," he would grunt, as the press-up count passed 50. If your backhand was weak, he would make you stay in the court until every stroke clung to the wall at high speed. We won the national Londonderry Cup 13 times. His invaluable contribution to Gresham's was that he taught people that if they wanted to succeed they must be prepared to suffer – and not only where squash was concerned.

He was not always an easy employee. In a state school, I doubt that he would have lasted more than a term or two. If a pupil offended him he would tweak their hair, or cuff them over the back of the head. And he tended to make remarks on the touch line or in the squash gallery which upset parents or masters of the opposition. There were times when I had to pour oil on the troubled waters, and if one or two parents had pushed their complaints any further, it would have cost either Malcolm or me our job. But he was saved by having a sense of humour and by his great success. Among his pupils were John Cordeaux, Captain of Cambridge squash, Gawain Briars, later President of the Squash Rackets Association and British number one, and three or four more prominent players. Bede was Durham University number one, Christie in the top 20, as were the Le Lièvre brothers from the Channel Islands.

His crowning achievement came after he left Gresham's when his son James became the world number one in 2012.

Tony Cuff was quite different but almost equally effective coach. Rugby was his game: a typical Welsh fly half from Exeter University. Tony also lifted us up to school-of-the-month in Rugby World and an unbeaten season. Whereas Malcolm used to condemn the myriad inadequacies of his pupils fiercely, Tony praised them and told them what a great job they were doing, until they believed him and became what he said they were. His unbeaten season included Nick Youngs as scrum half, (father of English internationals Ben and Tom of Leicester). Built like a tank, he played scrum half for England when they won against New Zealand. Nick Chesworth, fly half for Durham, when they won the University Championship, and Bede, centre three quarter for the same Durham side and, according to the Durham coach "the best three quarter never to play for Scotland." He had been Man of the Match for the Scotland B team, winning against France in France.

Tony was a good Housemaster, and took on the Junior School to which he made huge improvements. I know that one or two of the Senior School housemasters felt that he had got preferential treatment from the Governors, because he seemed to get money for all his projects, while they were still made to wait. Helen and he were a couple who brought a family happiness to the prep school and their staff, which is the most important thing at that age – and which brings success.

There were many other fine teachers on whose enthusiasm and loyalty the success of the school depended – so many, in fact, that I have described some of them in an appendix for fear of boring readers unconnected with the school.

The last ten years of my tenure were a happy time for me. The speed of growth of the school threw up a lot of problems, but they were rewarding. It was frantically busy: the constant building, the incessant appeals for money, the battle to try to ensure tolerable pay for the overworked teachers. I understood only too well how hard it was to make both ends meet, when a science teacher with an Oxbridge First earned no more than a police sergeant. I would have liked to pay the really outstanding teachers more, and I managed to bring about small changes in that direction, but recognition of special talent gets more and more difficult in a Britain in which envy is an increasingly dominating force. One of my chairmen once said to me "Logie, steady on, you're beginning to sound like a Trades Union leader". I suppose that was one of my important roles, and it was better than having the whole staff as members of the N.U.T. (I think we only had one!).

I suppose I shall be remembered for the growth of the school and its new buildings, and for the introduction of co-education. Sad, really, when I always felt that buildings were far less important than staff and staff-pupil relationships. I am much more proud of the loyal and supportive staff I left behind and their pursuit of excellence and of the many pupils who rewarded us by their enthusiasms and success.

In the early days of my Headmastership, Headmasters were free to organize discipline without undue consideration of governmental or legal views. As time went by, for better or worse they had to be more careful. I realized that times were changing when W, the son of a rather dodgy parent who was abroad, made copies of the keys to my office and that of the Bursar in our excellent handicraft department. He was caught searching the Bursar's office. I wrote to his father, saying that W would have to leave if he committed another serious offence.

No reply from dad, but at half term W went to London and picked up a Jaguar which had been left on the street unlocked. He hid it in a friend's barn, and used it to go out at night to such high spots as there are in Norfolk. He was stopped by the police and brought before the magistrate. It so happened that I had to be at a Headmaster's Conference on the chosen day, so I sent his Housemaster, John Coleridge, to defend him. Before I left I put up a notice saying that W was expelled for theft.

John defended W so well, not mentioning the previous offences, that the magistrate acquitted him, on the grounds that it was a first offence, and that there was 'intent to return the car.'

Father thereupon wrote to demand that I withdraw the expulsion, because British justice had cleared his son. I refused, suggesting that I might be prepared

Fiona (Pony) in Devon

Jenny

Dacre at the rock pools in Provence

Fire at the Cabanon

Alastair, Logie and Dacre at Thurlestone, Devon

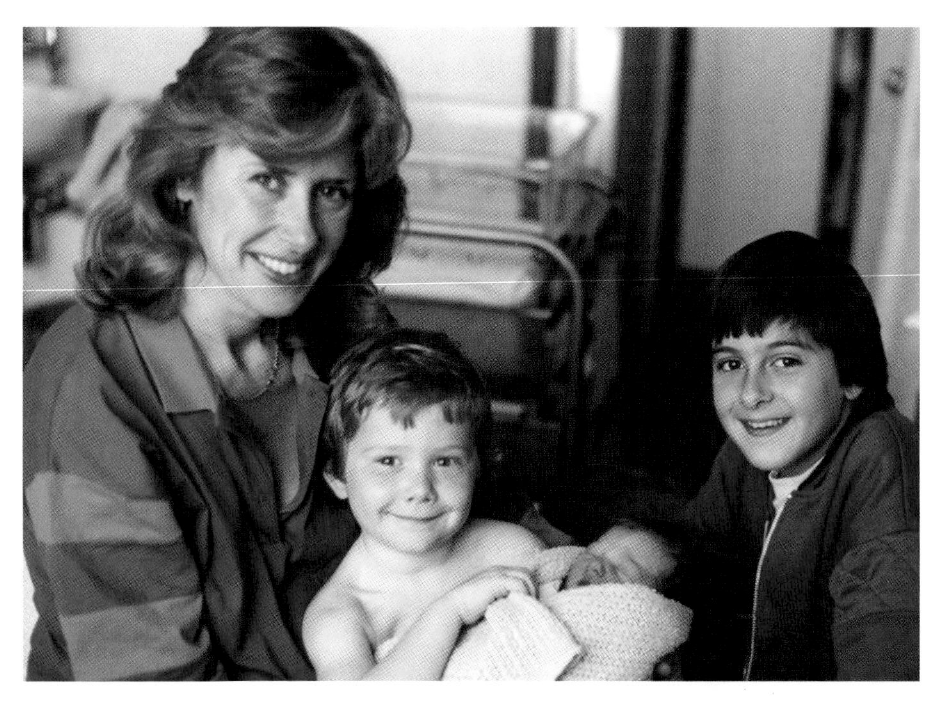

Philippa, Nicolas, James and newborn Chelsea at Norwich

My Mother, Mona

Sitting for Mrs MacDonald

Jo at the Cabanon, Provence

Family gathered to celebrate the Golden Wedding of
Reginald and Lulu Agnew

Bede, Dacre, Alastair, Jenny and George
Logie, Heather and Jo

Logie with Chinook Salmon at Langara, BC

Bede, Rhu and Logie at Holt

Bullfinches – an L B-L watercolour

Budgerigars – an L B-L watercolour

to change the notice to 'expelled for borrowing a car with intent to return, and considering previous offences.'

I reported the incident as I have related it, to the governors, adding that: "In some cases the law is an ass."

On the way out of the meeting a distinguished governor took me aside. "I think you should know, Logie, that I was the magistrate in charge of the case!"

After the first 15 or 20 years I wondered whether I should move on. I was tempted when Glenalmond became vacant, but realized that it would pay no more, and that I was influenced by false considerations – the proximity of good fishing, the Highland scenery and the pull of my Scottish ancestry. It would have been no fun for Jo and the family.

On the one hand you must lose a bit of zing after 20 years in the same place. If you haven't made most of the changes you wanted to, then it's probably time to move. On the other hand (I may be a slow learner!) it takes you 15 years to learn the job. Anyway I didn't feel I'd run out of energy and ideas, and, for better or worse, stayed on and left with few regrets. It was a great privilege and a happy time.

But I was young enough to enjoy retirement, to get to know my wife and family again, and to stop trying to be a good example, and to enjoy all the things I had not had time to do, and the next 15 years were wonderful.

*

What had happened to my parents and my brothers during my time at Gresham's? My father had died soon after the retirement he ought to have enjoyed so much. Before he died of leukaemia and of excessive smoking, he had a very successful exhibition of water colours at the Fine Arts Gallery in New Bond Street. It was acclaimed in the press and completely sold out. Mum went on living at Drum Mhor until she was about 80: as ever she was a tower of strength, putting her grandchildren straight, looking after her children in the holidays, uncomplaining and undemanding. When she began to be ill and found it impossible to look after herself, Rab and Pip who had retired to a remote house in the Lake District, adapted their house so as to provide a granny flat and looked after her, although they were both unwell, until she died at the age of 83. In the last few months she was bed-bound, and sent for us in turn to talk over the old days and open up about the things we had not discussed: sex and religion. She had become heavy and very sensitive ... how Rab managed to lift her and make her comfortable in bed I can't imagine. I tried it, and, to my horror, cracked one of her ribs in doing so.

John had gone on making a success of his M.I.6 career until one day he was stretchered out of an aeroplane almost entirely paralysed. Fortunately it was only temporary, but it was a sharp warning sign. Continual jetting round the world had taken its toll and it was an extreme form of jet lag. He was given three months' leave, and was told that he could choose between staying on with a good chance of becoming number one, or of getting paid off and found a job which would not need such excessive travel. John felt that, for the sake of wife and family as well as for his own safety, he would seek other jobs. He was never one to take his hands off the steering wheel of the world. He became Head of the Business Studies Council, introducing business studies to British Universities, raised money for Warwick University, became President of Rugby Rugby Club and Rye Golf Club, and personnel manager of Courtauld's. He continued to be consulted on matters of government policy – relations with old friends at the top of U.S.A. intelligence. Every month he met with centre politics big wigs for lunch at the Reform Club: Roy Hattersley, Roy Jenkins, David Owen and Bill Rodgers. He was always a village squire at heart, and loved shove halfpenny or skittles with the locals. At the end he came up to visit his daughter, Sal, in Norfolk, had a happy day walking with his grandchildren and rang me up. "Logie, I would love a day of simple all-male company. Can I come over and talk rugby and golf with you for a couple of hours tomorrow?" Alas, tomorrow never came. He collapsed on the way to the loo later that evening. An ambulance took him to the Norfolk and Norwich. I had to drive with his family to the hospital. It was clear that he was dangerously ill, but he was not in great pain and cheerful when we arrived. Suddenly his blood pressure fell, he lost consciousness and they rushed him away to see if they could do anything. They couldn't. He had a major cancer of the liver which had spread elsewhere. He must have known for some time, but contrived to disguise it. It was a grim night for us all. He left behind Mar, James, Sandy and Sal – no mean contribution to the world.

Rab and Pip had moved from Harrow via Appleby College, Wanganui as Headmaster, and, finally, to Loretto, where he became Chairman of the Scottish Division at about the same time as I was Chairman of the Eastern Division. Always generous and great company, I saw more of him than of the others during those years. He came to visit Jo and me at Church Farm House and we had a wonderful sunny day laughing about the old days. I watched him pause as he climbed the stairs to go to bed and remember being worried. Next morning he drove all the way back home to the Lakes, asked Pip to pour him a drink because he "felt a little tired" – had a heart attack and died. An example to us all ... I never felt that Loretto treated him as well as he and Pip deserved. Always concerned for others, he never asked for anything for himself, and I think (though he would never say so) that he was not well off in retirement. He had many difficulties: his own ill health, the loss of his talented eldest son, the responsibility for mum and a wife who had thyroid and heart problems too. Never did he show any sign of his troubles – unfailing in his help and hospitality. He was guided to the end by his admiration for the stoicism of Marcus Aurelius.

Pad returned from India to become a registrar in Bath and to patch up his marriage with Pat. Tired of waiting for a consultancy, he emigrated to Canada. Soon afterwards Pat got a brain tumour from which she died, leaving Michael, Simon and Ferelyth. Pad had married again, Eva Didychuck, an Ukrainian immigrant, who had 3 more children Tacye, Patrick and Logie (Paddy was not greatly original in his choice of names!) His fame as a consultant obstetrician and gynaecologist spread rapidly. All the most difficult cases were referred to him, and his years of finger exercises paid off handsomely. He operated still when nearly 80 and brought over 10,000 babies into the world, becoming President of the Medical Association of Ontario, then Speaker of Canada's Medical Parliament and an honorary Professor of Obstetrics of the London Medical School. I frequently met ladies who came up to me and said: "Bruce-Lockhart? I owe my life to a Doctor in Canada by that name."

Pad found time to teach his children to play the violin, and he composed romantic little tunes. He was also a victim to the fishing passion which has given so many of the family pleasure. At last, in old age, I was able to see him a couple of times and I have renewed contact with his children who remind me repeatedly of him in looks and gestures. "Do you mind what I'm saying, Logie?" he used to say, jabbing his forefinger towards my face. I've seen that elder brother approach and gesture in his sons, though not the words!

At his funeral he ordered that there should be no weeping and wailing. An old-fashioned wake was held round his coffin, while a son moistened his lips with a drop of the best Balmenach malt whisky from the family distillery, for which he had long cherished a certain fondness. A long life well lived and much loved.

*

Enough Death beds. This not a Russian novel. It's away to blissful retirement, a second honeymoon, and a full life in Church Farm House and France.

Chapter Thirty Nine
Paradise

In the 1970s our expeditions to France began to bear fruit. We concentrated increasingly on the area north of Cannes: Bargemon, Seillans, Draguignan, Fayence. Doctor Elliott lent us the use of his caravan at the very splendid holiday camp just north of Cannes: the 'Domaine du Pin de la Lègue.' There were luxurious central facilities: shops, bars, swimming baths, shows. There were also a number of hills each with caravans arranged so that they never looked directly over a close neighbour's plot, but had fine views over the lovely countryside. It was surprisingly inexpensive in those days. We were tempted to settle for buying a plot and caravan, but would still have preferred somewhere more private, rural and remote.

Doc Elliott and his family were close friends of ours for many years. Although he was the School Doctor he was not an employee. He was very human and humane – rather too much so where the fair sex were concerned – possessed of great Irish charm and a certain amount of contempt for pompous bureaucracy. At his best in a crisis (and we shared several) his judgement was always reliable. When Jo nearly died giving birth to Bede he had saved the day; when Jenny got a pea stuck up the top recesses of her nose he extracted it painlessly. When pupils had alarming injuries on the rugger field he always took the right action. I found that his opinion, whether on family problems or school issues was always worth listening to, even when he had drunk two or three glasses. He and his wife Dru and three sons shared a couple of holidays in the South of France. The three sons: pleasant Barry, helpful and kindly Nigel and successful and brilliant Giles were of much the same age as our four, and they had great fun together. The Doctor died, but we are still in touch with the rest. Giles made enough money to send six children through public schools and still holiday in Provence.

One happy day something happened which really settled our plans. We were camping in a wood near Bargemon, the property of Andy Mulligan, the ex-captain of Ireland's rugby team and an Old Greshamian. It was a very hot day in August, and we had run out of water. I spotted a farmer working at his vines at 2 o'clock in the afternoon – a time when most good French farmers are enjoying a siesta. I went up to him to ask if he could spare me a container-full. He replied, in French, that there was a tap of good drinking water a few yards from us. In spite of his fluency, there was something very British about him, and he was wearing British army boots. So I plucked up courage and asked him whether, by any chance, in spite of his good French, he was a Brit. He admitted that he was, and we embarked on a conversation, from which it emerged that we had much in common. His father had played scrum half for Oxford, when mine was playing stand off for Cambridge. He had just retired from being European manager of Shell. A brilliant linguist, he was an enthusiastic lover of National History and a very keen fisherman. He, Peter Cumberlege by name, introduced me to his wife, Shirleyanne, equally varied in her interests, and from that time on we have remained close friends. They proved to be generous, kind and hospitable, and she, especially, had a remarkable gift for seeing who would get on well with who. She introduced Jo and me to a circle of friends who made our life in the south a real joy. Peter's mild eccentricities in no way detracted from his charm.

A week after this meeting I was suffering from mild food poisoning and was in bed in Rhu's 13th Century Bargemon home. The phone rang. It was Peter Cumberlege. "I think there is some news that would interest you two. Just beyond the end of my property at the end of the track, there is a cabanon with a great view. It has a couple of acres of olives, and is backed on to the top of the hill. It is just an old shepherd's hut, with walls 5 feet thick, that has been made habitable by an English couple. If you make a quick bid, I think you could have it for £9,000. Jo had just been left some money by her parents. I rose from my sick bed and drove over with Jo to have a look. We both fell in love with it instantaneously. It was about half a mile from the Cumberleges. Its view ranged from the Esterel in the south to behind Toulon in the west and the hinterland of Nice in the east. It was indeed primitive, but the primitive devices worked. An outside loo. A couple of oil barrels on the roof which acted as water tanks for the shower and tap. The water was agreeably hot by midday. A couple of water tanks, from which we pumped up refills when necessary. One small room with a freezer, an oven, and wine and food facilities. One outside room with a roof, but only a low wall, where we could entertain 9 or 10 people. There was parking space beside it for our caravan. What more could we desire?

It was in 1974 that we started to take our holidays in the cabanon. From the start we found it a most exhilarating experience. Our village, Claviers, was about four kilometres east of Bargemon, and the cabanon was about five kilometres the other side of Claviers. So while we were settling in, we had Rhu's family nearby. James went to school in Bargemon, and Nicolas was born in Cannes, a town which was made popular by his ancestor Lord Brougham.

To leave work behind, however much you enjoyed it, is bliss. We were at last escaping from the total lack of privacy, which is almost the only disadvantage of being a Headmaster or his wife. You stop having to do the right thing and setting an example. Instead you can walk down the street eating an ice cream. You can roll out of bed, put on shorts emblazoned with flowers or champagne glasses (do you remember the Housemaster, who, on being confronted with my proposal that it might be permissible to wear coloured bathing trunks, said: "Headmaster, not only should they be black, but on no account glossy!")! You lie on a deck chair in the sun eating sweet peaches and good coffee. You listen to Bach or Schubert, as you watch the short toed eagle hovering overhead. There is never another human being in sight. I was able to fall in love with Jo again: to talk with her about the novel we had at last had the time to read, to plan where we would go for a midday picnic and swim, and a glass of our next door neighbour's good red wine at a ridiculously cheap price. You could fill up large containers from three roadside tanks at Fréjus. Red wine, 1 franc 10 centimes per litre; rosé 1 franc; white 90 centimes. We would plan the next "group of 12" meeting with our charming new friends in well hidden, carefully chosen beauty spots. We sometimes felt a little ashamed of being so happy. Should we not rather have been serving our communities by working on committees and keeping our hands on the tiller of the world either in France or in Britain. But we knew we had worked as hard as anyone could, and we felt we had earned our weeks in Paradise.

The best times were 8 a.m. to 10.30 and the hour before and after sunset. Until our retirement the time of our holiday coincided with the 'grande chaleur' – the end of July to the end of August. The middle of the day was often hot, too hot, although our hill top attracted what breezes there were. Our thermometer often registered over 90° – sometimes 100°.

The major worry was the danger from forest fires. Every time the mistral blew during the 'grande chaleur' there would be forest fires. By that time of year the maquis, the gorse and the pine trees were tinder-dry, and the 60 mile an hour mistral would fan any discarded cigarette or ashes left by careless picnickers into a blaze, which could reduce thousands of acres to black charcoal. The speed of the advance of these fires was frightening. We would watch as great clouds of smoke rose from the hills in front of and behind us, with 60 foot high flames at the edges. Every now and again there would be an explosion, like the eruption of a volcano, as a particularly big tree blew up. A number of the fires were caused by deliberate arsonists.

The French dealt with these fires marvellously well. When an August mistral was forecast there was a fire engine at every cross roads in the Var. The 'Canadair' planes were at once put on call. Sirens were sounded so that swimmers in the big lakes like Saint-Cassien could leave the middle clear for the planes to pick up water. Some of them had a special chemical mix which could damp down even the heart of the blaze. You could ring a special number, which would advise you, if you were in danger, whether to stay put or try to escape. The pilots were extremely brave, and they usually succeeded in soaking the ground round isolated houses. There were casualties every year. The pilots had to fly through smoke in hilly country, and the 'pompiers' sometimes found themselves cut off. The casualties among wild animals – especially the slow ones like tortoises and snakes – were grim. One fire went through our property, by strange coincidence, on our final speech day at Holt. Fortunately we had obeyed advice to clear our olive terraces of all shrubs. Our stone walls were all of 5 or 6 feet thick. All the same the olive trees were burnt and the ground was reduced to soot. Yet when we returned next year the olives, drastically pruned, were producing fruit again, and the ground was green.

I remember driving along the motorway from the Esterel to Nice, when for ten miles there was nothing to be seen but sooty ash on either side of the road as far as the eye could see. Every year, when the summer mistral blew, we would see smoke like a volcanic eruption, sometimes at a safe distance, sometimes alarmingly close. Only once were we seriously frightened. A major fire was advancing at great speed. We took photographs, as the planes managed to divert its progress. It passed us 200 yards away. Well done the French!

Those fires were the only minor drawbacks: they did not seriously interrupt our blissful lives.

The cabanon was surrounded by heady perfumes. Behind us there were thick banks of broom. Immediately round the building there were clumps of lavender, thyme, rosemary and oleander. In Britain I dream about my incompetence, rendezvous with my family when I forget the number of the house or the name of the street where I'm supposed to meet them. I lose my wallet, my passport and, eventually, my car and my wife. When the broom is in full bloom behind the cabanon, I at once start to dream about how brave and clever I am. The local children are not allowed to pick the broom for the Grasse perfume makers because it is too powerful an intoxicant. It suits me. I dream of a fire in the local village of Claviers. Three girls are screaming for help from a top floor window. I tie two ladders together and rescue them one by one in spite of the smoke and flames. An admiring crowd acclaim my astonishing prowess, and I am unanimously elected Mayor. I make a brilliant, but tactfully modest speech, and the villagers decide to put up a statue in the square, so that my courage and good looks shall be commemorated for ever.

Unfortunately the reality does not quite match. I drive over my specs, not once but twice. I lose my passport, only to find it hidden under the distributor on the next occasion that I open the bonnet.

Morning and evening were always a delight. The birds, even in August, were still singing and the butterflies busy everywhere. We would watch fascinated as nature's mass murders got under way in the lavender. At the bottom of the pecking order were the grasshoppers, crickets and butterflies. Lying in wait for them were the scarlet and black assassin bug and the praying mantis. The assassin bug would plunge its long proboscis into any nearby bee or wasp, hold it steady in its powerful pincer-like forelegs and suck it dry of all its juices. The praying mantis was lord of all the insects, shooting out its pincer-like forearms at any insect which understandably mistook it for an innocent leaf. It is called praying, because its huge forearms appear to be joined in prayer, but if it prays at all it is saying a grace 'for what it is about to receive'. It has a formidable appetite, and the much larger female doesn't hesitate to eat her mate, if his performance has not pleased her, or if she is in a bad mood – or just hungry. The giant hairy robber fly mops up any substantial insect which has escaped the assassin bug or the mantis. The gaudy bee-eaters are on hand to deal with the stinging insects, and there are plentiful lizards and geckos to dispose of the crickets, butterflies and moths attracted by the cabanon lights when evening comes. A big ocellated lizard competes with the southern smooth snake to eat any unwary geckos or smaller lizards. To complete the chain, the beautiful short toed eagle, which nests half a mile away, hovers 1,000 feet above the cabanon waiting for a smooth snake to leave its hiding place under the lid of the water tank and slither into the open. Beech martens eat anything that moves, as do badgers – as well as most things that don't . . . we once watched our local badgers, tired of plundering our figs, having a tug of war using a snake as the rope.

In the evening time there is more song and dance and less murder. The constant whirring of the cicadas, enjoying the sun after their 8 year spell underground, begins to fade with the sun, and more pleasant sounds begin to take their place. Nightingales, woodlarks and tree frogs greet the cool of evening: Bing and Satchmo. Complete silence is very rare, generally just before a storm. There is a persistent purring of nightjars and the repeated pee-oo, pee-oo, pee-oo of the tiny scops owl attracted by the food he finds coming to our outside light. Foxes are very common, and the startling cry of a vixen is another late evening sound. Wild boar are everywhere. One night, Jo said: "There's somebody outside on the path, see who it is." I got out of bed with a torch and opened the door only to find a large male scratching its back against the outside door. Sadly, I didn't have time to get my camera and flash.

The woodlarks nested nearby. Their lovely descending scale song went on as late at night as the nightingales. In the morning it was the scratchy rattle of the Sardinian warblers, the musical song of blackcaps and the fluting whistling of the bee-eaters or the still lusher notes of the golden orioles.

When we had settled in Jo and I were introduced by the Cumberleges to some of their friends. They had a great gift for spotting who would get on really well together.

If you leave the main road in this part of the hinterland of Provence, you will find a rough track without a sign post, apparently leading nowhere. Persevere. At the end of it there will be a picturesque mediaeval house, lovingly restored – usually by a Brit, who will be betraying his nationality by mowing his immaculate lawn in the midday sun.

These are not the kind of Brits who only seek each others' company, they have a network of all nationalities, especially Dutch, Italian or French. Amongst these we met a dozen or so charming people who became close friends and brought a variety of experience from all sorts of jobs in many different countries.

Guy and Pamela Jones. He a Devonshire farmer interested in Archaeology, politics and natural history. Almost a caricature of the tall English gent. She a rumbustious generous person formerly in M.I.6: widely travelled and of vigorous opinions.

Henri Denamur, one time top scholar of the Polytechnique, and then in charge of the engineering side of Air France. Highly intelligent, but modest, twinkle-eyed and with a great sense of humour. He had resigned (like my brother John and Sandy Smith) when asked to sack good employees just in order to ensure a bigger profit. He spent a lot of time trying to understand why the English were reluctant to join a Europe ever more closely integrated under the wise leadership of France . . . which I did my best to explain without being in any way tactless or rude. I still correspond with his now, alas, widowed wife: the formidable Trudy. A Dutch lady of good cheer, a legendary appetite and far-reaching intelligence.

There was an English Doctor, Mick Stonor, who, after attending Tonbridge School had worked for 30 years in Australia with his dynamic, small, partridge-plump Dutch wife, Leneke, the most generous of people, with a crust of cynicism failing to disguise the warmest of hearts. He was a fanatical enthusiast for Formula 1 racing.

Nano Pasquiou was a wonderfully witty Frenchman married to a half French and half American lady called Marion. Nano had spent half his life in Glasgow trying to persuade the makers of Harris Tweed to export to France and to pay attention to the vagaries of French fashion. He himself was always immaculately dressed in the manner of an English country gent, while his R.A.F. style 'wizard prang' moustache added to the surprise effect when he opened his mouth and nothing but the most elegant French emerged. He was at his best describing the eccentricities of the Scots. Alas he got cancer and died prematurely. His big competent wife still runs many of the events and fêtes in Bargemon and district.

David and Mary Erskine had a village house in Claviers. They were Scots who had spent a long time in China. More lately he was running a big country estate in Ross-shire, after a career in the navy and then oil. He was quiet, modest and efficient. She was talkative and sociable.

There was a retired English Ambassador, Francis MacGinnis, 6′ 4″, well travelled and well informed, with a First in P.P.E. He told me once that he had never disliked or been let down by any colleague or employee. He was a Roman Catholic – perhaps that had something to do with it. His American wife was a graduate of Berkeley with strong and amusingly expressed opinions. They were particularly kind to us. He was killed in a car accident, in which his wife sustained nasty injuries too. But she (Carolyne MacGinnis) soldiers on in Provence.

Liz Collins, among a number of striking characters, stood out in any company. Built like a burly, but good looking Brunnhilde, she had made good in the Marks and Spencers organisation. She married a wealthy man (Sutton's Seeds, and Yardley perfumes) whom we never met because he had died shortly before we arrived. She was the chatelaine of the castle at Bargemon, immensely hospitable to Rhu's family and to us and putting her swimming bath with its glorious view at our disposal. Periodically she would run eccentric fancy dress parties. She apparently felt she had a mission to convert homosexuals and had one or two artistic boy friends of that nature. Her family and friends were more alarmed when she took a self-styled Italian count under her capacious wing, bought a castle in Casablanca for him, which, when taxes and domestic servants were taken into account must have made a dent even in her considerable fortune. Fortunately she was eventually persuaded to drop him – he was exactly what, in one's worst dreams, one would imagine a suspect Italian fortune hunter might look like – all over-elegant dance floor twirls and exaggerated compliments, like a stage dancing master. Liz returned to being a benevolent presence in Bargemon and beyond. She was a genuine culture vulture and spent much time in Aix, where most of Provence's composers and artists ply their trade. We all loved her.

Our cabanon was only reachable via a rough track about a kilometre long. Despite the Citroën's ability to rise on tiptoe, my bill for repairs of its silencer was almost annual. I had two good neighbours: Peter and Shirleyanne Cumberlege who had found it for us and introduced us to all these people, and Georges Veronese. Of the infinitely kind Cumberleges I shall write later. Georges Veronese was a great-hearted Frenchman of Italian origin (there are many such in this corner of France). He ran a very successful plumbing business in Saint Raphaël, had semi-retired to a small plot adjoining the Cumberleges, and was enjoying growing his own grapes and a selection of Provençal fruits. On retirement he had gone round the world collecting all the strangest and strongest alcoholic drinks from the exotic countries he had visited. Every time I had gone shopping, I had to pass his front gate. It became quite a hazard. He would see me coming and come to the gate. "Ah! Monsieur Bruce, j'ai quelquechose de vraiment exceptionel pour vous aujourd'hui." He would seize me by the arm and steer me towards his outdoor table, put a giant tomato into a bag for me and reach for one of forty or fifty bottles, generally coloured blue or green. I would try to stop him pouring. "Ça suffit, Georges . . . c'est même beaucoup trop." Protests were of no avail. I would do my best and hoped for a moment when his attention might be distracted and I might pour a little away. He would regale me with tales of his visits to Twickenham (he was cracked about Rugby) and the riotous aftermath. When he learned that I had played for a Scottish side that had beaten France, he was overjoyed. He said he had never forgiven the referee, who, when France had scored three of the most glorious tries ever seen, awarded 6 penalties to England. I remembered the match well. He was quite right. The Gods of rugby must all have wept. He was a great help over the care of olives. When I had him round for a drink, he would inspect a tree I had just pruned. "Vous manquez complètement de courage", he would reprove me, seize my shears and, in a couple of minutes, remove the whole of the middle of the tree. He also asked Jo and me to a great bouillabaisse party. Alas, he was charged by a wild sow whose children he had inadvertently approached. His leg was badly gashed, turned cancerous and he died.

There were a number of other picturesque characters: Provence seems to breed delightful and slightly eccentric characters, whereas Parisians are so often stand-offish, arrogant and tiresome. Pamela Kerr, the very good artist, and her jazz trumpeter boy friend. The wonderful garage owner at Bargemon, Laffin, who undercharged for everything but could mend anything; if a part was missing, he would make it rather than wait for a part to come for Draguignan. The brilliant Doctor Calvet, whose father had cared for Paddy when he had developed a tubercular knee joint, and who came to the rescue in the early times of Jo's long illness. The nearest farmer, who helped us often and had an ambitious young wife with a good voice. She left him to go to Paris to make her fortune. She didn't, and came back with her tail between her legs. We took them to a film about a Provençal farmer . . . he was deeply moved.

Although Jo had by this time transformed the cabanon into a place where we could entertain with a kind of Arabian Nights glamour, cooking for large numbers was difficult. We solved the problem of how to return hospitality by forming a group of 12, who would meet once a month from May to September on the night of the full moon, in a pre-agreed beauty spot. It had to be out of sight, within reach of a road, but not visible from it or from any house. It had to have a wonderful view and be free of midges and mosquitos. Some of the glorious places we found were so successful that we repeated this year after year.

We were extraordinarily lucky. It seems that at full moon in Provence it never rains, and the mistral never blows. We always had sun, and shorts and play shirts were warm enough to see us through until 11 p.m.

We had to find a flat area about 8 metres by 5. It had to be within 20 miles of our homes. We met at 6.30. Each couple brought a lamp, although it was hardly necessary. It was the most delightful way of enabling friends to get together in idyllic surroundings, eat and drink extremely well and very cheaply. The glow left by the crimson sun, unnaturally magnified by the heat haze on the horizon, gradually gave way, as it sank behind the jagged peaks of the Esterel, to the moonlight. This used to soften the colours of gorse and heather with a wash of silver. It also hid our wrinkles, shone on our white hair or bald heads, and made us feel young again – for we were all over 60 and most of us over 70. It was almost light enough to read. The full moon whispered to the werewolf buried within the most civilized of us, and stirred the pot of our conversation in unusual directions.

When deciding on 12 people we had no apostolic example in mind; but Jesus knew what he was doing when he chose that number. It is small enough to avoid factions, big enough to ensure variety of experience. Above all everybody can talk to everybody. The organization of food and drink puts no undue strain on anybody. Each couple brings a small table, 2 bottles of Gigondas (which is a red wine on which we all agreed), and one course. One couple looked after the aperitifs and nibbles, another saw to the hors d'oeuvres, a third to the main course, a fourth to cheeses and rolls, a fifth to the sweet or dessert, and the last to the salad and condiments.

We enjoyed ourselves as only the old can do, when they are, for a while, free of pain, responsibility and worry. We drank to the moon and to absent friends and got down to the proper business of the old. Criticizing the young, setting the world to rights, flattering each other, and scraping away at the not quite empty sardine tins of our lives to see if there were any as yet undisclosed treasures left. We decided what should be done about the Great Problems, while rejoicing that we were still alive and almost kicking, and that we would not have to do anything about them.

In the meantime the glow worms still glowed, and the fireflies flickered. An eagle would fly over, a scops owl would start up its persistent cry, bee-eaters would flute their way to their nests, and the nightingales and tree frogs took over.

It took a bare five minutes to clear away, pack up, embrace, make arrangements for the next meeting and drive home. It was about 11.30. We always met exciting wild creatures by the roadside: beech martens, badgers, wild boar and foxes, but, fortunately, never the Police.

My eldest brother John thought he should warn me: "You will just go to seed and die doing nothing! People in Provence think the sun makes them immortal."

Well ... we are not doing our duty, dear brother, nor are we saving the world. But most of us have tried hard to do so for 40 years or more. Now it's time for a little gentle living before the lights go out.

We did, however, do things besides drinking in the sun and watching birds. Gresham's had given me as a generous parting gift, amongst other things, a magnificent camera with a zoom lens. Knowing that I had hardly ever taken a photograph, and that I was frightened of modern gadgets, my expert biology master explained in detail how to deal with different lights, close-ups and long range photos. At the time I understood him.

The cabanon was ideal for nature photography. The Professor of Lepidoptery at the University of Florence told me that we were in the best place in Europe for unusual butterflies and moths, and we were visited by Alpine birds as well as the exotics of the plains: rollers, bee-eaters, hoopoes, golden oriole, wallcreepers, blue rock thrushes, three kinds of eagle. I was eager to record the astonishing variety of lovely creatures, which surrounded us. I tried my 'prentice hand on my wife and daughters with some success. On the whole they did what I told them, stood still in the right place and avoided abrupt movements. Butterflies and moths came next: what dazzling beauty!

Three spectacular butterflies were particularly common. The swallowtail, the scarce swallowtail and the two tailed pasha. Not hard, you'd think, because they visited the lavender every day. My attempts to capture the two kinds of swallowtail were not too bad, but I wasted hours of time on the glamorous two tailed pasha. For some reason it was the only butterfly in my reference book which showed only the underwing. After an hour of pursuit I began to understand why. It must be the fastest flyer of the butterfly world. It settles for only a few seconds and opens its wings for an even shorter time. Not that it is shy: in fact it seemed to develop an affection for me, or perhaps it was the abundant perspiration in which I was drenched after I'd pursued it in the burning sunlight. Anyway it landed on me, my hand and even my camera before taking off on its high speed circuit again. I never got a photo of it until I discovered its taste for beer and figs. We had a fig tree, and an open bottle of beer proved irresistible.

The uniquely marvellous flight of the short toed eagle (otherwise named the cireaëte or the Mediterranean snake eagle) was another sight I wanted to commit to paper. It hovers more and better than any other big bird of prey. It hangs in the mistral effortlessly scanning the ground from a thousand feet up and spotting with its remarkable yellow eyes a small and well camouflaged snake that I couldn't see ten yards away. But although it nested only half a mile away and flew over us every day, it had a knack of hovering only when I was separated from my camera. Similarly we had an open air loo which doubled as a hide. Five bee-eaters and a golden oriole settled in a bush six feet away, but I hadn't brought my camera. A really good photographer must have the patience of a saint, and a bit of luck as well.

*

Another pastime for which the cabanon was ideally suited was, of course, painting. Dad had been a first-rate water colour artist, especially good at catching the atmosphere of Scottish skies, hills and water, owing much to Egginton, Russel Flint and Cotman.

I had nothing like his technical mastery, but had learned something about bird painting from Talbot Kelly. All the time I had been a teacher I had neglected the art. This was like a new start, and, to my great joy, I gradually got a little less bad at 85 than at 70. There are not many things of which that can be true! But I could never cope with the Provençal landscapes. For someone brought up in Scotland the light is so sharp and the colours so bright. The trouble is also that Van Gogh, Cézanne and Matisse set such impossible standards that they make one's efforts look inept and childish. Winston had a good shot at it. My attempts to depict olive trees turning from dusty green to silver as they dance in the mistral were garish and vulgar, but it was fun trying.

The height of my artistic ambition is to paint a tree, which looks like a tree: it is something that has baffled the greatest artists; only two or three have done it.

Chapter Forty

A New Sport

We occasionally went down to the Riviera coast. I am not really one of nature's beach boys. Lying in the sun is tolerable once in a while, if you can find a beach which is both beautiful and not overcrowded, and not backing onto a main road lined with souvenir shops and fish and chip dealers like any British seaside resort.

For my eldest son Rhu and his wife Philippa it provided something else. They had fallen in love with wind surfing while in Barbados. To my surprise, on Rhu's return to Norfolk in February he appeared to take leave of his senses. To pursue such sports in the West Indies or Côte d'Azur is fair enough, but he got into his wet suit, drove to Sheringham and disappeared into the North Sea in a force 8 gale, visibility of 200 yards and a temperature of 35° Farenheit. I was left to peer into the mist and the driving rain, stamping my feet into the squelchy grey sand to keep pneumonia at bay and praying for his safe return.

His move to the South of France gave him and Phillipa a great opportunity to sharpen their expertise. We and Rhu lived only a few miles apart near two of three splendid lakes, ideal for learning.

Water is not my element. I drink it seldom, swim in it only under protest, and when the temperature is in the high eighties. I am only really happy in it when in pursuit of fish. The sea frankly frightens me. However, I gave way to taunts, flattery and bullying and was finally brought to Var, confronted with plank, sail and rope and made to get on with it in spite of the mockery of some French girls.

There was only a gentle breeze. I took heart. All kinds of doddery, pot bellied ancients, little children and matronly females were gliding around effortlessly. What could there be to fear for an ex-rugby international?

> I soon found out. "Weight on your toes, Dad, and not on your heels!"
> Splash!
> "Get your feet balanced on both sides of the mast; in the MIDDLE!"
> Splash!

"Don't try to use your strength, just lean!"
Splash!
"Manoeuvre the sail round to the other side! Work your way GENTLY round the mast ... right foot further back!"

For the tenth time the water closed over my head. When I tried to clamber aboard an attractive girl was roaring with laughter. As I hauled my 16 stone frame onto the plank for the eleventh time, like a superannuated blubber seal, I wished I had given up gin for Lent. A childhood rhyme was running through my mind:

"A bear, however hard he tries,
Grows tubby without exercise.
Our Teddy Bear is short and fat;
It's hardly to be wondered at.
He gets what exercise he can
By falling off the Ottoman
But generally seems to lack
The energy to clamber back!"

When I at last managed to stay erect for 300 yards, I was totally unable to tack and sail back. Rhu had not warned me that I'd have to swim back against the wind, towing the wretched contraption behind me.

"Well done, Dad!" What hypocritical nonsense! I went back in a high wind and fared no better. On the third occasion, however, a miracle happened. The wind was neither too strong nor too weak, nor did it change direction. I stayed upright, more or less balanced. A couple of hundred yards from the shore, dreading another swim back, I tottered desperately round the mast, tacked and returned to base surviving only one or two clumsy lurches.

The aches and pains and bruises vanished. I felt a ridiculous rush of conceit. I was the conqueror of a new element, a pioneer of a new and thrilling sport. I understood Rhu's passion.

I shall never be good. 60 years old is too late to begin. But I got far enough to enjoy it and to realise that it has everything a great individual sport should have – skill, timing, balance, a struggle with the forces of Nature, fresh air, exhilaration, even a soupçon of danger. And it doesn't need great strength. It should become a major school sport.

*

The cabanon was a great centre for expeditions.

The most remarkable trip (about 1½ hours) as far as I was concerned was to the Gorges du Verdon. This is where the Verdon river curves its tortuous way through the sub Alps. It is Europe's version of the Grand Canyon, on a smaller but no less spectacular scale. There are two ways of exploring it: one by car. There is a road about 30 miles long winding along the top or near the top of the deep cliffs, from which one can see the beautiful transparent green water or white foam of the river a thousand feet below, or the Alpine swifts flashing in and out of the shadows. Here and there the gorges get wide enough to accommodate a wider pool with a small beach; enterprising ladies have found their way there and cast off their clothes for a dip which must be very cold even when the day is hot. You can even pick out large trout rising to the surface, when the white water canoeists have passed on. The bird life is exciting: wall-creepers like small crimson winged bats flutter up the cliffs, golden or short toed eagles soar along the tops and peregrine falcons nest on the cliffs. The first time we went, the gorges were at their magical best. It was a lovely sunny September morning. The gorges were full of cotton wool mist which came just as far as the edge of the road. We had the slightly alarming feeling that we had a cliff on one side and nothing but thick mist on the other. We might have been driving along the clouds. The mountains were bathed in golden sunshine, where they reared up through the mist. Gradually the mist disappeared and revealed the giddy depths. It was breathtaking.

The other approach is only for the fit. You leave the car near the upper end of the gorges and follow a mountain path which takes you down to just above the river where it enters the gorges. You follow the path which is cut into the side of the cliffs near the bottom, sometimes close to the river bank, sometimes in a tunnel, for 24 miles, when the path makes its way towards the road again. A lovely walk, but you are glad to see that your friends have got a car there to take you back to where you started.

Picnics beside rock pools were a favourite pastime. The Argens, the Durance, the Bresque, the Endre, the Artuby, the Nartuby, the Siagne and the Loup were rivers which offered wonderful rock pools, where we hardly ever found anyone else, and where there were flat rocks, deep pools, waterfalls and the purest of clean water. Birds and trout, lizards and (mostly harmless) snakes – and even no excess of aggressive insects. What wonderful places to enjoy a swim and a bottle of wine! Sunshine and shade according to our need.

The big lakes St. Cassien, Sainte-Croix and Carcès were other beauty spots where we spent happy days with friends or family. The first two are fairly recent creations and all three are popular centres for sailing and fishing. Our favourite was Sainte-Croix, which is a big reservoir lake on the edge of the mountains into which the Gorges du Verdon empty in a spectacular way. We used to hire a pedalo and seek out our own favourite beach. There are big trout to be caught in Saint Cassien, but, as in many big lakes, they are hard to catch.

We went even more often to Saint Cassien because it was closer. It is famous throughout Europe for the size of its fish: huge catfish, record carp and big cannibal trout. Although more likely to attract numbers of tourists, bathers and fishermen than the more remote Sainte Croix, it was beautiful and never overcrowded.

The third, Carcès, was further to the West and a little smaller. We liked it because it gave us a chance to visit Thoronet Abbey: not only a fascinating building, but somewhere where you could hear top class rendering of plainsong.

*

There are so many charming hill villages that it would be invidious to try to pick out the best. Mons has the most spectacular views to as far as Corsica. Tourtour is picturesque and pretty. Bargemon is a good centre, has good food: they say that if you drink in the main square there regularly, you will sooner or later see everybody who lives in Provence. St. Tropez is beautiful beyond the dreams of the average Riviera resort – and you might catch a glimpse of Brigitte Bardot. At Fréjus which is an old town by the sea rather than a resort there is a famous arena, where bullfights are held and, on one very special summer night, we sat entranced and watched Nureyev and Fontaine in their prime.

Behind Nice there are two or three villages full of artists and galleries: Vence, Saint-Paul and Tourettes. There are old streets reserved for pedestrians – and a great number of cats sleeping in the sun.

Don't miss the half ruined hill village of Bargème, explore the Massif des Maures, Cotignac, Flayosc and the Lubéron with its Cézanne-painted beauty. To the North Sisteron and Castellane are quite substantial towns on the border line between the high Alps and Provence … you can smell the differences. The capital is Draguignan. If ever you are involved with lawyers or the police or planning permission or a sudden heart attack, Draguignan will solve your problems. It reminds me of Norwich, but with broader streets and surrounded by hills.

What is there to say about the climate? Perhaps just that in four months we only ate under cover four times … during the August storms. April is lovely, May warm, but occasionally rainy, June and early July hot, July 10th – August 21st dry and very hot. Between the 21st and 25th of August, huge spectacular storms. Thunder and thunderbolts, hailstones the size of eggs and four inches of rain in a day. Rhu's birthday fell on the 21st, and for some years we had to drive home after a great meal to celebrate at the Hôtel de France through torrents. After the storms finished there were one or two after-shocks, and then September was always lovely, hot but not oppressive, while the ground was covered with flowers of a second spring. Prices were lower and the tourists had gone home: the best month of the year.

Chapter Forty One
La Chasse

Autumn generally brings
Lots and lots of lovely things,
Sun all day, no searing heat,
Vines with heavy grapes replete.
Fruit of every kind to eat.
Charming, bright, idyllic days.

August storms have cleared the haze,
Woodlarks now begin to sing
Welcoming a second spring;
From Avignon and Aix to Vence
Autumn shows the best of France.
Olives swell, the locals shop,
Tourists leave and prices drop.

Flowers grow, the grass gets green,
Eagles soar and hoopoes preen.
Badger cubs are fed on figs,
Squirrels play, and baby pigs
Are stripey, fat and squeaky clean.
One small cloud begins to loom,
Sunday brings a taste of doom.
Anything that grunts or flies
Is shot for paté or meat pies.
Now begins the dreaded Chasse!

Foreigners should never fuss.
Hold your tongue and hide your head,
Or, better still, remain in bed!
Tomorrow at the break of day

Shots will whine or richochet.
Men with fearful oaths or curses,
Armed with ancient bluderbusses,
Trample through your private grounds,
Puffing after baying hounds.

For all the talk of boars and hares,
Partridge, deer and even bears,
It's robins, orioles and tits
They generally blow to bits.
Luckily most bigger game
Escapes their wild, erratic aim.
Their bag last year was rather poor,
One villager, an old wild boar.
One hen, two dogs and … Merde! Ah non!
The window of my cabanon.

MORAL

Brits must try to live in peace
With Chasseurs, Mayors and Police.
If you want the midday sun
Shake the hand that aims the gun.

August thunderbolts were no joke. One night Jenny was sleeping in the caravan, which was a few feet away from the cabanon. There was a deafening crash of thunder which woke her up in time to watch a fireball the size of a football roll over the hill between her and the cabanon, leaving a trail of burnt vegetation behind it. On another occasion George was at the wheel of his land-drover and Jo, Pony and I on board. There was a tremendous flash and bang and George was horrified to see a thunderbolt pass a couple of feet from his window. Yet again, after sleeping in their camper trailer, during a particularly violent storm, Pony lifted the sleeping bag off her two sons. Alastair, eyes still shut in panic, inquired: "Are we dead?"

The journey down to the cabanon was almost as much fun as the cabanon itself. We used to drive from Holt to Dover, cross the ferry at half price and choose a good pub near Calais or in Montreuil. Then we would drive, sometimes by N.7 or sometimes by the motorway and choose a pub well south of Paris, but north of Lyons to break our journey. We found four or five good ones, by which we meant not too far away from our direct route, not expensive, good food and in a pleasant untouristy village. We found that the 'Logis de France' was the best guide to these. We didn't have one disappointment.

Bligny-sur-Ouche was good and so was one at Bèze and at Givry. There were a couple more very pretty ones in the Beaujolais country and the Côte d'or. But we finally agreed that the one we would always use was the Puys Enchanté at Saint Martin en Bresse, about 15 kilometres from Chalon sur Saône. The food was superb, the rooms comfortable and the village quiet. What made it stand out, however, was the personal touch of the host's family. They came to recognize Jo and me and always chatted about the fishing and the wild mushrooms. The patron always went out in the season to catch trout and pick mushrooms soon after dawn. When James and Flip took our advice and went there years later, they recognized the name and gave them special treatment. Sadly 'The Sunday Times' discovered it and ranked it amongst the top ten in France, but it didn't seem to go to their heads – they didn't put up the price and get pretentious. And Jo and I always made love there, which helps the good memories.

Sometimes, if the time was short, we could go from Calais to Provence in one day and spend just one night on the way only about 100 miles from the cabanon. A favourite place, especially in our camping days, was on a side road north of Sisteron where there was a massive farm and a lake in a lovely Alpine valley. The owner too always seemed glad to see us. How hospitable the French farmers are! They would join us in a bottle of wine, supply us with drinking water and show us the most comfortable place to pitch our tent or park our caravan.

Chapter Forty Two
Hospitality of the French Provincials

There are three incidents which stood out among many which show the extreme kindness of the French (the Parisians, although they think they ARE France, are generally excepted) to strangers in trouble.

Jo and I were returning from an exploration of the Alps and descending a steep corkscrew road, when our brakes suddenly failed. By sheer luck I managed to steer into a layby and come to a halt without damage. I was peering about trying to trace the source of the trouble, when a car drew up behind me.

The driver got out, asked what had happened and if he could help. It turned out that he was a Citroën mechanic on his way home for the weekend. He quickly found a leak in the brake fluid system, and he told us he'd got a new pipe at home. "I'm only a few miles away; if you don't mind waiting for half an hour, I'll be back." He was as good as his word and wouldn't accept any payment, although we tried hard to insist. "It's not every day one gets a chance to be a good Samaritan", he said. "You've made my day."

The second great act of kindness was when we were camping at the foot of the rock mountain of Roquebrune. We ought to have known better: it was the time of the great August storms. When we pitched camp it was a lovely hot day, and we had found a flat firm area just 50 yards off the road. The clouds suddenly closed in ... I remember seeing them pour over the shoulder of the mountains. Then the thunder and lightening and 4 inches of rain before dawn. No chance of sleep. Jenny heroically played her guitar and sang songs to cheer us up. When dawn came, the rain eased off to about the intensity of a bad day in the Western Highlands. We peered out. What had been hard standing the night before was a pond of muddy water in the middle of which our car was stranded. We tried to move it, fetching bundles of heather to provide purchase for the tyres, but couldn't move it an inch.

At that moment a Frenchman, making his way gingerly along the road, saw our state: four muddy figures obviously at the end of our wits. He hopped out stripped to his shorts, fixed a tow rope to the car, failed gallantly in his attempts to move it and told us to get in his car. He drove us to his home, fed us, dried us and gave us a drink and chatted amiably with us until the sun came out. He then took us back, managed to move our car and wished us bon voyage. Again he wouldn't accept any money, but at least was happy to take a couple of bottles of Gigondas.

The last example was, perhaps, the most remarkable of all. It happened when I was taking Jo and Rhu back to our old haunts in the Dordogne where she had accompanied me on that memorable rugby tour 13 years earlier. I went into the Café des Sports in Saint-Cyprien. The man behind the bar recognized us at once. Drinks on the house; he had played fly half against me. He handed over the bar and took me round to see Jean Ladignac, the President of the Club, who was now Mayor: still a bundle of energy despite his chain smoking. He managed to find ten of the fifteen players who had played in our last match, and M*me* Ladignac laid on a superb dinner for us all. He showed us with great pride the grandstand the floodlighting he had installed on the profit of that tour. Not only that, he produced a film of parts of the match and a recording of my speech of thanks. He has since died, but I'm glad to see that the main square in Saint-Cyprien has been renamed after him.

It is sad to think that this sort of kindness to strangers is so rare in Britain. Is it something to do with Roman Catholic traditions?

*

The village fêtes in Provence, the concerts and the visit of the circus were enormous fun. In high summer time there was something going on every weekend: sometimes a choice. All three squares in Bargemon would be full. It was all very dramatic: everybody danced with everybody else, everyone drank a lot, but drunken behaviour was either very rare or banished to a corner out of sight. Farmers with cheerful sun wrinkled faces dressed up in flowery shirts, competed at Pétanque or the usual fair type games and whisked Jo away from me. The music was generally well played, varying from rock and roll to Fred Astaire and Ginger Rogers, and old favourites from the Thirties.

There were concerts to suit all tastes. A friend from Bargemon turned out to be an excellent professional cellist, and performed Bach unaccompanied in one of the churches. Doctor Mick Stonor's Dutch wife took the part of Queen Victoria in a Seillans pageant representing the Queen's visit to the town. She was made for the part. The pageant culminated in the Nice Choral Society rendering the Gilbert & Sullivan 'It is a glorious thing to be a right down regular, regular regular Royal Queen.' Every year the Var Symphony Orchestra performed to a full house. It was a strange combination of the sublime and the ridiculous. There were some fine professionals: the leading violinist, a cellist, an Italian tenor, and a great pianist. Alongside these, an infant prodigy flautist, racked with nerves, a quite good trombonist, who'd had a drink or two too many and a second cellist, who cultivated her resemblance to Suggia. Their programme consisted of light, well known classics. What was unique was the informality of the atmosphere. The bald tympani player beamed at all the ladies. A press photographer prowled around on bended knees, looking like Groucho Marx, and popping up periodically to take close-ups of the performers. Nobody cared. A large village dog left its usual position in the middle of the road to jump up on the stage, lick the hand of a small viola player and pee on the bottom of the double bass. The trombonist spectacularly missed his entry, but, unabashed, came in with a confident forte a few bars later. In spite of everything, it was well played. It was all received with rapturous applause, and even genuine deep emotion, and nobody left at the interval, except for a refill of wine. If there were any policemen, they were in disguise. I hardly remember seeing one in the mountain villages. I thought they were hardly ever needed, until a great burglary was pulled off in, of all places, Claviers.

It was on the day of a prominent villager's funeral. The entire village turned up in the church. Meanwhile three large removal vans came and parked in the main street and systematically emptied the three most wealthy houses of all their most valuable antiques. I never heard that they were caught.

Why did those fêtes and concerts seem to be more fun than their English counterparts? Of course the climate gives them an unfair advantage. The hill villages can be miserable, cold and wet in October, November and February. But you can usually sit out in the sun at Christmas and there can be lovely days in any month. The fun of the fairs is perhaps due to the fact that they are not over-organized. One or two events are well prepared, but small groups can make their own arrangements, and part of the enjoyment lies in the unexpected.

"Dost think, because thou art virtuous, there shall be no more cakes and ale?" Falstaff enquires of his dull British companion. Perhaps not cakes and ale, but the Provençaux certainly love their olives and pastis. Their fun is not dressed up for tourists, nor is it the presence of the rich: it is the good tradition of Merry old France.

How long will it stand up to 'le fast food' and binge drinking? Longer than us.

But Rhu has founded and guided the Holt Festival. Who knows?

*

Those first years of retirement ('82–'91) in Provence were the best of our lives. Periodically our children, now grown up and, in three cases married, descended on us and enjoyed the life as much as we did. Our grandchildren, Nicolas (the spitting image of Rhu), Chelsea, Alastair and Dacre and James followed suit.

But nothing lasts for ever. Jo had recovered from having both hips replaced by the great Hugh Phillips, who did them so successfully that she was dancing within a couple of months. She had a not so brilliant sinus operation, but was fit throughout the Eighties, swimming nearly every day.

However, she was taken ill in 1990 when in the cabanon. She was in pain, and it was Saturday night. We rang our local G.P. who arrived at the cabanon within half and hour, although we had not previously met, and the cabanon was not easy to find. He gave her pain killers and arranged an appointment with a specialist for Monday morning. We drove over to the local capital, Draguignan at nine o'clock. The specialist rose from his computer to open the door for us (that was a surprise for a Brit!) and showed himself at once to be efficient, careful and helpful. He sent us along the corridor for an x-ray and drew up a report for the British doctors which we translated together. Then he arranged for an appointment with a different kind of specialist – in the same building – within a few minutes, complete with x-ray photos. He was equally helpful and added his bit to the detailed report.

They had identified polyps in the bladder, which, though still superficial might well become cancerous. We cut short our holiday, gave the report to our Norfolk specialist, Gaches, who was amazed at the speed and accuracy of the report. He operated, while warning us that while things would quieten down for a while, he would have to keep a close eye on developments. He was as good as his word and kept Jo going for 19 years, with his successor, the great Sethia. They held inspections every three or six months and periodical x-ray treatment and operations. It was no fun for Jo, but she continued to be brave and cheerful and returned to the cabanon with me to enjoy life until 1997. In that year we decided we could no longer manage the cabanon. The entire bill in France for G.P., two specialists and report and x-rays was 270 francs – of which 70% was recovered. All the time we were in France we never heard of any complaints about their medical services.

We sold our beloved Church Farm House to my favourite successor at Gresham's and the cabanon to Rhu. We bought a more easily managed little house on the edge of Blakeney. It was quiet, near shops, surgery, garage and church and only about seven miles from Rhu. We had bought Church Farm House for £9,000. It is now valued at 1½ million! The times they are a-changing. Jo's genius for homemaking turned what had been a rather dull little house into a charming cottage with a conservatory, walled garden and a pond with a fountain. She continued to make light of her troubles, but had to have carpal tunnel operations on both wrists and a new knee joint as well as her now regular operations and treatment with radiation and chemotherapy. In spite of all her troubles she still looked 15 years younger than her age, but in 2008 the troubles accelerated, her general health deteriorated. At last the dreaded day came when the wonderful Mr. Sethia said that he could operate no more. The cancer was breaking through the wall of the bladder. It might be possible to create a new bladder but at Jo's age and with all her operations, she might not survive. It might extend her life for a few weeks, but it would be a poor way of life. He would try the operation if we liked, but he would advise against. They could make the end reasonably comfortable. We asked him how long. "Months not years. She has already been exceptionally resilient."

She had been a marvellous mum; much worldly wisdom was hidden behind a mischievous sense of fun. She was always on the side of her children, especially when they got into trouble. She was a real lioness in defence of her cubs. I think that was the reason why, even as teenagers, they loved to spend the holidays with her.

Behind the fun and the sexiness Jo was always an earnest seeker. She had a close look at spiritualism, was attracted for many years by 'the work' and took a brief look at Roman Catholicism. There was a strong interest in spiritual issues on Jo's side of the family: Granny Agnew, Jo's Mum, was prone to have visions and was a half-believer in spiritualism. Jo's elder sister, Heather, is a different kind of person. A couple of years older than me, she discovered in her youth 'almost accidentally' that she had a gift for healing through prayer and the laying on of hands, and determined to explore spiritual issues. Her complete confidence, faith and infectious cheerfulness were of undoubted help to her in this, to which she increasingly devoted her life. She joined an organization of like-minded people: the White Eagle lodge. When we occasionally raised an eyebrow at the more extreme forms of her spiritual beliefs, she accepted with good humour our inability, for instance, to see fairies, or to believe in astral wandering.

Although she never lacked the company of admiring males, she never married. She followed a straightforward career in banking, and, in retirement, throws her energies into becoming the ideal generous aunt to two generations of our family. All of us, even the reasonably prosperous, profited from her inexhaustible benevolence. She spends little on herself: emphatically not a lady for Monte Carlo or the Ritz. In many ways she is shrewd and down to earth, and fully capable of getting her own way. A broken ankle at 92 and deteriorating eyesight have utterly failed to daunt her. A tough old bird, behind that sunny benevolence. Everyone (Bertie Wooster included) ought to have an aunt like her: few have!

Jo was caught between a conviction that there were aspects of religion which were of supreme importance and a sharply critical mind. She could see that there was so much trickery, exploitation of grief and wishful thinking in the Spiritualist Church that it was nearly impossible to accept any part of it. When the Roman Catholic Church told her that her beloved little daughter Kirsty would have to go to purgatory because she had not been baptized into the R.C. Church, she was so disgusted that she gave up all interest in that form of religion. She respected the Church of England and some of its priests, but felt that, while they told you what was good, they gave you little help with how to be good. This was where Gurdjeff came in for her and for Jenny. Her greatest gift was her ability to talk to anyone from the daily to the Duke of Edinburgh, to cut through social nonsense and to see what interested them, what made them unhappy and to understand and sympathize. Bishops would open up and talk of their doubts, divorced people would weep, Everest climbers would tell her that God was to be found in the Himalayas. Life with her could never be dull.

She was profoundly artistic. Her dancing had grace and rhythm: ballet trained and a born tap dancer, the war and marriage had cut short what ought at other times have been a successful stage career. Above all she had a rare eye for colour, flowers design and the internal design of houses. She could make the cabanon look like an Arab chieftain's tent when entertaining. The Church Farm House drawing room (formerly two rooms and a staircase) became a wonderful place to live, and Mead Barn was bewitchingly transformed. In some ways, like Jenny, she was surprisingly old-fashioned. Things had to be done properly, and traditions had to be preserved. The Haggis had to be addressed, the Queen's health correctly proposed and the family had to go to Midnight Mass on Christmas Eve, even if they were no longer believers. But she could not resist giggling at some private joke in chapel and was a great deflator of pomposity. The family tended to accuse her of gossip, but while she was intensely interested in what was going on behind the scenes in family life, I don't think she gave away secrets.

I was genuinely astonished to hear my daughter say that she thought Jo nagged me and the other members of the family. She was extremely house proud and tidy herself, while I, Bede and Jenny were never anything like tidy. She struggled bravely for 50 years to get us organized (Jenny and I were hopeless about bits of paper: with Bede it was clothes). She even had some success with me in the cabanon and at Blakeney. But I never felt nagged ... Jenny having spent long years living on her own is liable to interpret any domestic exchange as nagging. After the first 40 years of marriage Jo and I grew ever happier with our domestic arrangements: I can hardly remember any disagreements in the cabanon or Blakeney.

*

I suppose the three main changes in my life after 60 were leaving Gresham's, leaving Church Farm House and the cabanon and, finally, aged 89, learning to live without Jo.

Leaving Gresham's was a wrench. It will always have a huge place in my heart, and I still follow its exam results, its sporting achievements and the successes of its pupils compulsively. I feel that is still moving towards fulfilment of my dreams and in some respects exceeding them. I was, at the age of 90, asked to write an article for the H.M.C. Magazine 'Conference'. In a sense quite a lot of this book has been an attempt to answer that question, but I clearly know more about then than now. "What are the differences between the job of an HMC Head 50 years ago and now?"

The world has never changed faster, yet in some ways our job was, for the first post-war years, very similar. We discussed the same problems: Sixth Form timetables and exams, how to stop too much time being spent on external tests. We faced the same difficulties: how to stop raising fees faster than the cost of living, how to help able, penniless boys and girls, how to co-operate with a Labour government.

There was far less bureaucracy. We could rely on the support of our governors and our local authority – even the government didn't try to obstruct our decisions, or flood us with forms and complex instructions which were constantly changing. I had one secretary, and my Bursar another.

Nowadays eight ladies occupy offices of their own. Counsellors, public relations, press liaison, fund raising, relations with former pupils, a registrar, someone in charge of publications and another in charge of careers – and the Head's secretary and the Bursar's. All think they are hard working, but in a strange way increase the Head's work, because he has to co-ordinate, organize and consult them, instead of doing the more important part of his job; getting to know and to enthuse his staff and pupils and making quick, clear decisions.

While computers, the internet and television have opened up marvellous possibilities, they have also contributed to the feeling that our pupils are increasingly living in a push-button world where people can only be contacted through machines, and human relations have been for ever changed.

It is much harder for Heads to bring about reforms and to influence their staff and pupils without endless consultations, and it is harder still to cast the net of opportunity so wide that even the smallest talent can catch fire. Parents are more demanding, and one per cent of them, usually the parents of the most difficult pupils, can waste 20% of the Head's life.

One 1980s mum came to see me about her tiresome son. I hardly got a chance to say anything, and, after she had harangued me for over an hour she finished on a high note: "The terrible thing with John, Headmaster, is that he talks too much – I can't think where he gets it from!"

Frank Fisher's Headmastership of Wellington coincided almost exactly with mine at Gresham's. I remember him saying: "When first I went to Wellington I interviewed prospective fathers to see whether they were suitable parents. Now I am interviewed by a mother who pulls twenty questions out of her handbag and then puts her son down for Radley!" But rural boarding schools in remote Norfolk were relatively free from the more extreme forms of the revolution. The H.M.C in general fell in with the old saying 'We hear and we forget, we see and we remember, we do and we learn.' At the same time most of us refused to accept that competition was wicked, that good manners were a misguided attempt to spread middle class values and that our efforts to keep our pupils aware of a spiritual dimension and moral issues were 'meddling paternalism'.

I was then asked: 'What were the best and worst things that happened to me at Gresham's?'

Family life in a school's surroundings with all its facilities. Like all Heads I got great joy out of our achievements: winning the schools and Old Boys' national squash for 13 years. The improvements brought by going co-ed in art, music, drama and academic work and, three or four years later being chosen as Rugby World's School of the Month; winning the Ashburton Shield, and two Olympic gold medals for the captain of our winning hockey team Richard Leman; the success of individual pupils like James Dyson, a Nobel Prize, knighthoods, an Archbishop and three Bishops, distinctions in music, art and literature and particularly in the realm of creative inventing. Watching Ben Youngs follow his father (both ex-pupils) at scrum half for England and scoring two tries against South Africa, and his brother Tom, joining him in defeating New Zealand. Dancing and singing 'Two, two the Lilywhite boys' in Frank Fisher's rooms at midnight on his birthday at the H.M. Conference with the improbable assistance of my brother Rab and Michael McCrum.

Worst? The loss of my beloved 7 year old daughter run over outside the gates of the school.

On a different plane, trying to get a very rich Old Boy, a judge specializing in juvenile deliquency, to contribute to our appeal. My five year old daughter escaped from the bedroom where she had covered herself in chocolate and, stark naked, she chose to clamber all over the judge's Rolls Royce. The chauffeur was too embarrassed to cope, and my wife was not on the scene quickly enough to rescue the situation. Farewell, covenant for £10,000 a year!

I was equally unlucky when I took another wealthy prospective parent to watch a rugby match. His glamorous Parisian wife was admiring my normally well-behaved wolfhound, when it decided for some extraordinary reason to cock a leg and pee all over her silk stockings and priceless bootees: the son went to Eton.

Why did I become a teacher? Because I liked teaching, and I felt that all my interests and enthusiasms, family life, games, languages, art, music and fishing would be an asset. And what better place to bring up children!

It is heartening to see that the modern Heads are still cherishing the same ideals and especially that in a cynical, often negative and money-centred time, they are producing idealistic, hard-working, civilized and charming pupils – more successfully, I suspect, than some of us did 50 years ago.

Whereas we used to prepare our pupils to take over their fathers' estates, to run the Empire, to work in the Church, the Armed Forces, the Law, the Foreign Office or the Civil Service, they now prepare them for a new world offering a much wider choice.

Before the war ex-pupils served an apprenticeship and stuck to their chosen job. If they changed jobs twice by the age of 30 we assumed that they had put their fingers in the till or seduced the boss's daughter.

Now they travel and try their hands at several jobs, acquiring experience and a variety of skills. I believe that it is a better way. Our ex-pupils still stand out for their unfashionable skills: good manners a desire to give good service, to be punctual, to work hard and get on with other members of their team.

After the war our common rooms were full of people from the Armed Forces, who, perhaps, arrogantly, looked down on the 'children' who had gone from school to university to teaching. But the experience we brought to our schools was valuable. War, the sight of a concentration camp and the loss of my daughter did more to change me than my academic studies could ever do. Take risks and make mistakes and you go on learning, but an easy life and early success teaches you little more than self-satisfaction.

The things I fear most for the Public Schools are the possible loss of faith in their own cause, and, above all, the fear that bureaucracy will strangle their vital role of experimenting, and the watering down of the all important relationships between teachers and pupils by endless committees (often run by businessmen rather than teachers who know their job) taking up time on often relatively meaningless projects.

On a wider scale I fear a future in which the larger part of our lives are spent sitting hunched over machinery with a dozen buttons and switches and screens. All contacts will be via machines. We shall lose all closeness to nature, all contact with real people. Regular exercise will be confined to professionals, and games will be things you play on a computer.

But the huge improvement in the spread of ideas is also the source of hope. Extremism of all kinds may, in the long run, give way to common sense and human values.

The greatest achievement any schoolmaster can hope for is to open new horizons, discover new potential and encourage any worthwhile enthusiasm - not just for the obviously clever or gifted, but for ordinary girls and boys. It's pleasant to have brilliant pupils, but to some extent they can look after themselves. The real excitement is when the apparently idle or stupid children begin to change. It does happen, and is infinitely rewarding – be it in 2013 or 1930.

The last question was: "Have you enjoyed retirement?" Oh yes! At last a chance to wear bathing trunks, glossy and emblazoned with champagne glasses and chorus girls. Not to have to suck up to the rich and important, or sack anyone, or to disapprove of not very important misbehaviour. To have time for my wife and family, to read 'Anna Karenina' again, to write, read, watch birds, paint and fish. To top up intellectual tanks that have dried up for sheer lack of time, and to reminisce with others of my age including ex H.M.C. Heads about the fun we had and how lucky we were to be in a time of great change. To put the world to rights without actually being responsible for anything, and to laugh about the extraordinary incidents that made it such a challenging and thrilling job.

Chapter Forty Three

In-Laws

Any readers who have got this far may have noticed that I have avoided much mention of my sisters-in-law or daughters-in-law. This is not only because of my over-male upbringing, and the fact that I was the youngest of four brothers and therefore had little experience on which to base any judgements. It is because life has taught me that no outsider is in a position to know the reality or the rights and wrongs of someone else's marriage – especially in war time. Lengthy separations when two people are in their Twenties are very dangerous: the number of prisoners of war whose marriages fell apart was huge. Mar, John's wife, was a highly intelligent person, deeply interested in her chemical research and T.S. Eliot, and understandably unappreciative of the domestic grind, constant rain, cold and draughtiness of war-time Sedbergh, with its all-male culture. Strikingly beautiful in an aristocratic way, she never lacked for admirers. John was notoriously good looking. Their marriage was, for a time in the balance. John fell for a very attractive girl in Paris, and took the affair extremely seriously. It took great efforts from both sides to repair the damage: but by the time John's work took him to America, they had got together again. I am more inclined to admire their success than to join in any condemnation.

Rab and Pip never faltered. Pip was a rock of dependability. Rab wrote to her every day of their separation. When in Austria, Rab recorded nonchalantly that the barmaid in a hotel, where he spent one night, walked into his bedroom unclothed and cheerfully offered her services. Rab didn't hesitate, but explained apologetically that he was married and didn't go in for that sort of thing. I wonder how many of us in a far-off land and inflicted with a monastic lack of sex would have resisted? Not, I suspect, Paddy. Perhaps not I: it depends on the barmaid!

I saw little of Pad's two wives. Pat was fun: a mimic, a wit and a flirt. I cannot have met her more than two or three times. A three-year separation inevitably led to faults on both sides, but they were reconciled on Pad's return from India and before the tragedy of her early death. Eve was more of a maternal figure, interested in stocks and shares, she had a great sense of humour: again I only met her on a handful of occasions.

As for my childrens' marriages? However good or bad, it is not a department in which fathers should meddle. Jenny never married, and Bede's seven year venture with the sweet and blameless P.K. and two sad miscarriages ended very amicably. Pony's is still sailing, with the wonderful George, taking turns at the helm. Rhu's marriage to the beautiful, horse-loving Philippa, a fine rider who was chosen as a judge for the Olympics, is sailing into quiet waters. She is a much-loved and loyal Mum and has special gifts with animals.

Chapter Forty Four

Goodbye France

What did we learn from our time in France, and did the student revolution affect them differently?

The thing that struck us most forcefully was that France is a collection of very different regions – even more than Britain. Paris thinks it is France: the centre of world culture. Provence thinks that Paris and Parisians are responsible for everything that goes wrong and rank somewhere below Germans and Belgians. Britanny is more like Scotland, Wales and, especially Cornwall. The Basques are more different to the Alsatians than Yorkshiremen are to the inhabitants of the home counties.

The student revolutions had rather less impact, because the students in Paris have for centuries believed that revolution was their principal role. So it was less of a novelty. The great French Revolution of the 18th Century has left a country which pays lip service to equality, and so perhaps in some ways is nearer to that goal than we are. But on closer examination it is apparent that in place of rule by aristocracy, they have rule by educational meritocracy. The 'grandes écoles' have an even greater stranglehold on top jobs than Oxford and Cambridge have in Britain. Their education is highly organized. Far from valuing eccentricity and original thought they aim to produce well-informed scholars who all present the fashionable ideas in much the same elegant and well documented fashion. Their arrogant belief in the superiority of French civilization prevents them from learning from other nations.

Their democracy is slightly bizarre in a different way to our equally strange system. Nostalgia for Napoleon and de Gaulle leads them to want strong leadership, with the wish to see France guide Europe to becoming a single unit, whose capital will be Paris. No matter how left wing they are before their election, Presidents and Prime Ministers soon revert to type when they find themselves in office.

Of course there are those who view matters very differently, but the French press seems less negative than the British media. Sex scandals aren't particularly bad news for a President: they are expected of him. To be strongly critical of

French policies is thought to be unpatriotic. Whereas in England the press seeks out every slight weakness in the country's preparations for the Olympic Games and makes mountains out of molehills, the France press would brush anything under the table that might be prejudicial to France's reputation for efficiency.

Every country writes its own version of history, exaggerating the creditable aspects of its past. French history goes further in its ignorance of any distinction or progress elsewhere than most others. School History concentrates on their successes. Henry IV, Joan of Arc, the Revolution, Louis XIV, de Gaulle, le 'grand siècle'. Every discovery, invention, achievement and innovation of importance is attributed to France . . . the huge contribution of Italy's Renaissance is undervalued, the superiority of German music not understood. An art book which I picked up there listed Constable as "English artist of the cow and ditchwater school, imitative of the French". Undoubtedly true, but a shade out of proportion. And the great Russian novelists are often ranked behind their French contemporaries of obviously less worth.

Yes, they are a great nation. But they would be greater still, if they gave serious thought to the progress made elsewhere by the likes of Sweden, South Korea, Norway or even the U.S.A. Country people are generally charming in most countries. France must be awarded high marks for that. And the behaviour of their children and their teenagers is usually much better than ours. Old people are better looked after and respected. Granny often rules the roost until she falls off the perch. The standard of education among the bottom 20% seems much higher, and everybody seems competent to deal with modern machines and to carry out repairs for themselves. Art? Yes, it would be stupid to deny their contribution in that sphere. But music? Jenny taught piano and guitar for 40 years in Paris. Hardly any children can sing, and schools give no space for music teaching. For France to imagine it is on the same plane as Germany in that respect is ridiculous. But they are wonderfully hospitable and kind in a way which we are often not, and they have not caught our disease: belittling our own country.

Britain, too, is reluctant to learn from other countries; I have found this to be especially true in the field of education. Our greatest weaknesses since the war have been our failure to provide for the bottom 15%, our inability to produce good technicians and engineers and our decline in learning foreign languages or in providing people with any meaningful combination of Arts and Sciences. Yet excellent examples of how to tackle these weaknesses are close at hand – and in combination with a more successful programme of sporting activities. Is it beneath our dignity to borrow ideas from elsewhere?

Chapter Forty Five

The Move to Blakeney

Our move to Blakeney and our sale of the cabanon marked a big change in our way of life. We missed the spaciousness of Church Farm House and of our Provençal Paradise. It was our first concession to old age. We began to hesitate before undertaking long journeys or entertaining guests for a long time. The dreaded visits to the hospital became more frequent. We were, however, relieved at having a manageable sized garden and a house which, once Jo had made her inspired adjustments, was not in need of constant seriously costly repair. Our horizons shrank – or would have done so but for our children.

They must have come to an agreement that they would keep their ageing parents going by giving them treats every few months, to which we would look forward so much that we would be rejuvenated. Any occasion would provide an excuse: golden wedding, diamond wedding, Jo's eightieth birthday, my 80th and 90th, trips to Barbados, Egypt, Canada, Paris, Devon, Lamport, the Highlands of Scotland and Thailand. Dinners in top restaurants. We found ourselves swimming every day, fishing and painting and enjoying the wonderful company of our family and their friends.

Some Brits don't look after their old folk as well as most other nations. Now that I am 91 and see how thoughtful my children are on my behalf, I am extremely ashamed of my lack of care for my mum when she was in her eighties, immobile and almost helpless but still sharp minded. I should have done more.

I have been spoilt. By luck I have so far avoided the worst of the slow killing diseases. I discovered I had diabetes at 80, when I felt unwell fishing in the Highlands in a fierce spate river in the rain . . . blood sugar 27. I dieted, lost two stone and took pills as directed, and took what exercise I could. (600 pedallings on a bicycling machine, 100 stomach pull-ins, 100 stomach muscle contractions and 100 foot wagglings daily!). Now my blood sugar averages 6, my cholesterol 3.6 and my blood pressure 130/70, and my only bother is tingling legs, which make any walking over half a mile a bit wearisome. Well done the National Health! We all like to grumble about it – especially its communications – but when we get to the business end, at last, they are really good.

The one thing that darkened our generally golden descent into senility was Jo's health. She was still brave and uncomplaining and even bright and cheerful. But the six monthly visits became three monthly and the hopeful verdicts of Mr. Sethia became more ominously cautious. Arthritis was spreading and she had to have a new knee to add to her two hips. This was followed by two carpal tunnel operations.

Then another blow fell. It was found that Rhu had got Parkinson's. It seemed so unfair when he was at the peak of his powers. After a career in the travel business with Jack Coronna – a faithful friend in good times and bad – Rhu had become an expert in many spheres: restaurant management, European and Middle Eastern culture and history, every aspect of travel. When it came to putting his experience and ideas into practice, he always seemed to know more about accounting, tax, law and architecture than the professionals who were working for him. He had a great eye for property development, and bought a neglected area in the heart of Holt, already the leading little market town for North Norfolk. Initially he built some stalls, but soon converted these into a shopping centre with buildings that really fitted in with the old Norfolk style. For pedestrians only, it linked the high street to the supermarket car park. An office block, an art gallery, a book shop, a hairdresser, two restaurants and 7 other shops. He then became a town councillor and founded an annual festival week which brought all kinds of national celebrities to Holt in the realm of theatre, opera, art, comedy, classical and pop music, poetry and dance. It is now in its fifth year and commanding (with the help of Gresham's School) audiences and spectators of over a thousand for some of the events – the kind of activities you would be surprised and delighted to see in big cities.

All this, with the usual stupid opposition which any improvement involving change meets, took place when he had already faced Parkinsons for some years and was finding writing and manipulating a mouse increasingly difficult. He made light of it and was expert at concealing the symptoms, continuing to be generous and kindly and supported by many good friends. He continued to look after me and mum and see to it that we still had our treats. I like to think too that he regarded me as something of a partner in decline . . . we seemed to get tired when walking at about the same time, and when I started to find a round of golf difficult, we both transferred our father-son rivalry to the Scrabble board on which we were equally unscrupulous and merciless.

All my children contributed to the happiness of our old age. Bede rang me almost daily, was ridiculously generous as always and contributed hugely to our 'treats'. Jenny came to hold my hand whenever she had a holiday and was always eager to help – a kindness to which I responded with an almost childish resentment. Like all of us, she loved teaching and when she tried, from the best possible motives, to take over the household duties, she must have felt very hurt when I resented any attempt to run things her way. I just wanted to carry on my life and to look after her, even teach her, in *my* own way! But she brought with her always an unflinching belief in 'the work' – however much unhappiness some of its aspects caused her – and a completely unassailable kindness and reliability. And, I suspect, an example of high standards which the rest of the family respected even if they could not follow or understand them. I am just beginning to appreciate how difficult it must have been to live on a financial shoe-string by herself for nearly 40 years. It is hard not to become wrapped up in one's own interests. So I sit down and write this nonsense, while she tries to commit Gurdjeff's sacred movements to paper. Jenny would love to have a big open house in Provence, and to be a refuge for artistic people and weary Bruce-Lockharts of any generation. But money is a problem and decisions are emphatically not her strong point. She has been infinitely generous to Alastair and Dacre and to me. She has so much to give: musical, artistic with strong views about the future and the importance of the struggle to find a higher level of consciousness; but is finding it difficult to apply her vision to everyday life, and she has become dominated by a pessimism which makes her unhappy. I feel that her occasional quiet and diffident bits of advice will be good seed appreciated by the young in a few years.

Pony and George come over at intervals to bring me wine for my soul and plants for my garden, and are very tolerant hosts to me both in Devon, and Lamport Hall. They have a great knack of letting me get on with my hobbies, and taking me on one or two undemanding but exciting trips. I for my part enjoy the role of an old piece of furniture – until five or six in the evening, when omniscient George brings me excellent wine and keeps me in touch with developments in the worlds of science, farming, history and global warming.

At which point Pony and Jenny, both of whom think they are experts, take over the argument. They both agree really, but get quite heated . . . I wish a had their conversations on record.

Pony is a great hostess. This somewhat temperamental small girl of a few decades ago has become an efficient and unfussed matriarch: she rustles up excellent meals in a few minutes, washes up like a streak of lightning, shops like a whirlwind without either losing or having a shopping list and tends her garden with loving care, under the expert eye of George. She is a real enthusiast for literature, as the touching letters of her ex-pupils testify. I hope that in retirement she will manage to cash in on her very real poetic talents. She has also trained a robin to eat from her hand, although she is in danger of becoming its slave. Unfussed? That would be overstating it. She is occasionally fussed at the up and down fortunes of her two sons in the early and mid twenties. Their exceptional good looks and fundamentally idealistic hopes will doubtless bring rewards in later years, but it is a bumpy time for all the young.

Becoming old has not been as bad as I feared. When we are 30 and full of bounce, the sight of most seventy and eighty year olds sets our spines tingling.

Even if they have escaped nightmare diseases, they tend to look boring, helpless and hopeless, as seen from the other end of life. As we get nearer old age, it gets less and less frightening. We find that the conversation of old men, if we can hear it, is often entertaining. Because they are not part of the rat race any more, they don't have to kow-tow to the rich or influential. They can please themselves in matters of dress, if they can do up their shoelaces or deal with buttons on their trousers. They say what they think more often than the young and ambitious can afford to. Their eyes may be baggy and their faces wrinkled, but these are the battle honours of life, and a good life produces good wrinkles. Ladies who have devoted all their energies to conforming to the contemporary fashions of beauty may arrive at their seventies free of wrinkles, but also with faces devoid of character: all distinction erased by the beauty surgeon's scalpel. Sadly there comes a stage when all but the very best preserved become either overripe tomatoes or wrinkled prunes. The demanding, over-virtuous and negative tend to become the prunes: I have a personal preference for the tomatoes: more fun, forgiving and lovable.

SAD REFLECTION

Mirror, Mirror on the wall,
Who was the fairest of them all?
I know by now I'm not so hot
But I *was* lovely, was I not?

*

Madam, though you WERE less plain
Concealment of the facts is vain;
Even in your youth's hey-day
You never were in any way
Remotely of the kind of class
To use a magic looking glass
Committed to the truth – Alas!

It can, of course, be a grim time for those who are let down by their family or are faced with the horrors of long and painful slow killing conditions. I have had the great good luck to avoid that. I can even delude myself that I have not lost all my marbles.

Chapter Forty Six

Treats

The difference between family holidays and treats is sometimes blurred. On the whole family holidays are those in which Jo and I took members of our family away for somewhat primitive camping, caravanning or cabanon holidays in Britain or France. Treats were glamorous and expensive holidays for which our children took us when we showed signs of senility. I've already described some of the first category, which we enjoyed greatly. Now for some of the others.

Barbados. This came in two instalments. It was, like most of the world, familiar ground for Rhu, who, later, met and fell in love with Philippa there. Also our old friend Doctor Elliott's son Nigel was the excessively generous manager of one of the best hotels on the island.

Jo went there with Dru Elliott, the Doctor's wife, just after her hip operations and our retirement from Gresham's. It was a wonderful break for her after the strain of the final days at Gresham's with the pain of two arthritic hips. I have a photo of her dancing with an enormous black man and no signs of pain at all! She loved the sun and Nigel was very good to her. She slept under rather hard conditions in a hut on Jubilee Beach and enjoyed every sunny moment. I think that she was fortunate in going to Barbados on that occasion and the next, when we went together, before the island became rather too fashionable and overcrowded with tourists in the Nineties.

I must confess that I loved our joint trip there a few years later. Rhu saw to it that we should have every comfort, a little flat with a sunny terrace looking out onto a lawn, with forest on the far side and access to a swimming pool and table tennis and quite near Rhu, Philippa and James – who was in his element in the land of his birth. The scenery was wonderful, especially the wilder and less fashionable coast. We were introduced to some careful snorkelling in the brilliantly clear water, complete with multicoloured fish of every shape and size, and there were new species of birds, which came to our table, strutted on our lawns, or lurked in reeds round the edge of a small lake. Lizards, geckos, mongooses and monkeys everywhere. The food was first rate, and the people friendly and interesting.

Scourie was an eightieth birthday treat for me from my two sons. I suspect that they thought I was tired, perhaps seeing the early symptoms of diabetes before I did. They certainly chose the kind of holiday, which I have always found to be a healing experience. Scourie is a wee village in the remote north west of Scotland, with a comfortable and hospitable hotel with fishing rights over some 20,000 acres of lochs and rivers: salmon, sea trout and trout. A real wilderness, much of which was out of reach for an old man, except by a cross-country vehicle, which delighted Bede, who sang songs and gave Nazi salutes all the way over the moors.

Scottish landscapes at their best: the strange rock mountains of Quinag, Stac Poly and Foinaven and the wild coast line. Before long Bede and Rhu had charmed their way into the hearts of the hotel staff and acquired a new friend, Derek Rippengal, who sat with us at meals and whose dry sense of humour fitted in well. He turned out to be a Cambridge lawyer and a regular patron of the Scourie hotel.

The fishing was not at its best. It rained a lot, and the spate rivers were over-full. There was enough doing to keep us excited. We all hooked and played salmon: Rhu landed his, Bede and I lost ours, but caught one or two sea trout by way of compensation. It was cold and taxing; I was really rather ill, but only occasionally noticed it, when staggering among the slippery rocks of the river, or overcome with tiredness in the evening. In that glorious countryside and the uproarious company of my two sons, I had so much fun that I didn't suffer. We had quite an adventurous trip. The rods were stowed out of sight on the flight from Norwich to Aberdeen, but were not delivered. Rhu was indignant and told them that if the rods were not delivered to Scourie the next morning the airline would have to pay for new ones. They were delivered by taxi in time for our first fishing trip!

The return journey was somewhat hairy too. There was a gale blowing, and the aeroplane was bumping around alarmingly on the way down to its landing. I went to the Doctor a couple of days later to discover that I had diabetes.

Egypt was a different kind of adventure. We went with Rhu as a very knowledgeable guide and his family. We had a short spell in Cairo to see the museum which was thrilling, the City of the Dead which was bizarre, and the Pyramids, which I found a little disappointing. Of course they are an amazing feat of slave labour and of accurate construction, but they are certainly not beautiful, and are rather spoiled by the number of people wanting to sell unwanted trinkets or to take your photographs or to act as guides. I found the recently discovered boat in which the Pharaohs used to be taken up and down the Nile rather more intriguing on a smaller scale. Its construction out of beautifully fitted wooden planks was ingenious and elegant. The biggest surprise was the bewildering juxtaposition of Western style streets, with shop fronts which might have been in Paris or London with rough and primitive side roads crowded with chickens and goats and slummy huts. I was astonished too to learn that its population, already much greater than London's, was rising by over a thousand a day.

Then to Luxor, which we enjoyed even more thanks to Rhu's intimate knowledge of the place and its history. The choice of hotel was excellent: a breakfast spread offering a choice to suit every conceivable taste. Rhu took us to the kind of restaurant that the Egyptians frequent and an international tourist centre: much more expensive. Nicolas was the only one to suffer a 'gyppy tummy'. It was one of the few occasions when we went with the whole of Rhu's family and enjoyed the fun of getting to know them in a new and exciting land. The scale of the buildings, the beauty of the ancient sculptures and the elegant riches of Tutankhamen's tomb were a revelation not to be forgotten.

Nor shall I forget watching pied kingfishers dive into the sunset-red waters of the Nile, from the comfort of deck chairs on a lawn whose green surface would have done credit to the opening day of Wimbledon. In the background, classical music: Wagner, no less; good Italian wine. Real pampering does me a power of good . . .

Rhu is an inspired guide. He went down to the landing stage, hailed an Egyptian standing nearby and said: "Tell Tahib, I am here".

Sure enough Tahib turned up, a charming fellow whose boat Rhu had previously hired. He took us on a lovely expedition up the Nile and, better still, gave us the pleasure of being entertained to tea with his wife and family in his home, which was being smartly refurbished. Being a devout Muslim, he prayed five times a day, and continued to do so after depositing us at a downstream restaurant. Nicolas turned to his Dad and asked: "Why is Tahib kissing the boat?" We were grateful for this glimpse of Egyptian life – not granted to many tourists. Their English was excellent and the family very impressive.

The next treat was Corfu. I had read 'My Family and Other Animals' and had been entranced by that best of Mediterranean books. Jo was beginning to be unwell and Rhu, as usual watching for the chance to help, booked a villa not far from Gerald Durrell's house. It was ideally situated, only a mile and half from a small village with a very good and friendly restaurant and a pleasant beach. We were, however, nearly 1,000 feet up, with the mountains behind us and a glorious view from Albania in the north to Greece in the south, and along the Corfu coast towards the capital. We had an ideal swimming bath, which could be negotiated by Jo and me without difficulty, and a terrace with a wall, on which we could lean our sketch books to catch the sunsets over the sea.

The hill slopes were well wooded, and there were plenty of snakes, geckos, lizards, tortoises and birds to keep me interested. Rhu and Bede got hold of a boat (Rhu has always been a sea captain at heart) and took us for a great tour of the coast, stopping off for a swim and a picnic. Bede somewhat alarmed me later by setting off to swim to Albania – without landing, which, we gathered, might still be a politically hazardous business. I'd no idea what a good swimmer he had become, because I'd forgotten that he had taken to swimming nearly every day in London to compensate for the lack of exercise. (He also went to the gym most evenings). It took him an astonishingly short time. Both Jo and I enjoyed Corfu hugely. The temperature was equivalent to a hot summer's day in England, with one or two showers to freshen up the countryside and a faint sea breeze to keep us cool. And the people were kindly and cheerful. Definitely a treat for a repeat.

I had two trips to Canada. The first was by invitation of my dear brother Paddy and his increasing tribe, after we had a reunion to celebrate the Millennium at Lamport Hall. His children and their wives were mostly at Lamport: Simon and Joanna, Logie and Michelle, Eve and Paddy, Michael and Carole, Ferelyth, Tacye and Neil, were all present . . . a fun occasion, but all too short to get to know the Canadians again. One of the last things my mum said to me before she died was 'Keep in touch with the Canadians'. I had not been very good about that, and their numbers had increased so fast that it was a little hard to keep up. This was an opportunity to meet all (or most) of them.

It was a beginning of September visit. I landed in Toronto in summery sunshine. What a clean, spacious city it is! I was taken to Patrick's house in the suburbs, where the family made music. Patrick and Logie are both good violinists, and Pad still held his own on piano and violin. Their performance of Bach's double violin concerto was most impressive. At that time Patrick was still married to the daughter of the millionaire MacCain: it was a marriage that didn't last. Patrick is a strong and independent character. Marrying money is generally difficult . . .

Logie was married to Michelle, a pretty girl with plenty of brain: a psychologist specializing in the healing of stress trauma after shocking incidents. Logie is stocky and muscular, very useful at ice hockey. He has made his way in business with some success. Less laid back than Patrick, who has remained very British in his sense of humour, he struck me as being more Canadian, serious, efficient, energetic. Michelle and he didn't have a child for some time and took all kinds of advice, but eventually decided to adopt a super daughter, Julia. As quite often happens, no sooner had they adopted Julia than they produced a sister for her, Cayla: both very alike and very sweet.

Little incidents can shape your whole impression of a country. I went for a walk from Patrick's house and, typically, got lost. I was really perplexed, because I had forgotten both the number of the house and the name of the street and there were no conspicuous landmarks to help me retrace my steps. The streets were practically empty and the houses were tucked away behind extensive gardens. A Canadian man of about 60 saw me wandering around in a muddle and asked if he could help. I explained my predicament: that I was an aged British idiot. Fortunately he knew the name of the famous Doctor's son and guided me back. The next day I was shopping in the local supermarket, when he recognized me, came over to greet me and insisted that I should come and have a drink with him. I thereafter expected such generous and hospitable behaviour from all Canadians – and got it.

After the musical evening chez Patrick, I was conveyed to Pad and Eve's home in Sudbury. The abrupt change from Indian summer with blazing autumnal tints to vast pine forests was astonishing in so short a distance, but not as surprising as the abrupt change in the weather. It started snowing as we reached Sudbury, and the next morning it lay deep everywhere: it might have been deep mid-minter.

I soon realized what a great man my brother had become – through the respect and gratitude I found among all the people I met. He was still working full-time at Sudbury and as Speaker of the Medical parliament of Canada. He and Eve were immensely kind, pandering to my eagerness to catch a glimpse of bears and wolves, and Pad drove me round to see the local sights in spite of further deep snow. On a particularly cold day he insisted on driving me down to the town. There was ice and snow on the road, and I said: "Don't bother to drive down with the roads in this state". Brother replied: "What a very English reaction: we are used to this all winter and have tyres which are specially adapted." We accordingly got into the car. No sooner had we turned into the main road than he got into a skid right into the path of a car coming the other way. We missed each other by inches and passed each other on the wrong side of the road.

I managed not to say anything: an indication of a certain change in brothermanship, after a few years absence.

The impressions of a couple of fleeting visits should not be trusted, but they were reinforced by a later return. Canada is emphatically a great country for the old and the young. Wonderfully clean, very few slums and less visible poverty than USA. Abundant energy, without the ruthlessness and extremism which spoils some parts of America: they are more gently humorous. Above all they have space, none of the overcrowding which is making British life increasingly cramped. They also seem to have been cleverer than most in the way they have happily absorbed immigrants. They have also been quicker than most to embrace women's rights and to rid themselves of class divisions.

Of all the treats prepared for me, the most brilliant was Langara Island. I had often read of this ultimate anglers' dream, but had always dismissed it as an impossibility. But in June 2008, when I was feeling at my lowest, Rhu and Bede told me to get some warm clothes and a decent suit and prepare for a nine day break. We were to fly to Vancouver for a reunion with Paddy and some of his family at Simon and Joanne's house on Vancouver Island.

So off went Rhu and Bede and I. Jo was still, bless her, fit enough to be looked after by Pony for a few days. We met up with most of the family. Simon looking exactly like we expected a British Headmaster to look: large, booming voiced, cheerful and self-confident. Joanne was the ideal hostess, bright, thoughtful and humorous. When I got lost as usual, she guessed where she was most likely to find me, and she quietly steered me home. We had an uproarious evening discussing the changes in our beliefs and the surprisingly similar experiences we had been through, and laughing at the same kind of things. Pad was more or less immobile at the age of 90, but as elder brotherly, positive and humorous as ever. He still pointed his forefinger at me saying: "Do you hear what I'm saying, Logie!" We discussed God and everything related to good living and the how and why of all things, with a blend of frivolous humour and flashes of sincerity. We got to know Patrick, Rab and Kate better. Great people: Patrick's golf was great, Rab, at 14, a real enthusiast and Kate at 18 had it all; charm, good looks and obviously outstanding scholarly promise.

The next day I was spirited away to the airport and told to expect a helicopter trip to Langara. I was so excited that I tripped over the curb of the entrance road and sprained my wrist, so unpleasantly that I secretly thought I had broken it. Terrified of spoiling the trip I hid the pain and refused to go to the Doctor. I was shoved in the co-pilot's seat and off we went on a spectacular journey up the British Columbia coast, with a close view of the few villages and the many rivers and estuaries.

Langara Lodge is the only building for many miles. There is one track round the island, within sight of the Alaskan frontier. The lodge has its own helicopter pad and landing stage, from which you only have to walk 20 yards, which takes you directly to a lift – which takes you straight to the bar 150 feet up a cliff rising out of the sea. The pine trees clinging to the hillside provided roosting for up to seven bald headed eagles, keen to take every advantage of the discarded entrails of the salmon, which were cleaned and packed in ice in a hut attached to the landing stage. Otters, sea lions and ospreys also took advantage of the facilities.

Sean and his brother, two very delightful friends of Bede's, were experienced guides. They told us to be ready to embark at 6.a.m. the next morning. All equipment would be provided, and we would fish the best parts of the estuary from a boat. Before we went to bed, we had a chance to read the mouthwatering records of the recent fishing and to examine the cast of a salmon of well over 60 lbs caught in previous years and the photo of a Japanese beginner holding a 63 lb salmon caught the previous week.

We were not to be disappointed. I had fished for a lifetime without catching anything (bar a pike) of over 12 lbs, claiming that the pursuit of specimen monsters was a mug's game, and that the only true angler's art was dry fly fishing for trout. Rhu quite fairly pointed out that this was just an excuse. When all is said and done, the truth is that we all dream of catching big fish: fat ferox, sea trout of 20 lbs, record salmon. The method favoured at Langara was to cut herring in the right shape to twist and dive, to cast it and use it as a spinner.

Within three hours we had all got salmon of over 30 lbs; lovely game fish, which fought like demons on our 11 foot rods. Bede's was 29½ lbs, but, as he caught a halibut of 38 lbs and another salmon in the 20+ category, we agreed to shut our eyes to the missing ½ lb!

The Chinooks were big, heavy, silver fish. They were tough fighters, not spectacular, but boring deep and setting off again repeatedly, when you thought you could bring them up to the net. Its smaller cousin, the cohoes, fights in a much more spectacular way, skittering along the top, leaping frequently and tearing at the line faster. It is seldom over 15 lbs and runs out of steam more quickly, but is just as much fun.

Bede was puzzled when he hooked one that went deep, refused to run away at speed, but was very hard to bring to the surface. After a long battle he was astonished to see a big flatfish on the end of his line: a giant halibut. It proved to be almost immortal. In spite of sickeningly forceful blows from a 'priest', it continued to flap around with undiminished vigour. Halibuts have no necks, and their brains (if any) are hard to locate. But they are as good to eat as, or better than, any other fish.

The intervals between catching and playing fish were happily occupied by watching humpbacked whales, ospreys and bald eagles, and listening to Bede singing ecstatic songs from the Wild West, Nazi battle songs and 'Jesus Christ Superstar'. In four days of uninterrupted bliss we kept 10 salmon each, returned about the same number and lost roughly the same or a few more. Never a dull moment.

All my theories about the healing power of angling were proved correct. My wrist was entirely forgotten, even in the quite strenuous heat of battle with big chinooks, when I was staggering round the boat with the uncertain footing of ancient diabetics. It was still painful six months later, but the miraculous anaesthetic of unique excitement worked its magic completely. Strange how even quite minor housework stresses bring back pain!

How wonderful was the happiness that the trip to Langara brought us. A father and two sons with all troubles forgotten doing what they like best in pleasant weather and beautiful surroundings with no chance to think about health problems, income tax, house and home stresses, uncertain futures, difficult decisions. Pure escapism at its best. My sons have been the greatest of companions. How lucky I've been.

The fish that we kept were delivered to the cleaning and freezing shed. We discovered that we were only allowed to take 5 kilos of fish out of Canada, and so the enormous surplus was packed up and delivered to the various Canadian Bruce-Lockhart households, who are probably still eating salmon four years later!

If there is a Paradise and if St. Peter is still at his post at the gates, when Rhu, Bede and I knock on the door, I hope that saintly old fisherman will recognize us as fellow anglers, enquire about the size of our catches at Langara, forgive us a slight exaggeration here and there, smile and say: "Come in, and turn left for the Heavenly Langara".

*

Rhu and Bede didn't give up their policy of treats for Dad just because I thought Langara unbeatable. Both of them tried for some years to make me accept their offer to take me to Thailand. At first it was impossible. Jo was by now too ill either for me to leave her or to come with me. I did not especially like the idea of a country where I couldn't speak the language, and I was afraid of spoiling everybody's holiday by falling ill and being a nuisance. I've never been as much enamoured of sunshine and beaches as most people and was beginning to have trouble with a mild form of skin cancer caused by long days of sun in Provence.

Even in old age, circumstances and attitudes change. Jo's illness became clearly terminal, and I was emotionally and physically exhausted. Chelsea had a nearly fatal accident in Thailand. She fell from a zip wire crossing a river, and the girl coming after her fell on top of her. She damaged her head seriously. Her companions acted quickly and wisely, and she was conveyed to hospital in Bangkok, where she got superb treatment, saving both her life and her brain-function. They made a room available for Philippa, her mother, and made a full report from the specialist for her and for Rhu every day, informing them fully about decisions they were taking and the reasons for them. It had been touch and go; but the British specialists who checked her on her return were hugely impressed with the treatment they had given and its results.

In the meantime two things had happened. Bede, exasperated by his failure to find any thornless roses among British girls and at the end of his Scandinavian period (two Swedes and an Icelander), had found a delightful partner in Moon-tree, Bee or Wipanan: a small bright Thai girl. With Bede's help she started up an agricultural tool shop which prospered so much that she soon had 20 employees and was able to give them a party with roast wild boar and champagne. The second was that Rhu's old boss and friend, Jack Corunna, who had retired as a millionaire, when he heard the Rhu had Parkinson's offered him the use of his lovely house in Thailand for a year, together with as many friends and relations as he could fit in. Also a wonderful maid of all work, two gardeners and a swimming bath attendant.

*

Chapter Forty Seven

Jo's Death

March 2009 had brought her to the last slopes. Mr. Sethia had been quite right when he had told us in the New Year that her death would come in months, not years. We managed to carry on more or less as before, but it became clear that to make her dress with my help and to move up and down stairs even with the help of the 'Stanner' chair was just causing more pain. Her gallant attempts to conceal the even more painful and alarming symptoms behind smiles and even laughter could no longer deceive me. She became confined to bed, finding it more and more difficult to get to the lavatory and shower. Eventually I had to give up my aged attempts to move her around and to wash her, and had to call in the N.H.S. I cannot speak too highly of their care. Two nurses came in the morning to wash her and make her as comfortable as possible and returned to settle her in for the night. Dr. Chapman, Dr. Crawley or Dr. Hallidie visited us daily, adjusting the level of pain killing drugs with amazing skill.

Curiously enough Jo, who had always been frightened of death, seemed to lose that fear when it came to the last few weeks. She became doubly incontinent, which was especially difficult for her, because she had always been so meticulously scrupulous about cleanliness. But the relief from pain was a wonderful thing.

I took Dr. Chapman on one side and asked him whether it might make for an easier end if she could be moved to Kelling Hospital, where expert help would be available night and day. Might an operation, even at this stage, extend a meaningful life for her? Dr. Sethia had been willing to try it, but had advised against.

Dr. Chapman didn't hesitate. "No! It would only prolong pain and would bring a far less easy death. The cancer is now widespread. I think she will die on Wednesday evening and I believe it will be a peaceful death: more so if her family are with her."

He was exactly right.

The previous weekend had been the time of the Grand National. Jo had never been a gambler – except that every year she had enjoyed a flutter on that great event. Rhu asked her if she would like him to back a horse for her. She brightened up at once. "Yes! But I can't read what all the tipsters say. Pick one for me – not just the favourite!"

Rhu is no expert, but he spotted that a horse called 'Mon Mome' was running. The odds were 100:1 against. He put on £20. The rank outsider won, and Jo was able to rejoice in the glad news before she sank into a merciful coma.

We all took it in turns to sit at her bedside, until it became obvious that she was dying. There were none of the horrors one fears: no choking, gasping for breath, spasms or twitching. Bede held her hand and squeezed a message that we all loved her. He was sure that she responded – and then stopped breathing. Completely peaceful: a wonderful release. It was 10 o'clock on Wednesday evening.

We assembled in the drawing room, taking it in turn to say our last farewells. We talked about silly things in a silly way. I went into the helpless daze, which I remembered so well from Kirsty's death. The children spared me from most of the grisly accompaniments of death: the undertakers carrying her downstairs, the signing of the death certificate and the organization of the funeral and memorial service. I was too cowardly to be able to face talking about Jo at the memorial-funeral service at Holt. So I wrote it out and gave it to my old friend Dick Copas to read, which he did extremely well.

We had obtained permission from the Rector to bury Jo a few feet from Kirsty – and to leave room for me close beside her. At the same time as putting up the gravestone for Jo, we had Kirsty's cleaned up by the same sculptor … after half a century, as good as new.

Josephine
Bruce-Lockhart
Dearly beloved wife
Mother and grandmother
A constant source of joy
Love, courage and kindness,
Died April the 6th 2009 aged 86

In loving memory of
Kirsty Amanda
Bruce-Lockhart
beloved of all
died 15 July 1960
aged 7
of such is the Kingdom of Heaven

Space for one more!

It was a very moving funeral. Perhaps the nicest thing about it was that our granddaughter Chelsea, although it was in the holidays, managed to get eight members of the great Gresham's choir, who were used to singing with her, to come back, rehearse with Mark Jones, the inspired Director of Music at Gresham's, (also returning from holiday) and put up the most beautiful rendering of Miserere that I have heard. And Mike Allard as masterly as ever on the organ.

A strange thing, Death. I didn't want to go and see her in the Chapel of Rest: she wasn't there. Almost three weeks later I had a dream so vivid that it upset me for quite a while. I woke up suddenly (or thought I woke up) and put my hand out towards Jo's bed. I was convinced for a few seconds that she was there and had taken my hand and squeezed it. She had removed the tubes and rolled over towards me. Her hand was warm and firm. She smiled and for a moment I thought she was alive. I opened my eyes and she wasn't there: it was the creation of my own mind; but it left so vivid an impression that I wept – and didn't quite recover from the shock all day.

Chapter Forty Eight

The Blackbird

One Christmas card in twenty eleven
Inspired me with a breath of Heaven:
Not robins, though they're rather sweet,
Not turkeys, though they're good to eat.
The one that pleased me most of all
Was a blackbird on a garden wall.

*

It took me by complete surprise,
It ought to get a special prize:
Open the card, before too long
The blackbird's rich and fluting song
Bursts from its pages, loud and clear,
With all the mastery and ease
Which makes him charm, delight and please
More sweetly than the Nightingale,
Whose wondrous Pavarotti voice
Is too accomplished for my choice –
Silk handkerchief to mop his brow
And cull applause with practised bow –
He often seems to try too hard
To figure on a Christmas card.
It's great but over-complex Art:
The blackbird sings straight from his heart.

*

When my Jo was buried, it was spring:
By her grave I heard a blackbird sing.

How she loved that dapper bird,
Whose serenade we'd often heard
Together at the break of day!
Its song went far to soothe and heal
The worst that any man can feel.
The dark despair that made me pray
She might return on Easter Day –
Although
I know
It can't be so.

*

In winter, when I'm all alone,
I touch that magic Christmas card
And hear the blackbird's heartfelt tone –
And life's no longer quite so hard.

Written on receiving a Christmas card which portrayed a blackbird and incorporated, almost invisibly, a magnificent recording of its song, which, after 64 years of happy marriage, held special memories for me.

Dedication to Alison Denning, who was so thoughtful and a constant source of help throughout this difficult time.

* * *

The first months after her death, although I had for a long time known that it was coming, left me in a low state: a kind of trance, reluctant to do anything, lacking even the energy to go fishing. I was negative and shell-shocked. To be old, alone and trying to look after the house, do all the shopping, cooking and gardening is a common experience, but I was worse at it than most. To be a beginner in one's late eighties is not easy. A Headmaster's life is too busy to allow much time to develop suitable skills. The only good thing about it is that it helps to drive away gloomy thoughts which flourish on a diet of idleness. After a while I got a little better at household skills, but my early apprenticeship was littered with mistakes. I was tired and missed Jo terribly. I was in grave danger of becoming a grumpy and boring old man.

Rhu and Bede clearly saw this and they worked persistently at making me snap out of it. They painted an increasingly tempting picture of Thailand. They assured me that it would relight all my enthusiasms, restore my energy and even some degree of ambition. I would enjoy life again. My response was to raise all the silly and negative excuses for inaction which I have always condemned in other people: the journey was too long for an old man. I might get ill, or even die and spoil everyone else's holiday, the tropical sun would cause a return of my skin cancer. I'd get the Thai equivalent of 'Delhi Belly'. Even if fit, I'd be a nuisance.

They had an answer for everything. It was decided that February would be the ideal month. My feeble protests were swept aside, and they arranged for me to fly business class. I was to meet Jenny at Schipol, who would mother me and see to it that I didn't get lost. I was given instructions about the journey. All comforts: V.I.P. lounge, and Wut (Rhu's driver) to meet us at Bangkok ...

Even with my notoriously unreliability in matters of travel, and my genius for getting lost, nothing could go wrong – and nothing did, except that I managed to drop something down the narrow gap between my seat and my neighbour's, and in fishing for it got my arm stuck, narrowly avoiding having to call for the help of the stewardess after an undignified five minutes' struggle.

Bangkok airport surprised me. I had not expected such a magnificent modern layout. Wut proved to be a charming Thai, who understood most of what we said and made extensive use of a P.G. Wodehouse – Bertie Wooster language littered with phrases like 'Bob's your uncle', 'It's a piece of cake' or 'Righty ho!' The 200 mile car journey was fascinating for me, because I had never before been to a Far Eastern country. The road south from Bangkok is lined with villages, yet one gets the impression that there are very few people living in the hinterland more than a couple of hundred yards from the one good main road. As we got further from Bangkok towards Hua Hin the scenery became increasingly tropical and unusual. Very few flowers and trees of European appearance: everything was new. Especially the strange hills which suddenly reared up above the generally rather flat countryside. It was still winter (January – February) but the weather was like a hot English summer's day. I was there for 3 weeks, and hardly saw a cloud let alone rain.

The most charming surprise was waiting for us when we drove up to Jack Coronna's lovely house. Rhu and Bede were waiting outside the front door, kneeling as if on prayer mats and bowing in humble salutation until their foreheads touched the floor, and champagne was awaiting us in comfortable chairs looking out over a delightful view, which was to provide me with fun for the whole stay.

Nok was introduced to us as 'the maid of all work', who looked after us with maternal care. She was always watching to see if we needed any help. If either Rhu or I dabbed our brow with a handkerchief, or if we just looked hot, an iced drink would appear like magic. She was a great cook, giving us a splendid first taste of hitherto unknown fish and fruit. She was a little Thai woman of about 40, always smiling and apparently keen to do extra work. Rhu finally insisted that she should have a day off; it seemed as though that had never figured in her scheme of life, but I think she was very pleased.

The house was roomy and spotlessly clean: white floors and walls with a big central room, of which the wide glass side looking out over the panoramic view was rolled back from early morning to late at night. Our various rooms, showers and loos all led off that central hall. The dining either took place outside by the swimming pool, or on a slightly raised level to the side of the main room. The only trouble with this splendid arrangement was that the glass partitions and walls were so clean that they were sometimes invisible. Add to that a white floor with changes of level and a transparent glass table with sharp edges protruding just below knee height, and you have a series of hazards for unwary old men. I fell three or four times in the first day, and cut my shin on the table. I was lucky that I am still quite good at falling without hurting myself thanks to my long experience on the rugby field.

The house could not otherwise have been more perfect. An immaculate lawn led to the swimming bath, on the other side of which was a bench overlooking the lake and the mountains; where Rhu and I met every morning before breakfast to swim and look at the extraordinary variety of birds. I attempted rough sketches in pencil and then spent most of the morning trying to improve on my efforts.

The lake was about 500 yards long by 100 wide. On the right-hand side there was forest, then at the foot of wooded hills topped by rocky peaks, the lovely championship golf course of Hua Hin. Early in my stay there was a match in progress. With the help of my binoculars I could just see one green through a gap in the trees: Colin Montgomerie was just putting – successfully! The shore of the lake varied between rocks, reeds, mud and shingle. On the left-hand side the bank was steeper, but the hills less high. Above the bank was a field with various shrubs. At the far end was a mile of relatively flat valley leading to hills and then mountains. It was a perfect magnet for migrant birds to spend a few days and for residents to find a home. There was habitat and food for every species of bird.

Although I know my European birds, the great majority of the Thai birds were of kinds I had never seen before. It was like making a new start. Of the 70 birds I managed to identify, only about a dozen were familiar to me. I had had the foresight to buy 'The Birds of South-East Asia': a masterpiece which enabled me to sort out those species of which we got a good view. But the small warblers, which we glimpsed for three or four seconds before they disappeared, were a problem. The book listed thirty leaf warblers very like the chiff-chaff and the willow warbler, with only minor differences of plumage, and seldom obliging enough to sing in any recognisable way. The night birds were difficult too: they are often heard, but seldom seen. Recordings are the only safe way to identify bird calls or songs. Chiff-chaffs oblige by having a monotonously simple repetition of its name as a song, although the German version Zip Zap is better still. Attempts to render long or complex songs in words are bravely attempted in many bird books, but seldom successfully.

Most surprising was the number of birds of prey we saw. Black eagle, crested goshawk, kestrel, peregrine, merlin, pied harrier, osprey. The majority just dropped in for a few hours or a few days. But there were three different kinds of kingfisher nesting on the banks, purple herons, little cormorants and coucals, egrets, yellow bitterns and pond herons.

No shortage of glamorous tropical birds either: varieties of orioles and bee eaters, the Asian fairy bluebird, drongos and bulbuls. Later on we went on a coastal tour of the national park north of Hua Hin. Fans of James Bond will remember the spectacular rock towers guarding the entrance to his dangerous enemy's seaside lair. That was our starting point. The path along the shoreline was too steep and rough for us, so we missed the chance of seeing either of the two kinds of bear, or one of the last remaining Thai tigers. Lots of monkeys, however, and one elephant on the way there – apart from the tame one we saw painting a carefully planned abstract with bold enjoyment and good judgement, which put many modern human artists to shame. The shoreline was mostly rocky (home to a variety of fishing wild cats with specially adapted claws on webbed paws). Every two or three miles there would be a cove with a sandy beach, space for a little farm land, and one or two islands, small but mountainous. Wut drove us there and back including some marshy land with fresh water pools at the entrance to the park where there were many kinds of waders, including godwits and the scarlet wattled lapwing. It was a great day for Wut, because, strange to say for a 40 year old born and bred near the sea, he had never been in a boat before. Rhu loves nothing more than being at the helm, so we were a happy boat-load. One of the bays looked a bit different: bigger and flatter. It proved to be a mangrove estuary, the first I'd ever seen. Rhu took us about three miles up the river, which had no perceptible current. There were a number of boats moored at the sides, some of them inhabited, in spite of which there were all kinds of birds: yellow bitterns, pond herons, Pacific reef egrets, and all three kinds of kingfishers. On the way back Wut showed us another of his mild eccentricities. He was obsessed with a mission to clear Thailand roadsides of snakes of all sizes whether venomous or not. If he saw one on the road he would stop the car, hop out with a special club he took with him for the purpose, and, if he could catch it before it disappeared in the tangle of vegetation would bash it to death. He would then return radiant to the car obviously expecting praise for his macho heroism. In spite of his efforts the population of snakes seemed to be thriving: they managed to find their way into our house more than once.

There were lots of other high spots nearby. A huge statue of Buddha was obviously a centre for pilgrimage, and was surrounded by praying admirers. If you needed healing, you put an adhesive label on the part of the statue that was equivalent to the site of your trouble. As nobody could reach above Buddha's ankle it looked as though half Thailand had foot trouble – though I gathered that on payment you could hire a monk to deliver your label to the head. Anyway I had bruised my big toe the day before our visit. I duly adorned the Buddha's big toe with my label (among many others).

My big toe recovered; but I must confess it was only a tiny bruise and would have got better in any case.

The Black Mountain golf course was beautiful. One of Rhu's neighbours talked a very good game of golf, and Rhu and Bede were rash enough to challenge him and another member-neighbour. Fortunately Bede had one of his good days, when his 300 yards plus drives reached the right fairways, and Rhu directed his irons greenwards and sunk some putts. They won by a large margin, after having denied that they were any good, which did no harm to the local reputation of the family. The beautifully kept course was in a hollow in the hills, and eagles soared (perhaps symbolically?) above the greens at the far end.

Hua Hin was fine too. Twice a week we all went for a foot massage. About £8 for a full hour of bliss. Pretty girls with pleasantly perfumed ointments, restoring life to tired limbs. I have diabetic tingling of my feet and my nerves, as Bede has discovered to his great delight, which make me jump if too much pressure is applied. It was the cause of much amusement – but also improved the condition markedly.

There were three places where we ate out. One was a fish restaurant built out over the shore and giving the impression that the fish were hauled up directly from the sea. The service was swift and helpful, the prices very reasonable and the food delicious – if sometimes overspiced.

The second Hua Hin restaurant was an old fashioned Victorian hotel with outside tables beautifully kept lawns and trees packed with intriguing birds: mynahs, magpie-robins, orioles and Eurasian tree sparrows. Also a lovely private beach.

If we didn't eat at home, the compound had a good little restaurant of its own, 300 yards down the road where we could meet our neighbours and play a local form of pétanque.

Most remarkable of the Hua Hin attractions is its huge fish market. It has stalls covered with every kind of fresh fish and crustaceans, most of them entirely new to me, although I am a fish enthusiast. The soft shell crabs were especially tasty, and outsize prawns are 'what tiggers like'. The stalls are separated by narrow corridors which criss-cross the building. These corridors are the pathways for motor bikes which constantly deliver stacks of ice cubes to keep the fish on display fresh. How they avoid running over customers I don't know. I suppose you can get used to anything. The main railway line crosses one of the main streets of Hua Hin. No lights, no gates, and the crossing keeper asleep or watching television . . . casualties?

There is a red light district where the ladies of the night (and day) perform enthusiastic snake dances on the pavement outside their headquarters. Nothing furtive about it, though I read of the prevalence of a 'lady-boys' culture, which must be confusing for an orthodox skirt hunter!

As in most lands there is a considerable difference between the country village people and those who live in the few big towns. Bede's very nice girl friend, Wipanan (moon tree), more often referred to as Bee, is from a small village the other side of Bangkok, although she was staying with us for the duration of my holiday. She is a great girl, who increased our already considerable respect and liking for the Thais. Her community is full of friends and relations, who all seem to care for one another and to help one another whenever it is needed. They look after the old and the children especially well. The young ones are sent to a Buddhist monastery for two or three weeks every year to learn how to live a good life, and they are certainly a first-rate advertisement for the system. In addition to the valuable tool shop Bede and Wipanan are busy developing a beautiful property with half a dozen bed and breakfast bungalows overlooking a lake. As I write, Bede is working for the Germans and earning great money, but I suspect that he wants to move to Thailand to develop more small businesses there, when he has enough money to ensure a comfortable old age in Thailand, which he loves, as a farmer and property developer. The trouble is that, although he makes good money, he is terribly generous. His Thai home will become a refuge for senile or fragile friends and relations.

All the Thais we came across were cheerful, hard working and unselfish, but there are other sides to the relationships between them and the outside world. The Danes and the Dutch, mostly wealthy, cultured and retired after jobs of real importance, treated them politely as equals, often marrying them or taking them as respected partners. Sadly, English tourists were different: The English man would be wearing shorts, with a pronounced beer-belly hanging over them. His British wife would be looking sour and disapproving, as if she thought everything stank. Their Thai maid would be walking five paces behind carrying all the shopping. She would only be spoken to in order to be reprimanded, given orders or laden with new burdens. The English tips also tend to be mean, because "It doesn't do to spoil them!" That was something that Rhu with his great experience of travel, and Bede, with his ability to charm his way into the affections of all nationalities, would never be guilty of.

Rhu's friends, the Danes and the Dutch were great people – wonderful linguists and a sense of humour.

Rhu and I started a lifelong (or should it be life-short?) rivalry in Scrabble. We were very close in ability, but he had the advantage of internet experience and possession of the rule book and the official Scrabble dictionary with its ridiculous supposedly English incredibly rare words. [Dadguum, daimoku, daftar and dahabeah, with alternative spellings: dahabeach, dahabiah or dehabiyah or dahabige]. As there are some dozen such words on every page of an understandably large dictionary, the game can become somewhat esoteric. But we enjoy our unscrupulous rivalry, as we enjoy staggering down the increasingly steep slopes of infirmity at a comparable speed.

The whole trip was like waking up from a nightmare to find myself in Paradise. Jack Coronna's kindness spread to Rhu, who distributed it, as usual, much further. He asked Tess, who had only recently lost her husband – my nephew Sandy – and her son Simon, who has recently set up a jewellery business in Thailand and married a Thai girl of good family. I think Tess was tired out and very glad of a chance to put her feet up in the sun. Simon seemed to be thriving on his expertise in the sphere of Thai rubies and diamonds and was a very devoted father.

The only cloud on the horizon is that a lot of the contentedness and unity of the Thais is due to their adoration of their wise old ruler whose photo is in every home. He is now very old, and his heir does not command the same respect. This may well lead to unrest when the old man has gone.

Those three weeks made me a different man. My two sons had restored my confidence and zest for life. The journey back was incident free, except that a man of about my age in the nearest reclining seat had the most alarming coughing fits and required medical care for most of the night. When we left Bangkok the temperature was 85 Fahrenheit. When we landed at Norwich it was minus 1°! A little hard to decide on the right clothes for the occasion!

What Thailand had given me was a renewed interest in painting and drawing, a lot of fun and laughter and the pleasant if somewhat ridiculous illusion that I should resume my hobby of writing. And I looked forward to meeting people again instead of retreating into my hermit-crab shell.

On my return I was surprised to find that Thailand was followed by a number of great holidays in Britain.

Chapter Forty Nine

Back to Britain

I was quite pleased to get back to Blakeney. I rearranged it so that a large photo of Jo smiled down upon anyone having a drink in the drawing room. She was holding a glass of Gigondas as if toasting a guest, and the people behind her were obviously attending a Provençal fête. It was a wonderful likeness: welcoming and cheerful. I no longer felt lonely and had lost my desire to run away from the world. A number of my favourite ex-pupils started to call and have a drink, or, even better, to bring a bottle. There was much laughter over the old days, and fascinating careers and interests had often developed, which was most rewarding. I also had great fun following Jo's last instructions to me to try to keep contact with some of our old friends, who had fallen or were falling into difficult times ... Betsy Rogers, the gallant wife of Dr. John Rogers, lived until last winter on her own only half a mile away. Isobel Bateman a lively 100 year old, still a formidable bridge player and, although very blind and rather deaf, still enjoys a trip to the restaurant and a glass of wine. She was a follower of 'the work' and loves to talk about it. And dear Pru Duncan, who was so kind and generous to us, but lost her husband and became ill and died. That is the saddest thing about old age – all one's friends fall off the perch. Of our Provence group, three-quarters are now dead. But there is something very rewarding about trying to bring a little cheer and optimism to those who are surviving bravely and without crippling illness, but are becoming lonely and exhausted.

On the other hand, some of the Clan closed in. Sal and her two brilliant daughters lived quite near and were kind enough to come and chat with me about family developments and the changing world: always a fresh view. James and Flip kept in touch too. They seem to have so much in common with me: birds (on which Flip is a real expert), writing, drawing, painting, German culture, fishing, music and, the sound of their own voices. We have long chats on the telephone every month.

Opportunities for holidays within Britain started to come. I was rashly asked (aged 89) to talk to the Holt Rugby Club, on the 50th anniversary of their foundation with me as President. To my delight and astonishment I found that I had not lost the knack of public speaking, and I had the couple of hundred guests in fits of laughter and found I didn't need the notes I had prepared. It was a great boost for morale. The Holt club had enjoyed a remarkably successful season again.

Then I spent some holidays again with Pony. Jo and I had joined them at Lamport, and in Devon, and I now enjoyed trips to both. Pony and her remarkable husband George gave me a fortnight at Lamport Hall, equidistant from Northampton and Market Harborough, and then at their home in Devon to which they will gradually retire. George is an expert on most things: surveyor, gardener and horticulturalist, builder, agricultural economist, historian. He would be a star in the quiz world. When he and Pony periodically come to spend a weekend with me, his eagle eye spots everything that needs attention in the way of damp patches, loose tiles, leaks and cracks. They are great hosts in the lovely homes. Lamport is a wonderful place to bring up a family. Their sons, Alastair and Dacre, two tall blond and handsome young men, have been surrounded by space and beauty. George was looking after the Peak District National Park, and then moved on to Lamport: a big stately home with splendid gardens and two farms and two villages attached. "Celts Corner", Thurlestone is in the most attractive part of Devon: half a mile from the sea, with half a dozen not too touristic beaches within easy reach. Lovely rivers, scattered farms with glorious views, good birds, nice people. Their home has a lush garden with all manner of rare flowers, and it enjoys a warm, mini-riviera climate – although it is wetter than Norfolk. They provided us and then me with a little granny flat, and spoiled us in every way. Pony, that fairly temperamental child, has become a highly efficient and intelligent housewife as well as an inspiring teacher, named 'trail blazer' by the press. Her pupils continue to write excellent poetry. I am able to relax, paint and write to my heart's content. Every now and again they take me off to some exciting place: the Eden Project, The Oyster Shack, the glorious gardens of Overbecks and Coleton Fishacre, a trout stream with an ancient bridge, kingfishers, buzzards and kingcups. Meanwhile my weary old brain is brushed up by George's latest book – often on the World Wars – and my fossilized views are shaken by Alastair and Dacre, and Pony holds forth enthusiastically about Cormack McCarthy, Faulkner or all the latest films – subjects about which I know absolutely nothing.

I had one nostalgic break: an invitation from my old friends Tommy MacPherson and his wife Jean to their home in Speyside. I had met Tommy two or three times since we played rugby together: notably at a reunion of the Oxford and Cambridge sides of 1947, which was attended by all but about four of the original players. Not bad after 50 years; none of us was under 70, some were over 80, and two had flown back from South Africa.

Jean was as lively and charming as ever, and Tommy as humorous and laid back as in his prime, in spite of having suffered a small stroke. It had the effect of making him unable to speak a word every now and again, so that he had to resort to a pencil and a sheet of paper. But he was clear-minded otherwise and was busy with the editor of his book 'Behind Enemy Lines' going through the proofs. It is a record of some of the most astonishing feats of gallantry of World War II, or of any war. They must make a film of it soon. He still walks a good distance every day. I took the opportunity to visit my Bruce-Lockhart grandfather's home town of Grantown and, more lengthily, the Granny MacGregor distillery of Balmenach, now taken over by a distiller, who has married the granddaugher of one of the many MacGregors of Balmenach. A charming lady showed me around and presented me with a vintage bottle of the best single malt. From there we went to watch the ospreys at their nest and the crested tits in the Abernethy forest and the golden eagles nesting on the cliff overlooking their other house.

It was lovely weather in a lovely place. The only snag was the journey. Leave Sheringham at 7.49, change Norwich, change Peterborough, miss the connection, change York, change Edinburgh, change Perth, arrive Speyside 6.30 ...

I learned some unpublished details of my heroic friend's exploits, although he talked very little about them. I asked him whether he was terrified of betrayal, when he had such near misses and a £300,000 reward for his capture. He admitted being very scared at times "but I always loved blowing things up, and still enjoy fireworks more than anything else!"

Apart from the treats my children gave me and the company of my grandchildren, there were several other factors which helped me to recover a zest for life.

In 2009–2010 I had my cataract operations on both my eyes. I've always been a coward about any encounter with surgeons, and the thought of needles and knives prodding those particularly sensitive organs is unpleasant. Though I had to wear spectacles for reading the deterioration had been so slow that I hadn't realized the need. A couple of friends reassured me, saying that it was completely painless.

The doctor recommended that they should be done one after the other 'to ensure that, in the unlikely event of there being any snag, you will still have one fairly good eye.'

The surgeon covered the other eye so that I couldn't see any instrument. I had a vague notion that some liquid was washing out my eye. There was no prick of a needle, no discomfort of any kind. I was feeling mildly sleepy and wondering when he was going to start, when he told me it was all over. I went back home with a dressing over my eye. Although he had told me to leave it on for a night, I lifted the corner and was astonished to see the world in bright, clear colours. For the next week I spent my time looking at flowers first with my new eye then with my cataracted eye. The second operation was just as successful, and I now see as well as I did in my forties. It really transformed the world.

That, together with a book by Winston Churchill, brought new life to my efforts to paint, draw and write. "Painting as a Pastime" is a very short book, but is the best and most delightful thing Winston ever wrote. It tells how at the most depressing time of his life, when his 'black dog' was threatening to rob him of all zest, he would put up his easel, which would infallibly bring him pleasure to accompany him to the end or nearly the end of his life and save him from the 'relentless advance of surly decrepitude."

All you need is courage and the delight of looking at beauty and seeking to convey it. Even at 80–90 you can hope to do it tomorrow better than today – of how many other pursuits is that true? If I feel a little disconsolate, I look at a late impressionist painting by Monet. He had cataracts in both eyes and was rather over fond of good wine, but his ability to render atmosphere was far better than anything he painted in his youth. So there is hope for us all.

At the same time I recovered my interest in reading and writing – and, like most old men, in light gardening. Living in Britain should make gardeners of us all ... constant contact with beauty and the joy of creation. Instead of becoming a grumpy old man and hermit, I began to feel that the days were just not long enough for all the things I wanted to and enjoyed doing. Bede introduced me to Scharma's book "The Monk who sold his Ferrari". He talked with enthusiasm about it and had been so impressed that he bought a copy for all his senior employees. When I went to an office party of his in London, no less than six of his staff came up and told me how that book and Bede had changed their lives.

So I read it. To begin with I had the typical reaction of an educated Brit confronted by a wealthy American telling him how to conduct his life. That lasted only for the first 20 or 30 pages. Then I realized that this was no Billy Graham or Bible-belt preacher. His story was set firmly in the modern world: the central characters were an over-successful, too hard-working lawyer, who became a victim of the rat-race and had a heart attack, and an old friend, who had seen the danger and travelled east (like the Beatles and countless gap year idealists) to a special monastery in the foothills of the Himalayas where the monks had made a profound study of how to live a rewarding life in the materialistic West. All a bit over familiar; but the teaching passed on to the lawyer is brilliant. All the best teaching of Buddhism and Christianity, shorn of superstition and the non-historical mythical elements, which so many of us find impossible to accept. The originality lies in the practical advice of how to plan a life of service. Many people tell us what is good and advise us to be good, but few tell us how to be "inspired, determined, disciplined, organized and to spread love and laughter wherever we go."

The advice is practical rather than theoretical. Hard physical exercise every day and meditation including mantras, targets and plans for the coming day and week and sorting out the most important thing to be achieved. Write it down together with other targets in a forward planning diary to ensure that they are accomplished. Make time for a spell in a beautiful place. If negative thoughts come into your head, replace them at once with positive ones. At the end of the day, play or listen to some great classical music before you go to sleep. Review the day. If there is a target you have missed ensure that it will be put right on the next day. Either in the morning or at night consider the words of the sermon on the mount or of the noble eightfold path and see whether your plans fit in with these ideals. Scharma makes the point that if you can do these things for three weeks conscientiously, they will become a habit. Make sure that you have fun and that help for others is a regular feature.

He has nothing to say about or against sex. If you are fit in mind, body, emotions and spirit, sex relations will benefit. Or, if you are my age, it is not a matter that will disturb you excessively.

The proof of the pudding is in the eating. Although half of me laughs at the stomach exercises and deep breathing of the other half, and mocks my enduring failure to find keys, wallets and passports, I have no doubt that it has cheered me up and helped in all sorts of ways.

It has been fun to return to the books which influenced me as a young man. Thomas Mann's 'Buddenbrook' and 'Tonio Kröger', Goethe's poems, 'Anna Karenina', Thomas Hardy, Aldous Huxley, Rousseau, Hermann Hesse, Rilke. The stories of Esther and Job and the New Testament, especially St. John. They all fit in in a strange way – as does the most sublime message: the language of music, which means more and more to me as I get older, and my fingers get increasingly unwilling to follow my aspirations on the piano.

*

If I felt that much was changing inside me it was even more true of Britain and the world.

My retirement had come just in time to save me from the internet, tweeting, computers and the whole world of gadgets and communications. Spending that blissful time in France had removed us from many of the advances of modern science. Our return to Blakeney hardly prepared us for the 21st Century: it is rumoured that one inhabitant voted Labour at the last election, and I am only fractionally above the average age. What are the main changes?

Medical science has, whatever your opinion of the N.H.S., made huge advances. There is a real chance that our grandchildren, if they escape death by drought, flood, Tsunami, fire, starvation, pollution or war, will survive to be walking around at 120 years old, even if it will be with someone else's vital organs. We are even beginning to conquer pain.

We are more open, more tolerant, and more kind. Most of us are less superstitious, less liable to believe things without proof or evidence. We love games, sport and exercise – or, to be more exact, most of us love to watch a minority of professional experts performing. The number of competent and enthusiastic performers may increase as a result of the Olympic Games, but we are a long way behind nations like Sweden, where one in twelve adults is qualified to teach some form of sport, and 75% of the adults are members of weekend sports clubs.

A preliminary look at the statistics is likely to convince us that official religions are in decline everywhere, except in Muslim countries. Certainly Roman Catholicism, Protestantism, the Church of England and most of the branches of Christianity are attracting fewer followers, or are split between desperate clinging to traditional creeds and forms of worship and attempts to change them to bring them closer to modern ways of thinking.

But it would be a mistake to believe that people are less concerned with moral behaviour and spiritual values. There are attempts in France by the government to provide an education in civic virtues to replace the sorely missed influence of the Catholic Church. People of influence in all the democracies are eager to be seen promoting the new key virtues: equality, freedom, tolerance, human rights – and sometimes rejecting the more Victorian virtues of hard work, elitism, competitive success, marital fidelity, complete trustworthiness in business affairs. There is a new curiosity abroad about heightened levels of consciousness and often untapped sources of energy connected with the human brain. And there is a new Puritanism at work in some governments, which tends to regard any branch of the fashionable standards as a sin. But as soon as religion or moral values are taken over as legal matters to be guided by the state, they become tainted. Behaviour is not a matter for enforcement unless it clearly harms others. Power corrupts most quickly in religious matters.

People who long for firmer values are often attracted to the vigorous certainty of the Muslim religion, and believe that its confident belief in what it thinks are god-dictated standards will drive it to become more and more assertive and bring it into conflict with all other beliefs or ways of life.

I believe that this will become less likely. However strict the censorship, ideas will no longer be able to be kept from spreading. Modern communications mean that issues like freedom of thought and expression, women's rights and humane justice will spread more quickly and effectively.

And, whatever Richard Dawkins says, and accepting all the truths which science is revealing, it will become more widely understood that there are spiritual forces at work in the world, even if they are the creation of man, which provide a kind of electricity of which the best human beings are the light-producing bulbs. And these, although they must never refuse to acknowledge proven scientific facts, cannot be judged by purely materialistic standards.

The most obvious changes in Britain are often puzzlingly contradictory. Sometimes it seems that we have overcome racial prejudice and that the dream of a multi-national Britain united in a society of shared ideals, but without the jingoism of the past, is becoming true. The Olympics showed what a great contribution the best of our immigrants are making. And then the figures showing the high levels of unemployment, poverty and crime in some immigrant ghettos paint a quite different picture. Or Muslims openly preach the use of violence and we have to spend millions on countering terrorist plots. Our government, whether from right or left cannot seem to give up the idea that we have the right to be the world's policemen and to meddle in the complex affairs of far off countries. You'd have thought that the results of trying to draw a new line to create a new state of Israel, or of a new line to define Pakistan and India, or of interfering with the affairs of Afghanistan more successfully than all the previous invaders of that country, would have made us think twice before embarking on fresh adventures.

The disappearance of the British Empire has confused us in other ways. We spend our time apologizing for the crimes of colonialism and the insensitivity of the Victorians, but miss the energy, confidence and determination which kept them at the top. We think that we are a superior society; yet our quest for freedom, equality and justice does not seem to have brought success. It has been too often based on envy of success, avoidance of hard work, the growth of an ungovernable underclass of under-educated unemployed, and the spread of unreliability and untrustworthiness in the 'higher' levels of society.

But is the Establishment really riddled with self-seeking and corruption? Our press gives us a picture of a country where crime is rife, immorality is rampant, policing ineffective, and which is sliding towards the bottom of every measurable achievement of the western democracies: financial, educational, teenage pregnancies.

And yet . . . I do not seem to meet or to see any of these villains of whom the papers write. I get civil and helpful replies from the officials I write to, even if their English is not always immediately comprehensible. If I leave my wallet in a shop, it is returned to me complete with contents. The builders, plumbers, electricians and gardeners are efficient, honest, likeable and hard working. You would think that the Press lives in a sort of Blunderland where everybody is wicked and all enterprises doomed to failure, while the rest of us live in a Britain, which may not be faultless, but is on the whole as good a place to live as any in the world.

There are plenty of reasons for the pessimism and gloom which is so widespread. Global warming makes it clear that there are formidable difficulties ahead. Rise in sea levels, disappearance of rain forests, increase in human population; climate change followed by droughts and famines, floods and fires, earthquakes, eruptions and Tsunamis, pollution and crop failure, water and oil wars. Britain is in recession and faces losing its markets to the great developing nations who work harder for their money. The young can't find jobs: the mysterious 'balance of nature' will ensure that the world's population will be swiftly and drastically reduced so that its shrinking resources will be sufficient to supply the small remainder of human beings.

Yet I think that the almost universal pessimism is wrong. I don't deny that disasters lie ahead, although I suspect that the speed and scale of them is often exaggerated. If some of the extreme doom merchants of the Nineties had been believed, most of the world would have been wiped out by 2012: genetic manipulation of our crops would have been counter-productive, New York and London would have disappeared under the rising sea. Methane escaping from melting tundra would have poisoned the atmosphere, the vast explosion of Yosemite and of the Californian fault would have wiped out the greater part of the U.S.A. The contents of the sea would have been poisoned.

There have been disasters before: quite recently, we have produced disasters of our own making: two horrific World Wars. And we have suffered the two ghastly outbreaks of the Plague, which caused as much suffering in as short a time as any of the probable trials ahead.

The times of greatest trial are also the times of greatest opportunity. Lord Gummer was right when, in a recent speech, he told his audience of teenagers and their parents: "You are the luckiest generation in history: all the greatest advances of mankind have been made in times of formidable challenges . . . you will have those, but you will also have unprecedented means of meeting and overcoming them."

Scientists of great skill and determination in all nations are increasingly working together to find global solutions to global problems, and as the dangers get closer, their countermeasures grow faster and more effective. You may remember the quarrel of Tweedle-Dum and Tweedle-Dee. When the monstrous crow turned up "it frightened both our heroes so, they quite forgot their quarrel." Both the means and the motives are there for the world's best scientists to get together – and even (which is the most difficult bit) for the political leaders and their followers to take their advice.

Often the would-be do-gooders obstruct the very aims they support: genetic improvement of crops is the only way to combat mass starvation, yet many campaigners for better food oppose it on semi-scientific grounds based mainly on fear of change. No less that the Nobel prize winner for genetic science said that these fears are groundless. Everybody loves a beautiful rose. Nearly all the loveliest are the result of genetic manipulation. Yet when a big glistening tomato is produced it is at once proclaimed as tasting inferior, and dreadful consequences are prophesied.

There is an inspiring world-wide battle to be waged, and it can be bloodlessly fought by biology teachers and geographers, physicists and chemists – but also by national and local governments, waste disposal planners, fishermen, farmers, oil companies, water experts, builders. If the young can make up their minds in what way they can help and pursue that aim single-mindedly, the chances of a rewarding life are better than ever. It must also be done internationally – it might help if the teaching of languages were to be taken seriously in Britain.

*

What other major changes are affecting the young, in the early 21st Century?

'Education, education, education', cried Tony Blair: a heartfelt cry which helped to sweep New Labour to power. But not much has changed for the better. Some universities have produced excellent new faculties. To turn so many excellent grammar schools into comprehensives did nothing to help. There was much talk of new technical schools and colleges, but very few emerged. The Conservative government has not done much better. The Alice in Wonderland recipe for improvement was to make universities offer places to students from bad schools at a lower grade than to those from good schools – not a great incentive for good teaching. Nor have either Labour, Conservative or Coalition governments spent enough money on the education of the bottom 15%: the underclass from which many of our troubles stem.

Which leads to the most dangerous change of all: the disappearance of any character training from most homes and schools. Mention the hated words 'discipline', 'hard work', 'ambition', 'sharing the housework' and you can expect to see a modern parent and even teachers shudder. You are at once categorised as a right-wing extremist.

Of course it is an exaggeration to say that such standards are never aimed at or achieved. A few solve the problems facing them: two full-time working parents, a do as you please nursery school or primary school, a computer and T.V. set at the child's disposal, the pressure to keep up with the Joneses, and the general perception that a child's life should be a perpetual round of 'fun' parties, with intervals invariably filled with the television or friends chattering.

There are indeed problems. I hope that, after the Olympics, more will join sports clubs and that schools will give more time to a wider variety of sports and activities. The early end to afternoon school made that side of education difficult. Music has an equally important part to play: mastering an instrument improves academic work and is a training in all kinds of important ways. From the start the idea that you must choose between pop, jazz or classical music should be discouraged: you learn from all types of music. There is nothing wrong with a teenager writhing to rock like Mick Jagger on Saturday night, and taking the part of Jesus in the 'St. Matthew Passion' on Sunday – both performances will probably benefit! The key to restoring happy homes and successful children is co-operation between parents and schools to ensure that creative enthusiasms are in every way encouraged, and that our children learn that there is no fun so satisfying as achievement through hard work – and there is no better way than sharing those enthusiasms and the work that success demands. The reward is immense for children, parents and teachers. To see a formerly bored child catch fire in pursuit of some ambition; whether it be dancing, football, playing the clarinet or helping old people, is what makes teaching such a wonderful job. Sadly this – the very essence of good education – is often neglected. Many teachers think that education is confined to the classroom and many parents think that it should be confined to the school. Enthusiasms arising from personal contacts outside the classroom have a habit of spreading to academic work as well.

How did all these changes affect my own interests and those of my family? I've already detailed the decline in fishing. Gardening is to some extent threatened by the more extreme changes in the weather and the alarming reduction in the number of bees. Nobody seems to have chronicled another alteration in the fertility of the British countryside: the number of edible fungi. Many species which were widespread and easily found have done badly – especially from 2010 to 2012. This may in part be the result of the increased number of immigrants from countries where they are a stock item of diet and the growth of interest and knowledge among native Brits. Another factor may be the erratic pattern of rainfall which makes some fungi appear at different times of the year; the comparative shortage is undeniable.

Writing? There is little doubt that the instructions to examiners not to take off more than 3% for bad spelling and grammar did lasting harm, although they have been rescinded. E-mail jargon and texting hasn't helped. Among the highly literate journalists there seems to be too much effort to be original and striking regardless of whether the similes and metaphors are apt, and it is not worthy of them to lard their articles with 'strong' language, which has become tedious through overuse. But some modern slang is vivid when effectively used. I am probably biased by the advice of the first editor to accept a contribution from me. "This has much promise, but you do not need to dazzle me with purple prose. Just say what you mean as briefly and clearly as possible!" How few of us achieve that laudable aim.

Painting and new art? Again, too much desire to shock and too much sheer commercialism. I remember that Picasso confessed in his old age: "I am not a great artist like the old masters. I am just a good technician, who has played upon the weaknesses of successive generations to my own great amusement and profit." Tongue not entirely in cheek!

Once again there seems to be a division between those artists who convey a genuinely original vision with skill, and those who aim to shock or surprise by crudely elementary means and with an eye to what will bring in the cash . . . or has that become the sole purpose of art? Or has it always been so, except that the rich of the 21st Century have very different tastes? I always thought highly of Taine, the distinguished French art critic of the late 19th Century, who said that every artist is the product of 'Race, milieu, moment': or, as we might put it: 'genes, environment and the time', including the stage in the historical development of the art. He also added that any work of art must seek to convey the original intention of the artist clearly enough to be understood by the majority of sensitive and intelligent viewers . . . Food for thought!

I find that my drawing and painting get better with old age, whereas writing gets worse. Perhaps this is partly due to the fact that drawing and painting were bad to start with, while I used to write quite well. Writing, except in short bursts, requires organization. Old men are disorganized, repeat themselves more and more, are obsessed by the out-of-date causes for which they fought half a hundred years ago. Their prose tends to be old-fashioned and loses passion and conviction. We are no longer so sure that we're right.

On the other hand the mere fact that we no longer write to please other people, to make money or even to gain a reputation for brilliance or produce world-changing ideas gives some advantage. If I aim at none of these things why on earth do I sit down for three or four hours a day of the precious short time left to me in writing my memoirs? I think it is partly because I love writing, and love comparing the outlook of different generations. In old age one becomes more and more convinced of the huge influence of our genes and our upbringing and of the characteristics repeated within families. At the end of 90 years you forget much, but tend to remember and learn something from the important things.

As I come towards the end of these rambling memoirs and of my life, I begin to realize that most of the valuable lessons I have learnt – in spite of my career as a Headmaster – have been firstly from other people, mainly my family and from my children in particular, and secondly from my mistakes which have been many and varied.

From my father, the importance of enthusiasm and hard practice and of helping others, and the passing on of most of his enthusiasms. Love of sport.

From my mother, calm and courage in the face of difficulties. Imagination and the way to influence and interest children without fuss. Forgiveness.

From both of them: a reluctance to discuss the fundamentals; religion, sex, death and disease and poverty.

From Uncle Bertie, a fondness for drink, travel and journalism.

From my paternal and maternal grandfathers: a reluctance to spend money unless absolutely necessary.

From the MacGregors: enjoyment of spending money even when quite unnecessary.

From my children: an example of how I would like to live if I were them.

From Jo: the supreme importance of love. The whole of the feminine side of life, which had been so lacking in my upbringing, the importance of colour and beauty. The importance of spiritual issues: where does truth lie? The role of sympathy with the suffering of others. All the concerns, which I had felt were missing from my own education. The need for elegance in internal decoration of houses. And the example of undaunted courage and cheerfulness beyond belief.

And Tidiness. She waged a life-long war on the untidiness of Bede, Jenny and myself. Clothes lying in heaps, papers scattered all over the tables. It must have seemed a hopeless task; but in retirement I improved a little – and it was not an issue in France!

It is strange the way that tidiness has suddenly reappeared in Pony, to a lesser degree, and in Alastair, her son, as an obsessive virtue.

And generosity. Jo passed it on to her children, though she never quite managed it with me.

From Jo's sister, Heather, an interest in all spiritual forces.

I share with five generations of my family a desire to teach – which, I believe, is the main reason that Jenny and I occasionally clash. We both want to teach the other and find it difficult to accept the role of student meekly. For instance, when she is anxious to advise me how to (or not to) conclude these memoirs, my reaction is that they must be mine, and how does she think she knows what conclusions (if any) I have reached.

From Jen I get deep seriousness about pursuit of a higher level of consciousness, [well, not really deep, it's a bit of a lie!] which she shared with Jo, and derived from joining 'the work' pioneered by Gurdjeff and Ouspensky. I have read many of the books explaining 'the work' and find a lot of them full of good ideas and insight into a new way of thinking and looking at the Universe. But I could not commit myself to an organization that tells me that I cannot hope to achieve real progress and understanding without years of following their schooling. I cannot undertake such a programme, and, have not long years left. There are other wise people apart from 'the work'.

Jenny is unselfish, artistic, generous and utterly reliable. She must be lonely, for Parisians are not generally hospitable, and she gets little practical help from those for whom she has slaved away for long, largely unpaid hours. But she knows right from wrong and will always help others without asking for anything in return. It is not every single lady of 67 who sets out on her own to explore the South East Asian countries.

From Rhu I get infinite generosity and tolerance, combined with occasional obstinacy. He lives by Christian standards while rejecting all talk of miracles or God. Above all he has organization, clear thinking, wide intellectual interests, a mastery of accounts, planning, the law, tax and everything to do with entertainment, building and festivals. He keeps our family feet on the ground. He has a gift for friendship. He is less at ease with women, suffering from the same all-male education as me and being a little impatient with the often more emotional and intuitive approach of the female sex. But he is attractive and responds to affection and sympathy. His passion for travel has spread to Nicolas and perhaps, in lesser degree to Chelsea, who, I suspect, has inherited his gifts for organization.

Rhu has helped me hugely at times of crisis by stopping me from turning in on myself and dragging me towards his treats in foreign parts. His courage in the face of Parkinson's, and his remarkable achievement in creating the Holt Festival, have been a source of great pride to me.

Pony in her childhood had something of her maternal grandmother in her: a taste for the theatrical in life and on the stage, Miss Piggy when crossed. She always had a huge energy and resilience and a vivid imagination. This became more controlled; she did well at University and her marriage to the impeccable George brought out the best in her. She is hugely successful in her job as a teacher of English – above all poetry, for which she has a true gift. Some of the thank you letters she has received from ex-pupils are really touching. Like most teachers she finds common room politics rather tiresome – she always was keen on getting her own way! But she is efficient, drives like a Formula One winner, helpful, decisive, and is full of ideas and a devoted mum, a good producer of plays and is not afraid to have a go at anything.

When I say 'from Heather or Jenny or Rhu I get' I mean that I feel the influence of these people in various ways; I certainly do not infer that I have acquired their various virtues.

I was almost in danger of omitting one of the most powerful of all these influences. My naughty but beloved son, Bede. Jo and I always felt that he was given to us as an answer to our prayers that the gap left by Kirsty's death might in some way be filled. So we loved him as he set about proving my contention that we learn all the important lessons of life by taking risks and making mistakes. Certainly he made some spectacular mistakes: wild parties, climbing Mont Blanc without training, not working until the last minute before exams, telling the Scottish selectors they didn't know their job, getting in a muddle by obliging too many of the girls, Icelandic, Swedish, Dutch, English and Chinese who sought to share his bed.

He was for about six years a very good sportsman and games player. Many of his rugby playing friends have remained close to him and loyal throughout his life. The last days of amateur rugby were a world-wide source of companionship.

But it was in life that his influence on me is strongest. Training at Rank Xerox he found he had a gift for salesmanship and soon rose to the top, moving to the financial markets. He charmed people and they trusted him and he took the job seriously and helped two or three companies to turn their fortunes around – ending up with the Commerzbank after a spell with the French, who were not quite so reliable and trustworthy. By this time he had acquired a following of fund Managers from whom and for whom he raised vast sums of money. He didn't really enjoy being the boss, he preferred doing the job himself, which is strange, because all his employees love and admire him.

He is one of those rare beings who light up the room, whatever the company they are in. Children and old ladies love him and women adore him, because he is always positive. Not that he had always felt cheerful: he had periods of anxiety about his health and even bouts of depression. I often think that that is the reason he was so good at understanding other people's troubles. It is strange too that this man, who was so bad at maths at school, came to have such good judgement in matters financial.

The clue to his success lies in an unexpectedly serious approach to the art of living. In spite of all the 'laddishness' and the games playing heartiness he had always been interested in what he would hesitate to call spiritual matters and would rather call them secrets of kindness, love and courage. Bede was fascinated by two books "Zen and the Art of Motor Cycle Maintenance" and "The Monk who Sold his Ferrari".

Now I'm sitting in my drawing room as summer makes a bold decision to change to autumn, and I wonder whether I can afford to turn on the heating. The generous government has decided to pay a heating allowance, which lasts for about six weeks. They also promise free insulation of my attic. Unfortunately when their man comes and looks at my long low attics, he tells me that he is not allowed by Health and Safety regulations to work in an attic of the roof angle and height of mine for free. I will have to pay a worker who does not belong to the 'organized scheme'!

I realize that I'm in something of a panic about the last chapter or chapters. My life is not quite complete, but I've got to stop writing. I have contemplated writing an amusing and scurrilous appendix, in which I record not only all my most disreputable moments, but an honest and open assessment of those few people I have thoroughly disliked, leaving it to my four children to decide whether to make it more widely available. But what for? It would be cheap vengeance and would benefit none. In any case dislike is usually the result of insufficient understanding.

Once a teacher, always a teacher. So I shall not avoid the danger of pomposity and conceit, which haunt most of those of my profession, and I shall write about what it is like to be very old, why I am happy, and what 91 years have taught me and what I feel that parents and teachers should try to pass on to the young to fit them for the new world.

What is it like to be very old? Of course, it can be bloody awful. We all know old people who are suffering from Alzheimer's or cancer with all their attendant horrors.

Before writing a collection of doggerel verse: "Now that we are very old" I wrote a cautionary warning to myself:

"Advice to Grandpapa".
Last birthday you were 89

Congrats! O.K. Well done, that's fine!
But, please! Don't give us more advice,
Your thoughts on Virtue or on Vice
Command no interest any more –
Old men's views are just a bore.

Who's Lady Gaga? Who is WHO?
The modern world is not for you!
If there's one thing that you should learn
It's that you have had your turn.
For comedy it's far too late
Your sense of humour's out of date.
Romance at ninety's just a jest
Gone are passion, wit and zest.
Don't make matters even worse,
Please don't try your hand at verse!

As usual, I didn't take my own advice. I tried to take off Kipling's "If" as a dedication.

If you stagger putting on your sock,
If your neck has lost its youthful look,
If you're dim of eye and short of breath,
If you're dizzy, tired and scared to death,
If your face is puffy, pink and baggy,
If you're wrinkled, pallid, thin and scraggy,
Unattractive, stout and hard of hearing
Ugly, full of aches and pains past bearing,
Lose your specs, forget your pen and paper –
It's you for whom I write this creaking verse.
Enjoy a glass of wine before the end.
Before the surgeon reaches for his knife
Join us on the rubbish tip of life:
Laugh with us a while at all one fears
Before the laughter turns, perforce, to tears!

There are sadnesses one can't avoid. Friends die almost every week, and my social life centres on funerals, not weddings and baptisms. The loss of Jo was a shock. The news that Rhu had Parkinson's was intolerable. I know that I am no longer in a position of any importance. I can't bend, and physical skills are failing fast.

Chapter Fifty

But

I am lucky in that I am not suffering any really nasty pain, I am still mobile enough to do most things I want to do. I've not completely lost my marbles and I find much to enjoy in life.

I get visits and/or letters from ex-pupils or ex-colleagues every week. They take the trouble to come to Blakeney bringing a bottle of wine and saying nice things about what I'd done for them at school. They helped me enormously with a little judicious flattery, appearing to forgive or forget all the nasty things I did and remembering (or inventing) the good things. It has been hugely rewarding to see ex-pupils who have become famous and successful and, even more pleasing, who have become experts in the art of living.

It has been a delightful surprise to find how many people of all ages take time and trouble to come and spend a cheerful hour or two with a ninety one year old – even Old Tonbridgians, who haven't seen me for 65 years, or the secretaries who struggled to organize me 40 years ago, or other retired people from the North Norfolk coast with a huge variety of interests and experiences from all round the world. There is no excuse for boredom or depression. It is a great pleasure when they bring their children, or I see my nephews and great nephews and nieces, who show me that the new generation is as lively and well mannered as any of their predecessors. Or old rugby playing friends' children who claim to have seen me playing all those years ago.

I had always believed that poachers made the best gamekeepers. It is the mischievous and unorthodox who often make the outstanding 40 year olds, rather than the virtuous schoolboys and girls. As Headmaster, you cannot let this be too widely known, but the years have proved it to be generally true. Of course the top scholars are needed to make the wheels of society run smoothly, and the genuinely brilliant come in all shapes and forms; but it is the risk-takers and those who make mistakes in youth who learn the most valuable lessons of life.

After 64 years the loss of Jo was a hell of a wrench: as though I had been torn in half. Looking after Jo in those last weeks had given me a sense of purpose: then, suddenly, nobody needed me. It was our children who restored me to sanity, who convinced me that I shouldn't just turn to the wall and give up the ghost.

However, I remembered something Jo had asked of me. "When I'm gone, do keep in touch with those of our old friends who are in trouble". It seemed to echo something my own dad had told me at the end of his life "If you're feeling down, find someone who's worse off than yourself and help them." So I started to get in touch with four or five old friends who had lost their husbands, or were ill and finding it hard to look after themselves, or had been obliged to move into old people's homes, and I took them out for a glass of wine and lunch ... all were over 80, and one is 100. I don't know if it cheered them up, but it certainly cheered me. The courage of a lady is a fine example. She is too blind to follow the television or to read, and so deaf that I have to shout to make myself heard, not only by her but by all those who are sharing the restaurant with us. She delights in quite saucy reminiscences and still laughs more than she weeps. She still hosts a group of bridge players and generally wins, although she has to have a special pack with very large clear cards to save her from confusing spades with clubs. Nine years older than me, she is a survivor of the British Raj and, rather surprisingly, an enthusiast for 'the work'.

I still see something of Pam and Paul. Pam was an outstanding au pair, who helped Jo look after the family in the early hectic days at Gresham's. She was a good looker and married Paul Girardot, a charming ex R.A.F. officer with a 'wizard prang' vocabulary and a moustache to match. Their daughters have been the pin-ups of Norfolk (and well beyond) for many years. Sadly one died, we suspect unnecessarily, in childbirth. Paul has had a stroke and Pam is unwell and rather deaf. Fortunately one of her daughters lives next door; even so it must be a hard life. Paul is as endearing as ever, though a little rambling in speech and very blind. Yet they are as welcoming and kind as ever. I often think that some of Britain's old and unwell are truly brave, not the heroes of war.

Millie, John and Chris Monckton. He was a distinguished, but charmingly modest and humorous eye surgeon. Millie was unfailingly kind and cheerful, but, alas, lost John a couple of months ago. Chris, a gifted linguist, pianist and singer, now runs a musical tour firm with his friend Simon, which is a great success. He now lives in the Canary Islands. He was in our House at Gresham's in the early days and is wonderful company.

Betsy Rogers, the widow of dear John with whom I used to go fishing, was a shade younger than me and was still in possession of most of her faculties. She had all the best characteristics of the war-time generation and lived on her own less than a mile from me. She found the time to be generous to the Blakeney church and community. Her daughters visited her frequently, especially since she had an alarming fall. If either of us was without company we rang each other up and arranged tea, drinks or lunch and watched Roger Federer or a Rugby international together. Sadly and unexpectedly she died this year.

I have already described the great part played in recovering my zest for life by painting, writing and gardening. I should add the periodic get-togethers with old members of my staff at Gresham's and my successors as Headmasters, all of whom were exceptionally tolerant of me and kept me in touch with developments. John and Jean Arkell, who were distant relations through the MacGregors, were particularly close because they bought our dearly loved house: Church Farm. John was very much the kind of Head I admired: a real schoolmaster who knew and charmed his staff and his pupils and cared for music and the arts. The governors were pretty shrewd in selecting my successors: each appointment seemed to excel in the particular aspect of Headmastering which had not been the strongest of his predecessor. [If this should fall into any of their hands, they should not puzzle over it for too long: there were exceptions!].

I also got together with Liz Savory whom I had appointed as my secretary early in my Headmastership. It had been a good decision. She was highly intelligent and organized. I seem to remember that she knew the Christian names of everybody in the school. She was also extremely pretty: I remember the Bursar giving me a quizzical look, when I told him I had appointed her. "She's rather young, isn't she, Headmaster?"

She married well and became the source of reform and rescue of village life initiating a scheme, which attracted the attention of the Television and became widely imitated throughout the country. She lost her husband at about the same time as I lost Jo. Still good looking. It was a shock to learn she was over 70 – it didn't stop her travelling to the Antarctic. We had some good laughs about the old days and some tears for our departed other halves.

One of the things I miss is the help of a full-time secretary. I was lucky to find two ladies to help me part time, Julie Higgs and Sue Buck, the first of whom was a teacher and therefore (it was a long time ago!) could spell. The other had worked at the BBC and was able to read my tiny and usually illegible scrawl.

In the holidays, I used to write for a great many magazines and newspapers. It was great fun. Occasionally I aroused heavy correspondence, particularly for an article on selecting doctors for the 'Lancet' which attracted over 100 letters of approval from doctors all over the world – I had not set out to be controversial.

In old age I wrote far less for magazines and newspapers, because I tackled three or four bigger undertakings. "Stuff and Nonsense" was a selection of my articles mostly in the Eighties and Nineties. Then I wrote a short biography of Dick Bagnall-Oakeley, and finally I translated Robert Mengin's "Pour Helen", a French romantic war-time novel. I was handsomely paid for it by François, his son, but have been unable to find a publisher. I found it fascinating – but very French. Fifty years afterwards it was perhaps unreasonable to expect English publishers to take an interest! I also spent a little time on doggerel verse in a feeble imitation of Hilaire Belloc "Now we are very old", completed a few months ago.

And now this. Every time I think I am coming to a fitting conclusion, I go off at a tangent. What started out with the intention of being a crisp analysis of family life and education Then and Now is fast becoming a collection of rambling thoughts about Now. But life is fun again. All the same something is missing. I am, perhaps inevitably, getting increasingly incompetent. The business of organizing an ordinary life lacks organization and direction. As Headmaster you have to make important decisions several times a day, every day. As a retired old man, I find it difficult to make less important ones once a week. Everything takes longer: dressing, shopping, cooking. Time is wasted looking for the specs you have pushed back over your forehead, or looking for your wallet and keys. Because there are no deadlines, you fall back on the Times puzzles. Time rushes by faster and faster, and less and less is achieved.

This brings me back to the Monk who sold his Ferrari to which Bede introduced me. I re-read it and made up my mind that I would follow the invaluable practical advice it contained. I had seen the impact it had had on other people's 'art of living', and have now followed it for about a year. It not only restored a sense of purpose and direction, but I felt fitter and younger and happier. By sticking to half an hour in the morning and half an hour at night, by having a framework for meditation and planning of targets, I have recaptured a clear purpose. I know that I have made some improvements, and I am happier. I have added touches of Marcus Aurelius and a sprinkling of Goethe, and I at last feel that I know in what ways I would like to do better and how I might do it. If you say something often enough and wish for something hard enough, you stand a good chance of it coming true.

Most of us don't fully realize, when all our energies and ambitions are taken up with our official life's work, that we are so busy coping with the immediate difficulties, that we have lost sight of the stars or the compass which should be guiding us. It has been distressing in my lifetime to see how what began as a rejection of the superstitious and irrational elements of religion has ended for some in a rejection of everything that makes life meaningful. They suppose that kindness, love and courage are merely mechanical reactions in the struggle for the survival of the fittest, and thus "all lifestyles are equally valid".

What I have always wanted is happiness and success for my children and grandchildren, which is the nearest approach to immortality of which one can be certain. And, secondly, to know what I ought to be doing and to do it.

That is the difficulty with Christianity. There is no doubting the teaching of Christ was inspired in many ways. For me, however, and I suspect for many of my contemporaries, it is impossible to forget that it was aimed at a different world and recorded by people who had no doubts about the miraculous. The services of a church seem sometimes more concerned with hierarchy, incense, stately robes, power and tradition than with the lot of the poor and suffering in the modern world. They don't feel generally like a search for spiritual enlightenment. How can I pray to an 'Almighty and most merciful Father', who allows Belsen and Auschwitz? He cannot be both Almighty and Merciful. And yet, although we cannot believe in a benevolent old man in the sky, there is everywhere a force for Good, perhaps just the highest standards that we can conceive within or outside ourselves, from which we ought to be able to gain strength.

Advanced household skills were however initially beyond me. Ironing, folding, proper discriminating shopping, and cooking for important guests were generally beyond me. Running the whole household for yourself and by yourself is different. You have to do these things. No-one to say: "Well done!", or to tell you that "You've overdone the Worcester sauce again!" You get lazy and start buying supermarket boxes: 'Admiral's Pie', 'Mariner's pie', 'Ocean pie'. Some modern passion for equality has resulted in these all being the same price and tasting similar. Everything is packaged for two or more people. So you buy too much and either eat too much or eat a smaller stale portion later. My fridge is full of out of date food, and my cupboards with jars years past their sell-by date. My shopping bag is defiled by unwrapped raspberries or tomatoes squashed by potatoes which should have been at the bottom. My wallet is so often left in the Fish shop that they reserve a special shelf for it, while next door in the Spar they regularly enquire whether I've got my car keys because I repeatedly leave them beside the till, while searching my pockets for change or my shopping list. I really had no idea how much efficiency was needed for everyday shopping – or how much can be wasted by senile novices.

The joy of living in a village, however, is that the shopkeepers are kind and forgiving, even rather amused or pleased at your idiocy, and can help you. At 91 you have to accept that old ladies, when you drop money on the floor, are quicker to bend down and pick it up. Don't feel upset, just accept it with good grace!

When I get home there's lots to keep me busy: the usual things which drive away gloomy thoughts; painting, writing, fishing, watching birds, music. But there's always something missing. When you've lived with a girl for 64 years, she may be critical of you at times, but how you miss it; how you realize that she also shared all the little successes, all the nice things that happened, and how that doubled the pleasure. Hearing our blackbird sing, seeing the startling green of a larch tree in spring, hearing about one of our children's successes, watching Roger Federer play a sublime shot to win another tournament – against all the odds and the ravages of advancing age. Like most old couples we didn't talk a lot latterly, because we knew what the other thought or felt and could convey most things by nods, smiles or grunts. Once a week we would talk in the conservatory about the fundamentals of life or the changing situation of our children and grandchildren.

Without her my absent mindedness and disorganization got much worse.

In the last page or two, when I set about the dangerous job of trying to pass on the secrets of happy living to my children and grandchildren, I make no claim that I have achieved wisdom and virtue and success. It is just that I have lived long enough to see some remarkable people who have achieved some of these things and others who have not, and that has helped me to identify the things that really matter, in 2020 as much as in 1920, and should be passed on from one generation to the next by parents, teachers and all those in a position of influence.

*

I'm very aware that Grandfatherly advice is out of fashion. It probably always was in the West, where novelty is thought to be synonymous with Good, and old age may be pitied, but seldom respected. Nevertheless, here goes!

First and foremost: if you want to have a happy life find something worthwhile to be enthusiastic about.

Secondly: find a job which is of real value to your community, gives opportunities to pursue your enthusiasms and gives you time to devote to your family. Marry someone you really fancy, to whom 'in sickness and in health' and 'in good days and bad' mean just that, and who has a sense of humour, harbours no grudges and will excel at life's most skilled job – bringing up a great family.

Build a close-knit family to share the good things of life and help to cure the mistakes that children will make by your unconditional love. Teach them ideals of service and spreading joy to others.

Try to nourish your spirit as well as your mind and body. It is important to cultivate what is highest within or outside you. It does not greatly matter whether you think of a God as the creator or of man who creates God. There are powerful forces for good and evil at work in mankind. It is in any case the lot of mankind to show the light. Don't deride the Church because you don't share its beliefs and because it makes mistakes. It is too easily mocked, but it is a force for good and deserves respect.

Value fitness and health. Enjoy exercise, games and sports and the wonderful companionship they provide.

Learn the importance of hard practice, which can bring almost any achievement within reach and can be fun.

Bear discomfort, pain and disasters with courage and even with humour, but be helpful and sympathetic when these things strike other people.

Seek a hobby which will keep you in contact with beauty: music can be stronger than words.

Learn to distinguish truth from falsehood. Support the good in all people.

When difficulties arise, look for the faults in yourself and the best ideas of others.

Honour your parents and teachers, and, as parents and teachers, try to be worthy of that honour.

Dispel negative emotions by laughter, kindness and praise.

Welcome new ideas and techniques and develop creative inventivity and imagination.

Cultivate disciplined habits, giving time every day to planning your priorities, setting targets and achieving them.

As a parent or teacher cast the net of opportunities so wide that the smallest talent may find scope for enthusiasms and success.

Seek to build bridges of understanding between all the warring factions of the world: rich and poor, black and white, old and young, management and workers, religious fundamentalists and atheists, men and women, nation and nation.

Aim at excellence, and take risks. Don't worry about failures – just learn from them. In the end you will regret the things you did NOT do – seldom the things you did.

So have a go, have fun and love good friends.

How lucky I've been! In spite of so many horrific and unjust sufferings, in which no-one can hope to avoid some part, it is an unbelievably beautiful world as long as we can treasure it instead of contributing towards its destruction. We live in a country full of brave and kindly people, however much the media try to persuade us otherwise. I've had great moments, three wonderful brothers and a worthwhile and rewarding job, which I thoroughly enjoyed. I loved sport and music and fishing, I had lots of love and laughter, a fair share of cock-ups, good friends and, above all, the supreme and undeserved blessing of a supportive, forgiving and unreasonably affectionate wife and family.

Nothing, in the end, matters more.

Appendix I

Rugby

It is hard to be objective. The English press were certainly puzzled that I was dropped for what they saw as my best three years, and repeatedly urged my case – headlines to the effect that the best fly half in the south was a Scot. To be fair I had not been at my best in my first three internationals ... I had made one or two breaks, but had not quite the pace to round them off successfully. It was a time when Scotland's forwards were seriously outweighted, so we got very little of the ball and when we did we were usually going backwards and in our own half. As I have previously explained, the selectors could not see me until after Christmas every season from 1948–1956.

When I finally played myself back into favour, I was 32 and my speed over 30 yards which had been sharp was somewhat blunted.

They were truly enjoyable days, and I had some memorable games, some with brother Rab in the centre. He was still a lovely, unselfish player with magical hands, but was past the peak of speed which he reached as the war began. Especially satisfactory was a game in which we beat the Harlequins by a large margin, when they were England's best club and had the entire English international back row. I scored three times. Some of the occasional matches during the war were memorable, because they gave me the chance to play with some great players of other nationalities: as partner to Wales' great Haydn Tanner for a war time Barbarian side against a reinforced Leicester: a delightful experience against the R.A.F. In an Army match I kicked two penalties from my own half. While I was a reliable drop kicker and once dropped three goals in a county match, my place kicking seemed to come and go. 18 months reliable, 18 months erratic. Also the occasion when the Rugby Union made peace with and played against the Rugby League. We just lost in a high scoring game, but I had quite a good day. There was a great game for the Midlands against the New Zealand forces with several well known Kiwi internationals on view.

My strength was in attack: I had worked hard at side steps, swerves and dummies, and reckoned that if I was given four or five yards, I could beat anyone. Very quick off the mark and good at acceleration, I was not as fast after 50 yards as I should have been. I was a bit selfish in my early days and not a great defender; but I improved in those respects after 1950. I liked playing on hard grounds, which was why I had some of my best games on French tours. The peak years for me were 1950–1952, when London Scottish were a side which really enjoyed throwing the ball around. T.G.H. Jackson, 15½ stone and 6″ 2′ on the wing specialized in vast crossfield spin passes (he was a champion discus thrower). These took everyone by surprise, fortunately our opponents marginally more than ourselves, although they gave away some tries, they brought us more. Doug Smith, later to be in charge of a successful Lions tour, was a ferocious, stocky runner who ran through or over any opposition, whenever he was given an opportunity near the line. Cunnie Ranken was the secretary of the club who organized everything in the background, quietly but efficiently. Other characters from the last generation who helped in the background were Dave Thom and George Horsburgh, who, when he accompanied us as assistant manager of a French tour, was christened by the French as 'L'homme Cro-magnon'. George had been a rugged second row forward. I remember him having a disagreement with someone at the bar after a match. He threw a powerful right hand punch. Fortunately it missed its target, but in drawing back his elbow he caught Rab and knocked him over . . . an unworthy memory of a charming man!

Another memory of George: because of my swerve, opponents often managed to grab my shorts, and, although they failed to bring me down or stop me, clutched at and sometimes tore my shorts. On one occasion I lost them altogether, but managed to score a try. George bellowed, his huge voice audible all round the ground: "Logie, it's hanging oot again!"

Looking back through old drawers and albums to try to stimulate my failing memory, I came across some 60 or 70 newspaper cuttings. I was surprised at how glowing many of them were: perhaps I was better than I thought, or the press was kinder then than now!

I've picked out a few. It seems that I had three periods. The first was from my last year at school to my last year at Cambridge, including the war years when there were no international matches (1940–47). The second was 1948–50, when I played for London Scottish and got my first three caps. The last was 1950–1955, when I played my best rugby for London Scottish. During this time I was generously allowed to play for the Scottish after Christmas, as I had promised to coach the Tonbridge rugby side for the first part of the season. I think that this was the main reason I didn't play for Scotland for my best years (1950–1953). They relented and selected me again in 1953, but I was 32 by then, which is a touch ancient for a fly half!

1943 Army v. New Zealand forces. "Bruce-Lockhart not only opened the way for his side's only try, but kicked both penalties".

1946 "L. Bruce-Lockhart the Cambridge stand off was in a class of his own at the Final Trial. His all round play was the best yet, and an inspiration to his backs."

1946 Varsity match (won 11–8) "Bruce-Lockhart went through the whole team opposing him, being only overhauled by Pearce 10 yards short of the line. A gallant run indeed. In the 18th minute passing went from Lowden to Kirby to Bruce-Lockhart to Fairgrieve, who just got over in the corner."

1947 Sir W. Wakefield's English international side v. The co-optomists Scottish side (a centenary match). "In the Scottish three quarters Charlie Drummond and Logie Bruce-Lockhart were outstanding."

1948 Glasagow Herald headline. "*Ace Bruce-Lockhart sparkles in eclipse of the West of Scotland* ... Personality man of the game was Logie Bruce-Lockhart. The flying stand off, with the excellent handling and eel-like running, time and again cut through the home defence. He capped an excellent display by converting all 4 tries."

1948 Final trial at Murrayfield. Sunday Dispatch. Headline "*Selectors puzzled, but Bruce-Lockhart had a great game*" ... 'Personality of the game was Logie Bruce-Lockhart, switched to stand off, he and Dorward were largely responsible for the 4 tries scored by the Rest in the first half. He has all the dash and verve associated with his family name. He has the nose for the tiniest opening, and the brains and tenacity to exploit it.' The Scotsman added 'Bruce-Lockhart was the outstanding player of the game'.

1950 Times. London Scottish v. United Services. Headline "*Great tries by Bruce-Lockhart.*" ... "The match winner was Bruce-Lockhart who can still beat the best players with his body swerve and induce them to accept his dummy."

1950 London-Scottish v Rosslyn Park. "The inspiration of all their attacks was Bruce-Lockhart."

1950 London-Scottish v Clermont-Ferrand. "The fly-half is of the very top class, and he at times toyed with our defence."

1951 London Scottish 22 Harlequins 9 (when the 'Quins had the entire English International back row) "Logie Bruce-Lockhart was in his very best form in attack and defence, and his brother Rab also played a leading part."

1951 v. Richmond (London Scottish 24 Richmond 5). "It was only the class of players like the brothers R.B. and L. Bruce-Lockhart that made the difference. The passing and running of the 2 internationals was delightful and each scored two tries."

1952 Times: London-Scottish v United Services. Headline: "*Bruce-Lockhart at his best*" ...United Services will play as well as they did in this game on many occasions and win. Logie Bruce-Lockhart can never have played better in his life."

Telegraph: "Logie Bruce-Lockhart was the inspiration of his side, there appeared to be no answer to his dazzling runs."

Evening News. "There was nothing to offset the remarkable exhibition given by Bruce-Lockhart. Everything he did came off. There were stirring runs which brought the onlookers to their feet ... He showed a fine turn of speed."

1952 London Scottish v Blackheath (the Times). "Bruce-Lockhart was the inspiration of the outsides: he is still the same elusive runner and seems to have lost none of his former skills. One wonders that the Scottish selectors can afford to overlook him."

1952 London-Scottish v Gloucester. Headline. "*Bruce-Lockhart has the class*"... 'A 35 yard drop goal by the invaluable Bruce-Lockhart. A minute before he had hit the post with a long penalty and he brought the few touches of class. Always in the right place, he kicked great lengths in defence and ran fast and cleverly in attack. It seems strange that in recent rather barren years, Scotland have needed him so little."

1953 Times headline. "Bruce-Lockhart earns cap ... Logie Bruce-Lockhart of the lion heart returns to the Scottish team after an interval of three years. If ever a man deserved his place, this former Cambridge blue does."

and lastly (*Times* 1956) Headline "*Bruce-Lockhart shows the way*" ... in an 'Old Timers' match between London-Scottish and Rosslyn Park to mark their last match at the Old Deer Park, London-Scottish won 12–3 largely through the artistry of Logie Bruce-Lockhart, whose form was such that one can only regret and marvel at the fact that he is no longer playing first class rugby. He did more in this short game (15 minutes each way) than anyone in the full time match which followed – which the Scottish would probably have won if he had been playing.'

*

There are many similar ones including some quite kindly ones about the international matches, played behind a lighter and usually retreating pack with very little ball. We won two (against France and England) and lost three (against England, Wales and Ireland).

It was all huge fun and the basis, above all, of enduring friendships.

Appendix 2
The Staff on my Arrival

It is time I returned to a very brief picture of some other staff I found at Gresham's on arrival. Paul Colombé was another powerful mathematician: Gresham's never seems to have had any difficulty in attracting them. He had the not always easy job of looking after Old School House: the house in the middle of the town, on the site of the original school of 1855. Because it was half a mile away from the main buildings and facilities of the school, it was less easy to be involved in all the legitimate spare time activities, and there was more temptation to substitute clandestine pub visits. Paul's great strength was as an administrator and organizer. He was also a genuinely good man, perhaps too good to run this particular house; he was inclined to hold one or two not very serious incidents against boys, thus ignoring the rule that poachers make the best gamekeepers. So his prefects tended to be the virtuous (I can think of one or two exceptions!) rather than the dynamic. As a second master he had a great head for timetables and the arrangements for examinations.

Peter Corran was another exceptionally bright scholar with a First in Chemistry at Oxford. Also a useful games player. I was lucky to have him and Paul: they had all the mastery of detail and ability not to lose bits of paper that I lacked. Bruce Douglas, my first second master, of whom I have written elsewhere was appointed to Gresham's in the year of my birth (1921)! The others who I found on arrival include David Addleshaw, that most hospitable of men; to be invited to dine with him was the greatest event possible . . . a wonderful chef. He and Dick Bagnall-Oakeley set up Gasché, the great Swiss, who ran the restaurant at Weybourne for so many years when it was famed throughout the East of England. Hugh Ramage was in charge of Biology; a great scholar and the author of a book on how to teach, but stronger on theory than practice because he had difficulty latterly in keeping order. Jan Day: an inspiring chemistry master with three sons all scholars. He was Housemaster of Woodlands and subsequently Headmaster of Queen Elizabeth College, Guernsey. Bernard Sankey, Housemaster of Farfield and second master, whose wife was a great friend to Jo. To my secret delight and official disapproval he hit a certain lady over the head with a frying pan – not, I hasten to add, his usual behaviour. Stoney-Smith was a good teacher of Physics, and a rather solemn house tutor in Howsons, who left to become a very successful coach for university exams in London. Stuart Dodd the French teacher, combined this with high grade golf, good trout fishing and most attractive water colour landscapes. I have a collection of 6–7 Christmas cards painted by him which I value highly. Laurie Taylor combined junior school teaching with a nice touch for jazz on the piano. Stuart Webster who looked after the art and painted in a style not unlike Dodd. Then there was Dyson as classics master, famous now through his son James, well known for his vacuum cleaner and other inventions. Sadly he died young of cancer, so, as we were able to help James with his fees, and, as he was the same age as my children, we saw quite a lot of him. Jumbo Burroughs was the charming handicraft master, who had spent a large part of the war planning practical devices for escapes from his German P.O.W. camps and who looked after our woods and open-air theatre. Phillip Simon only stayed with us for a couple of years before promotion to look after biology elsewhere. Dr. Wilf Andrews was our Chaplain, after Douglas Argyle, and became Housemaster of Woodlands. Douglas was one of the five sons of the Rector of Tonbridge – all of whom became Headmasters or Chaplains of public schools (The sixth child was a daughter and became a matron at another). A great hockey player and a good tennis player he was a lovely man of simple faith, although not of the intellectual nimbleness to deal with the more rebellious products of the 1960s. Wilf was a complex personality: a good history teacher, but he lost some elements of his faith, and asked me to relieve him of the duty of preaching, which he no longer felt capable of carrying out with honesty. Dan Frampton was Geography master and ran the corps, while his wife, as my secretary, ran me. Dan was another fine hockey player. He struggled against cancer for much longer than he admitted: a very brave man.

Bill Thomas was in charge of Farfield for many years, and of cricket. He had had a testing war, swimming across the Irrawaddy, hanging on to the tail of a mule, as I remember it. He was very much of the old school: insisting on high standards. A fine left arm bowler and a good batsman, he found time to play for the county on occasion. He was also one of the only masters to criticize me to my face – quite rightly. He might be surprised to know that I very much respected him for it. Bill also volunteered, in the interest of the common room, to be the victim of an experiment. Knowing that there was a lot of pot smoking in a local town, we thought we ought to know what it smelt like. Bill crammed some into his pipe and puffed away, while all the masters sniffed him. When we asked him what effects he felt, he just said, "Absolutely none!"

The Junior school was in the hands of John Williams when I arrived. Tall and athletic, he was a quiet and gentle man, which didn't altogether conceal a powerful will. He ran the corps most efficiently, for which he got an O.B.E.

He also ran the Holt Rugby Club of which we were founder members ... me as the idle President, he as the active Chairman. It is now an outstandingly successful club.

Neville Jones was another gentle kindly man teaching mainly in the Junior school. His wife Nancy was a strong character, a good musician and scholar. Michael Hughes worked with him closely under difficult conditions, before moving on to another Headmastership.

So I was, on the whole, lucky to find a fair sprinkling of good staff, round whom I could dream of building a happy school which would give opportunities for real excellence in every possible way; academic, artistic, sporting.

Well! One must always dream!

Appendix 3
Fishing

I fully understand why that great Welsh scrum half, Gerald Davies said that to land a big salmon was even more exciting than to score a try for his country at Cardiff Arms Park. I also understand that many people incomprehensibly find it boring, and so I have relegated my gushing about this greatest of sports to an appendix.

Size is not all that matters. A two pound trout on an eight foot rod and a 3 lb breaking strain leader, caught with a perfect cast under a difficult overhanging branch after careful stalking in a fast stream, can be as exciting as a big salmon caught in deep, still water with a powerful rod.

The attraction of this most enthralling of sports does not, of course, lie in killing the fish. As time goes by, most anglers return the majority of their catch to the water unharmed. The joy lies in the number of skills involved and the magic of the British river and lakesides.

And Timing! Timing is the secret of success in all sports: the timing of a side step or of a short pass on the rugby field, the timing of a drop shot in tennis or squash, the timing of a late cut or an off drive in cricket. In none of them does timing play a bigger part than in dry fly trout fishing.

I say trout rather than salmon. Although a good fisherman may thrash a famous salmon river 8 hours a day for a week, if the river is the wrong depth, the weather wrong or if the fish are just further downstream or have already passed through – or if they are sulking or just absent, he may catch nothing. Or he may fish for only one day and catch 4 or 5 in the same place with the same technique.

Trout too can be temperamental and affected by all kinds of circumstances. But they are always somewhere around, and the experienced fisherman will nearly always be able to catch one or two if he is skilful.

Timing! The time of the year, and what insects proliferate, where and when. Most trout streams reach their peak for only 3 or 4 weeks, and that varies with the weather and the nature of the river.

The time of day. The trout rise to hatches of their favourite flies on Tweed or Don for about 2 hours a day in the early part of the season. You may catch a few before or after that prime time, a dozen when they are really feeding. This usually happens in the hottest part of the day in March and April – but the temperature of air and water and the weather may alter the time. In the late season the timing changes and the morning and evening produce the greatest excitement.

Timing of the cast. With some anglers it is instinctive, but it improves with experience. There is real joy in the perfectly timed lifting of the rod tip to enable the line to clear the water, the backward and upward flick, the short pause and then the deft throw forward, sending the fly leader straight to its destination with leader and line in a coil-less straight line. Watch an expert. He doesn't wave his rod much behind the perpendicular, and he times the release of the line gathered in his free hand to perfection. It looks effortless even in a high wind.

Timing of your lunch. Be sure you don't take it when they're taking theirs.

Timing when playing the fish: when to apply pressure, when to let it run, when to bring it to the net.

Last, but not least, all the timing which comes into play when you manage a boat on a windy day on a Highland loch. The Oxford and Cambridge boat crews think timing is the basis of their sport, but they should try managing a leaky tub in a Sutherland gale, when both anglers are playing good fish, and you are liable to be blown onto the rocks. I remember my father and I hooking and landing two good sea trout (4 and 5 lbs) simultaneously in a gale on Loch Mudle with no boatman to help us.

Another of the delights of fishing is that it opens your eyes to so many other relevant fields of knowledge. You must know about your beloved opponent, the trout. Exactly what is his field of vision, whereabouts in a pool he is likely to be feeding, how deep he will be lying in search of what insects? What edible insects are to be found in what kind of water and when? You must become an entomologist and can hardly avoid becoming an ornithologist. You soon learn that a dipper feeds on the same insects as a trout, and are rightly encouraged if your river has a good population of dippers. Moreover trout streams and lochs attract some of our most delightful birds: grey wagtails, blackcaps, willow warblers, chiffchaffs, sedge and reed warblers, reed buntings, curlews, sand-pipers, oystercatchers, greenshanks, buzzards, ospreys, kites, eagles, divers, lapwings, golden plovers, goosanders, mergansers and smews, dabchicks, moorhens, coots and grebes. Always there is the miraculous healing music of the waters and, for most of the season, a background of bird calls and bird song, taking the place of the Naiads and Dryads of the ancient world.

For some fishing is a social activity. They like meeting fellow enthusiasts, comparing notes and exchanging advice, discussing tactics and timing. Not for me! I like one member of the family or even two provided they don't chatter all the time. I have no wish to hear people babbling about television, news, money, health, family troubles, the tax man or global warming. It is because angling banishes such concerns that I love it.

It heals so skilfully and surreptitiously. It demands all your attention, but imposes no strain. It surrounds you with nature at its best, in a country which is overpopulated and becoming less beautiful decade after decade. It provides you with fresh air and exercise, which can be as challenging or as gentle as you wish. It brings back all manner of half-forgotten delights: the smell of gorse in full bloom; the sight of bluebells, daffodils, marsh marigolds and wild garlic massed along the banks; the sound of waterfalls and the feel of early summer sunshine warming the waterproof jacket across your shoulders.

It has been said that, if you include the myriad islands and the indentations of the sea lochs and the hill lochs, Scotland has longer shores than the rest of Europe, excluding Scandinavia. What infinite variety it all offers. Although tourism is making some inroads into the wilderness, the great majority stay at the bottom of the glens, or leave them only in order to climb the more famous peaks: the Munros. The majority of the hill lochs are beyond their sight, tucked away two, five or twenty miles from the nearest road. They offer a whole range of pleasures: the scent of bog myrtle; the company of herds of deer; banks which can be precipitous crags, reed beds, heather or pebbles. One loch with no substantial outflow may have lots of small dark trout taking on the colour of their peaty surrounds. Only a mile away another loch may have a substantial run of sea trout alongside beautiful yellow trout with red spots, which live along the edge of reeds. A third and bigger loch may surprise you with a ferox: a large, mainly cannibal trout, which may seize your tail fly if you fish deep. The trout are as varied as the nature of their habitat and their food. Some are nearly as silver as sea trout; pebble-bottomed waters produce elegant spotted beauties; big lochs often harbour ugly hunchbacked hook-jawed monsters.

But the most fun is to be had on rivers, each with its own character. For me the Don before the war was ideal. My father found a private hotel with 3 miles of prize trout and salmon fishing, a nine hole golf course, a large sitting room with a grand piano, a suite for him and another for me, excellent food for – it now seems quite impossible – £6 a week each. We went for about 10 days for two years in succession. It was lovely water, clear and fast but with big, pebbly pools. The bank was varied between farmland, woodland, heather, grass and rocks. The trout were big. We never failed to catch one or two of over 3 pounds. The best week for the big ones was usually the first week after the melting snow had mostly cleared from the water. Then the edges of the main stream into the big pools and the tail end would dimple hectically with rising trout.

Anglers are divided into those who regularly fall in and those who wade carefully and don't. I am emphatically one of the first group. So it was that I nearly always preferred wading in shorts and gym shoes. It was much safer than waders which always filled with water and could be dangerous if you slipped into a deep pool. But it had its drawbacks. I remember one day in particular, when there were still bits of ice on the edge of the river. My knees were no longer pink with cold, but were ominously turning purple. I told Dad, comfortable in his dry waders, that I was going back. He said: "I think the cold wind is dropping and the sun's coming out, I'll stay on for a bit." I returned to a warm fire. Dad came back an hour later with 6 beauties. The most exciting thing about the Don was that the 'Professor', the best trout fly, also attracted salmon. Dad got one of 15 lbs on his 9 foot trout rod. What a battle!

The Tweed at Bermersyde was my happy hunting ground from Drum Mhor for the second half of the Easter holidays. Like the Don, there was always the chance of running into salmon or sea trout. On one glorious occasion I caught 3 sea trout in one pool on a dry greenwell. The river was about the same size as the Don, but it ran at the bottom of a gorge and was more dangerous and swift running. The bottom was mainly of large, slippery rocks, often loose. It was full of trout, but not so big; anything over 2 pounds was unusual. But blank days were very rare and the profusion of flowers along the bank made it startlingly beautiful. It could be Heaven, Hell or Purgatory in April. One day, hail and snow and only the odd foolish trout. The next a wonderful hatch of flies and as many trout as we thought it respectable to keep. And on the third day another wonderful hatch: but for some reason the fish wouldn't look at me.

Two days I remember. The first was when I took Bede down with me. I was so excited at the beginning of the season that I broke into a run down the very steep slope leading to the big boat pool – all 16½ stone of me. I fell and skidded for the next 10 yards. We fished for a while in rather too cold conditions only getting a couple of small trout. I then went up to a pool where I saw a big fish rise. It was just within reach, if I stood on a tricky rock at the bottom of the pool with water 5 feet deep on either side. By a supreme effort I landed my tail fly in just the right place, and the big fish took it. It took my line out, and it was sometime before I was sure what it was. It passed near me, and I saw it was the biggest trout I'd ever seen on the Tweed, certainly over 5 lbs. I bellowed for Bede to come and see the fun, or perhaps to net it somewhere downstream of me. I got it near the net two or three times, but it went off again each time, at last brushing past my legs on the way down to Bede. I hauled him back, leaned forward with the landing net. I must have exerted too much pressure. My rod straightened, I slipped. The great fish made its escape with the tail fly, and memories of my 8 year old loss of the salmon flooded over me as I fell in up to my neck in cold water. As I recovered my rod and net, I looked for Bede to offer a little sympathy. He was roaring with laughter.

Another famous Tweed day was on the golf course pool above Mertoun Bridge. Bede and I had made an appointment to meet my dear nephew Kim, a crazy enthusiast if ever there was one. The fish were rising furiously, and we called to him to hurry up and join the fun. He broke into a run, splashed into the water at the bottom of the pool, started 'shadow' casting, slipped, fell into deep water. All we could see was the rod, sticking out of the water, but like a hoop with the weight of a fish that had seized his fly at his first cast! He landed it safely. I understood why Bede had laughed at me earlier. There is nothing funnier than seeing your friend fall off a roof, as Confucius may or ought to have said.

One of the incidental joys of fishing is leaning over bridges. Britain has a wonderful array of old bridges, ranging from the great engineering feat that is the Forth Bridge to plank or log bridges, mediaeval stone bridges and perilous amateur constructions to enable local Lairds to cross their river. Best of all are those like Mertoun Bridge which has parapets about stomach or fifth rib high and a number of convenient alcoves, where an angler can lean over and see the water in comfort with his rod and landing net alongside. Before he starts his day's fishing he can see the colour and depth of the water, where the fish are lying, and how deep; he can even spot what kind of flies are floating or drowning on the surface, or whether the fish are nymphing. Time spent on reconnaissance is seldom wasted. I often wished I had the patience and delicacy of touch needed for tying my own flies. My brother Paddy with his surgeon's fingers and sharp eyes was very good at it.

Good anglers need to be experts on weather and on pollution: to know the minimum water temperature at which trout can swim and the temperature above which they get sluggish and off their food; to know the PH number at which acidity begins to affect the trout, to know what chemicals and farming practices pollute the water, to know what weather and what water favours what kind of insects, and when those insects are likely to be a significant part of the trout's diet.

In my old age I was introduced to an altogether different level of fishing, which I have described elsewhere.

Before leaving fishing I must bear witness to the decline of British fishing over the years, in spite of the great efforts of conservationists which have had some success since the Millennium.

Records show that the 1880's were about the peak years for salmon and trout. The salmon fishing on the Grimersta in the Isle of Lewis was miraculous. As late as 1921 (year of my birth) Cecil Braithwaite enjoyed 17 days of holiday on the Grimersta river and its lochs. He caught 178 salmon up to 21½ totalling 1,134 lbs. This included one blank day (it was in August, usually not the best of months), and another day on which he only caught one. The best day yielded 34!

At the turn of the century an angler fishing the Thames near Richmond caught literally hundreds of trout between 3 and 5 lbs in weight over the course of a few years.

The decline became clear between the wars and accelerated after the Second World War.

Overfishing was a major factor: the royal family made Highland fishing a fashionable pastime for the rich, more concerned with breaking records than with conservation. Salmon netting grew, as did the number of salmon farms. Agricultural pollution, acid rain and increased demands on water resulted in a decline in the quality of water, a change in the amount of insect life and the vegetation. Global warming has changed the flow of the gulf stream and, with it, the feeding grounds of the salmon. Sand eels, which form a large part of salmon diet, have been overfished. Then there came outbreaks of salmon disease. South westerly winds brought acid rain pollution from the big cities of the north to Scottish trout waters and the proliferation of sitka forests made it worse. Salmon, escaping from the farms, infected sea trout with their lice and interbred with wild salmon with uncertain results.

There is still time to save the fishing. The east coast rivers have done better than the west, and netting has been reduced. The pollution from factories is being tackled. The great southern chalk streams still yield lovely trout, if you can afford to fish them, and if the owners continue to stop too much extraction of water. And, for the old and for beginners, there are numerous reservoirs and trout farms, with big fat trout easily caught. But it is not quite the same thing as pursuit of the wild fish.

Global warming is a factor, but need not affect the trout fishing as much as the salmon. Thank goodness the many bodies concerned with clearing up our waters and conserving our trout are getting together and taking action. I want my grandchildren to be able to experience the same delights as my father, uncles, brothers and children.

Appendix 4

The Staff on my Departure

Richard Peaver was a quiet man of many gifts. A fine organist and pianist, he was always ready to take over at services or concerts. The important tradition of Gresham's taking its choir to perform abroad was started by him taking them to Nice Cathedral. He was at the heart of our most successful C.C.F. and a good linguist. His quiet, gentlemanly manner was most effective in our new purpose-built girls' house. You knew that anything entrusted to him would be well done.

Michael Allard was a fine musician: pianist, organist and composer. I still remember my astonished delight when, at interview, he played some Brahms on a second-rate piano, as if he had been the composer himself. A sensitive and religious man, I always felt that he should have been teaching at the College of Music: he was exceptionally good with the talented, but not a popularizer of classical music with the very young or not very musical. Fortunately in David Harris he had a colleague who was strong in this department and whose performances of the Messiah or the Creation were enjoyed by staff and pupils.

Ken Taylor and Avril were a great couple. Ken had combined Art with first class football and cricket and a single figure golf handicap. It all seemed too good to be true: I was too slow to recognize that Avril was also a good teacher of art, and let her escape to Beeston. Ken was a joy to see bat in hand. He was always over-modest. He was primarily very good with pencil and ink: great drawings of houses and landscapes, and he saw to it that his pupils understood perspective . . . and helped my amateurish efforts with advice on this. Colour and modern abstract art were not his things, but they are different spheres. There were so many good teachers, some of whom moved on and some who stayed. David Gregory was regarded by many pupils as a really inspiring teacher. John Walton was a disciplinarian and a geography teacher, who made an immense contribution to the strong 'outward bound' traditions of the school and was especially successful with boys who were not shining in other departments. He married Dick Bagnall-Oakeley's daughter Jane Anne.

Ron and Jill Coleman were a talented couple who ran a good house: I was always surprised that he did not get a Headmastership. He kept to the syllabus and got pupils A grades in Geography, which had not always been Dick Bagnall-Oakeley's priority. John Mainstone brought wider experience from the oil world. He created our careers department from virtually nothing and eventually broadened it to a valuable national organisation and made good money from art prints, especially Lowry's. There was Mike Chesterman who taught German well for a few years. He came to us as a Headmaster from Africa, where he had run a remarkable school for blacks and whites. Tall and imposing and very confident, I was sometimes a little uneasy as to which of us was the Headmaster of Gresham's, but he was, on the whole, very tactful. I appointed a great trio of Biology masters. Oliver Barnes, Tony Leech and David Horsley, all experts in different departments of Natural History and worthy heralds of the David Attenborough era. Tony shared my passion for mushrooms, Oliver my fondness for fishing and humorous verse, and Dave's wife Liz became my diabetic nurse in my old age. I was lucky too in a great trio of Lab assistants: Harold Cooke, ex P.O.W. of the Japanese and an ambulance man, Arthur Lewis who turned his hand to everything including cricket and football, and David Olby who rose to be the Bursar's right hand man. David Beeby was a great Christian Housemaster who moved on to a Headmastership. Graham Worrell a splendid rugby coach and Housemaster. Michael Hughes and Nevill Jones who ran the Junior School; Martin Crossley Evans, Michael Barrett and Mike Runnels who made sure that culture was not eclipsed by games. Graham Lynn was an inspirational teacher whose stay was all too short. Keith Ashby: linguist, great walker and sailor and Ron Cox and Patrick Thompson who ran an invariably successful Physics Department. Ron ran the sailing and Patrick eventually became a hardworking and independent M.P. – he would have become a minister if he had not had the unusual courage to oppose the party line from time to time. Richard Brearley and his wife have provided another guarantee of excellence for Gresham's Prep School which has attained a new peak since I left.

Oh! I nearly forgot Richard Mansfield. His father used to play against me in the veterans' Norfolk squash competition. He was a gifted actor (in 'Journey's End', as a boy in Howson's). He took up modern dancing, professionally, but had to give up following injuries in a car crash. He then became the rock on which the improvements in the prep school were founded, plays, administration and all. Fiona Gathercole returned to us to introduce some continuity and inside knowledge as a teacher and Housemistress, and Sue Smart was for years saddled with the most responsible job of looking after the girls, which she accomplished with quiet acceptance. Her husband John was a dynamic English master, who, on retirement, looks after the Old Greshamian magazine. In the Senior School there was a sprinkling of more unusual but lively birds of passage like Duncan Hill, Graeme Fife (who wrote an authoritative book on the Tour de France), and John Harrison, rugby coach, and teacher of Russian and Classics. He married Amrei, who was with us as an au pair, moved to Oundle, and then retired to near Holt, from where he still produces plays.

And John Bates an ideal sergeant-major for our flourishing C.C.F: unflappable, organized and a dependable man in our tremendous record of success in Duke of Edinburgh expeditions.